New French Feminisms

New French Feminisms

An Anthology

Edited and with introductions by
Elaine Marks & Isabelle de Courtivron

Schocken Books · New York

First published by SCHOCKEN BOOKS 1981

Copyright © 1980 by
The University of Massachusetts Press

All rights reserved under International and Pan-American
Copyright Conventions. Published in the United States
by Schocken Books Inc., New York. Distributed by
Pantheon Books, a division of Random House, Inc., New York.

Published by arrangement with The University of Massachusetts Press

Permissions acknowledgments appear on pages 281–82.

Library of Congress Cataloging in Publication Data
Main entry under title:
New French feminisms.
    Bibliography: p.
    Includes index.
    1. Feminism—France—Addresses, essays, lectures.
I. Marks, Elaine.   II. De Courtivron, Isabelle.
HQ1617.N43   1981   305.4′2′0944   81-40413
                                              AACR2

ISBN 0-8052-0681-7

Manufactured in the United States of America
9 8

Contents

Why This Book?   ix

Introductions   1

1   Discourses of Anti-Feminism and Feminism   3
2   Histories of France and of Feminism in France   10
3   Contexts of the New French Feminisms   28

Beginnings   39

SIMONE DE BEAUVOIR   Introduction to The Second Sex   41

Demystifications   57

FRANÇOISE PARTURIER   An Open Letter to Men   59
FRANÇOISE D'EAUBONNE   Feminism or Death   64
BENOÎTE GROULT   Night Porters   68
DOMINIQUE POGGI   A Defense of the Master-Slave Relationship   76
ANNIE LECLERC   Woman's Word   79
CLAUDINE HERMANN   The Virile System   87
HÉLÈNE CIXOUS   Sorties   90
LUCE IRIGARAY   This Sex Which Is Not One   99
LUCE IRIGARAY   When the Goods Get Together   107
MARGUERITE DURAS   Smothered Creativity   111

Warnings   115

ANTOINETTE FOUQUE   Quoted in "The MLF is you, is me"   117
DENISE LE DANTEC   From an interview   119
MARIA-ANTONIETTA MACCIOCCHI   Feminine Sexuality in Fascist
   Ideology   120

ARLETTE LAGUILLER   From an interview   121
MADELEINE VINCENT   A Basic Fact of Our Time   125
CATHERINE CLÉMENT   Enslaved Enclave   130
JULIA KRISTEVA   Woman Can Never Be Defined   137
SIMONE DE BEAUVOIR   From an interview   142
SIMONE DE BEAUVOIR   From an interview   151
EVELYNE SULLEROT   The Feminine (Matter of) Fact   154

Creations   159

XAVIÈRE GAUTHIER   Is There Such a Thing As Women's Writing?   161
JULIA KRISTEVA   Oscillation between Power and Denial   165
CLAUDINE HERMANN   Women in Space and Time   168
MARGUERITE DURAS   From an interview   174
CHANTAL CHAWAF   Linguistic Flesh   177
MADELEINE GAGNON   Body I   179
VIVIANE FORRESTER   What Women's Eyes See   181
CHRISTIANE ROCHEFORT   Are Women Writers Still Monsters?   183

Manifestoes—Actions   187

Women Arise! / Debout les femmes!   189
Manifesto of the 343   190
SIMONE DE BEAUVOIR   Introduction to "Les femmes s'entêtent"   191
Editions des femmes   193
Rape Is an Abuse of Power   194.
The Women Prostitutes of Lyon Speak to the Population   196
C.D.   For a Materialist Feminism   197
XAVIÈRE GAUTHIER   Why Witches?   199
NATHALIE RONCIER AND CLAUDIE LANDY   After 48 Hours of Women's
      Films in La Rochelle   204
"Defense of Violette C."   207
GISÈLE HALIMI   The Common Program for Women   208
Research on Women   211
Variations on Common Themes   212

Utopias   231

SIMONE DE BEAUVOIR   Liberation: The Independent Woman   233
FRANÇOISE PARTURIER   An Open Letter to Men   234
FRANÇOISE D'EAUBONNE   Feminism or Death   236
ANNIE LECLERC   The Love Letter   237
MARGUERITE DURAS   From an interview   238

vii   Contents

MARIA-ANTONIETTA MACCIOCCHI   Feminine Sexuality in Fascist
    Ideology   239
JULIA KRISTEVA   Chinese Women against the Tide   240
JULIA KRISTEVA   About Chinese Women   241
MONIQUE WITTIG   *Les guérillères*   242
SUZANNE HORER AND JEANNE SOCQUET   Smothered Creativity   243
HÉLÈNE CIXOUS   The Laugh of the Medusa   245

Bio/Bibliographies   265
Selected Bibliography of New French Feminisms   269
Index   271

Why This Book?

"We translate what the American women write, they never translate our texts." This complaint by Hélène Cixous, one of France's leading women writers, is accurate. There are exceptions,[1] but in general the texts that have been produced in France since May 1968 around and about the women's liberation movement are not known in the United States. Our book is therefore the beginning of an exchange.

What is going on in France has certain surface resemblances to what has been happening in the United States. There has been a temporary working together of diverse women's groups on such central issues as contraception and abortion; a split between reformists and radicals; a development of tensions, often ruptures, between homosexuals and heterosexuals; a formation of early links, later shattered, between feminist movements and other political, social movements whose goal is also to change both consciousness and the quality of life. Although the proportion of women involved in the women's liberation movement is significantly higher in the United States than it is in France, although consciousness-raising groups on the American model are virtually non-

[1] The exceptions include: Hélène Cixous, "The Laugh of the Medusa," trans. Keith Cohen and Paula Cohen, Signs, 1, no. 4 (Summer 1976): 875–93; Hélène Cixous interviewed by Christiane Makward, Sub-Stance, no. 13 (1976): 19–37; Hélène Cixous, "La jeune née: An Excerpt," trans. Meg Bortin, Diacritics, Summer 1977, pp. 64–69; Marguerite Duras, "An Interview with Marguerite Duras" by Susan Husserl-Kapit, Signs 1, no. 2 (Winter 1975): 423–34; Julia Kristeva, "On the Women of China," trans. Ellen Conroy Kennedy, Signs 1, no. 1 (Autumn 1975): 57–81; Julia Kristeva interviewed by Josette Féral, trans. Jane Kritzman, Sub-Stance, no. 13 (1976) pp. 9–18. We should also mention the occasional, often truncated interviews with Simone de Beauvoir by Alice Schwarzer, trans. Helen Eustis, in Ms., July 1972, pp. 60, 62–63, 134 and July 1977, pp. 12–13, 15–16, and a dialogue between Simone de Beauvoir and Betty Friedan in Saturday Review, June 14, 1975, pp. 14, 16–18, 20, 56. The only longer works of importance that have been translated are: Monique Wittig, Les guérillères, trans. David LeVay (Avon Books, 1973); and Julia Kristeva, About Chinese Women, trans. Anita Barrows (Urizen Books, 1977).

existent in France, and Women's Studies programs are just beginning, tentatively, to develop, the concern with blatant acts of oppression against women and with the institutionalization of sexism is the same among feminists of both countries. In France, as in the United States, groups of women are committed to arduous daily work on feminist issues. We do not wish to suggest that all French feminists are theoreticians and that all American feminists are activists. That would be a gross oversimplification of what has been and is happening in each country. But there are important differences. We hope that by examining differences and specificity, by confronting modes of writing, thinking, and acting, we will be able to enlarge the scope of the discussion, to enrich our understanding of women and feminism, of words and acts. We would like to share with our American readers some of the excitement we have felt in our contacts with new French feminisms.

Women concerned with the woman question in France use the words "feminism" and "feminist" less often than do their counterparts in the United States. The ridicule to which "feminists" were subjected has always been more aggressive in France; this may be one reason why the words do not appear as frequently. But there is a more profound reason. The desire to break with a bourgeois past—with the inadequacies and fixed categories of humanistic thought, including feminism—has led to a vigorous attack against the labels by one of the most influential and radical of the women's groups (known originally as "Psychanalyse et Politique"—"Psych et Po"—and more recently as "politique et psychanalyse")[2] as well as by Hélène Cixous. We have nonetheless decided to place "feminisms" in our title because there is as yet no better word to account for the phenomenon we are presenting. We define feminism as an awareness of women's oppression-repression that initiates both analyses of the dimension of this oppression-repression, and strategies for liberation.

The term "radical feminist" raises other problems. It is not always used cross-culturally or within a culture to refer to the same ideological orientation. In *Woman's Estate*, Juliet Mitchell proposes the following distinctions: "But the need is clearly for a specific theory of women's oppression. There are currently two tendencies within the movement directed toward this aim: Radical feminists who are developing a new theory of sexist society; and those Socialists who recognize the inadequacy of past socialist theory of women's position, but who believe in the viability of its methodology for providing this analysis and for whom

[2] Capitalization has been rejected and "politics" precedes "psychoanalysis." See Carolyn Greenstein Burke's article in *Signs* listed in our bibliography.

the class theory of society and the demand for revolution (based on this theory but giving unprecedented prominence to women's oppression) is paramount." [3]

These well-formulated discriminations between the two tendencies do not quite correlate with the French experience. This is true, first of all, because Marxist theories of oppression have influenced so many women in France and, secondly, because psychoanalytic theory, more than Marxist theory, is the center of current debate. But that is not all. Many women who refer to themselves as radical—Marguerite Duras, Christiane Rochefort, Claudine Herrmann—are convinced that the will to theory is the most pernicious of male activities. They militate against the dangers of theoretical paradigms at the same time that other women who are also radical—Simone de Beauvoir, Julia Kristeva, Catherine Clément, Hélène Cixous, Maria-Antonietta Macciocchi—militate on behalf of a rigorous theoretical stance. We therefore use "radical feminist" in a different sense, in order to account for the French scene; a radical feminist is any woman (whatever her relationship to whatever theory) who believes that women's liberation is inseparable from radical change.

In the United States, the texts of the new feminisms are influenced by women trained in the methods of inquiry of the social sciences, by women with a strong religious background (whether it be in Christianity or secular Judaism), many of whom were originally active in the civil rights movement and in anti-Vietnam War groups. American feminists are interested in going back, in resurrecting lost women, in reevaluating those who managed to survive, in reconstructing a past—"herstory." They are engaged in filling in cultural silences and holes in discourse. The assumption is that women have been present but invisible and that if they look they will find themselves. American feminists tend also to be focused on problem solving, on the individual fact, on describing the material, social, psychological condition of women and devising ways for improving it. Their style of reasoning, with few exceptions, follows the Anglo-American empirical, inductive, anti-speculative tradition. They are often suspicious of theories and theorizing.

In France the most stimulating texts of the new feminisms are being written by women of letters, intellectuals, professors of literature and philosophy, psychoanalysts, formed by a radical anti-bourgeois bias, steeped in Marxist culture, trained in dialectical thinking. Some were active in the "revolution" of May 1968. Their tradition, resolutely atheistic, loudly proclaims the death of God, the death of man, the death of the privileged work of art. It concentrates on the acts of reading and

[3] Juliet Mitchell, *Woman's Estate* (Vintage Books, 1973), p. 75.

writing as subversive, political. The points of articulation between this
tradition and the new analyses of women's oppression-repression are
many; they have proved fruitful. Such writers as Hélène Cixous, Julia
Kristeva, Catherine Clément, Luce Irigaray, and Claudine Herrmann
have assimilated and are now deconstructing Western philosophical and
literary discourse from Plato through Marx and Freud with important
intermediate stops at Mallarmé and the avant-garde of the nineteenth
and twentieth centuries. They have profited in varying degrees from
Kojève's and Hippolyte's rereadings of Hegel, Lévi-Strauss's rereading of
Saussure, Lacan's rereading of Freud, Althusser's rereading of Marx,
Derrida's rereading of the Hegelian, existentialist, and structuralist traditions. Their own analyses "of the status of womanhood in Western
theoretical discourse"[4] have led them to a variety of startling conclusions,
among which the most frequently shared and propagated is that only
one sex has been represented, that the projection of male libidinal economy in all patriarchal systems—language, capitalism, socialism, monotheism—has been total; women have been absent. These writers are
engaged separately, and in some cases collectively, in an attempt to
formulate a theory that would account for women's specificity. They
take from the Hegelian and Marxist dialectics those modes of thinking
that allow them to make the most connections between the oppression
of women and other aspects of their culture, from the most concrete to
the most abstract. They take from psychoanalysis the imperative to
know the unconscious. They are less interested in therapy than in lucidity, less interested in bolstering a wavering ego than in the relentless
pursuit of displaced desire. Some accept the notion that desire is different in women and in men; they explore woman's libido, woman's fantasms, and woman's texts as a first step in discovering what might be
the relationship between woman's body, as she interiorizes it, and woman's language. Others have moved from a critique of the ways in which
men have oppressed women to a critique of the totality of male culture
which they describe as a "pederastic society." This expression is used
to designate the primacy of male bonding, the exchange of women in
the general economy of the Occident as if they were merchandise in a
market place. Still others, like Monique Wittig, wrestle with and within
the language which they feel is alien to them. The styles in which they
have elected to write and speak (we have used several interviews) oscil-
late from the intricate semiotic analyses of Julia Kristeva, to the Joycean
and Lacanian punning of Hélène Cixous, to the more conventional syn-
tactic sentences of Françoise Parturier and Françoise d'Eaubonne, to

[4] A phrase used by Shoshana Felman in her brilliant article "Women and Madness:
The Critical Phallacy," *Diacritics*, Winter 1975, p. 3.

the political pronouncements of Madeleine Vincent and Arlette Laguiller. Our selection includes those for whom language is an expression
of thought and those for whom meaning is located not in the thoughts
of the enunciator but in the system of signs itself, those for whom language is communication and those for whom language is signification.
The distinction between reformist and radical in France is often most
blatant in the deployment of words.

With the exception of *The Second Sex*, we have chosen texts that
reproduce the spectrum of new French feminisms since 1968. We have
arranged them in a dialectical order: their *beginnings* in Simone de
Beauvoir's *The Second Sex*;[5] the *demystifications* of official male models
and categories; the *warnings* about the dangers of marginality and pro-
vincialism inherent in the assumption that there is an exact correlation
between sexual and linguistic specificity; the *creations*, in spite of the
warnings, of women writing, not *about* women or feminism but writing
woman, writing feminist; the *manifestoes-actions* that accompany the
launching of journals or groups and which translate the presence of
feminisms in France today; the *utopias* toward which all feminisms tend.
It will be immediately evident to the American reader that the greatest
discrepancy between French and American feminisms is in the realm of
psychoanalytic and linguistic theory.[6] For the initiated, theory and practice are united in the writing and the reading. For the uninitiated, some
of the texts will at first appear impenetrable. It is hoped that in com-
paring French feminisms with American feminisms the reader will try
to evaluate intellectual strengths—the most cogent analyses that lead
to or emerge from the most comprehensive theory—and tactical suc-
cesses—significant changes and possibilities for change brought about
within the culture. Our goal is to illuminate the difficult and exciting
feminist inquiry.

[5] The translation or nontranslation of French titles and expressions is deliberately
inconsistent. When a text is well known in English (e.g., *The Second Sex*),
we have used the English title. If the book is less familiar, we have given the French
title and provided a bracketed translation—those that are our own are not italicized
or put into quotation marks.

When a French expression is easily recognized (such as "liberté, égalité, fraternité"), we have used it. When the French is less familiar, we have given both the
French and the English.

[6] For an excellent introduction to linguistic theory see David Crystal, *Linguistics*
(Penguin Books, 1971). For an excellent introduction to psychoanalytic theory see
Juliet Mitchell, *Psychoanalysis and Feminism* (Vintage Books, 1975).

Introductions

*I. Discourses of Anti-Feminism
and Feminism
II. Histories of France and of
Feminism in France
III. Contexts of the New French
Feminisms*

Introduction I

Discourses of Anti-Feminism and Feminism

The recent French interest in discourse (the relation between language and the object to which it apparently refers) has made it easier and more difficult to write about how women have been written about. Easier because we have provocative models, more difficult because their analyses relate discourse to discourse and divorce it from experience. The unwillingness to move outside the text, to move from the word to the referent is unacceptable to most feminists. We cannot believe in the reduction of reality—oppression, suffering—to language. Still it is no simple matter to present a brief history of French feminisms. Any coherent narrative would falsify the relation between outstanding events, texts, and the subjectivity of millions of women. In a sense there is no history of feminism in France until the French Revolution of 1789 when feminist texts written by women and a feminist movement conscious of itself came together.

What preceded this configuration was the sad history of women's daily oppression punctuated by the solitary outcries of a certain number of writers to whom we refer today as feminist: Christine de Pisan, Martin Le Franc, Marie de Gournay, Poulain de la Barre, Condorcet, Olympe de Gouges. Punctuated, too, by moments of revolt: women of the lower classes, who could stand it no longer, said no; women of the bourgeoisie and the aristocracy came together to write against the brutality and the tyranny of men in matters of love and learning. Many questions remain. Was witchcraft, as Jules Michelet and others after him have claimed, a revolt of women-as-serfs against their condition? Women did indeed participate in the urban emancipation at the end of the eleventh and the beginning of the twelfth centuries, they did participate in the crusades, and Joan of Arc did lead the French armies to victory. But they were fighting for their men, or their king, or their God. And how can we weigh sophisticated language reform and literary texts on the same scale as domestic enslavement or wife beating? How shall we evaluate the actions of these women in terms of a feminist consciousness? We do not understand them now the way they understood themselves or the way they were understood by succeeding generations. We read differently. The same is true of the texts. Christine de Pisan, highly regarded at the beginning of the fifteenth century, was considered an insufferable blue stocking by the great pundit of French nineteenth-century literary history, Gustave Lanson. Marie de Gournay was subjected to ridicule during her lifetime and was then remembered not as a writer but as Montaigne's *fille d'alliance* and the editor of the definitive edition of his essays. Poulain de la Barre was largely ignored in his own day and continued to be until Simone de Beauvoir resurrected him (and the whole feminist problematic) in *The Second Sex*. We are just beginning to discover such important feminist activists and writers of the early twentieth century as Lydia Pissarjevsky, Hélène Brion, Nelly Roussel. Only now do we have enough information to bring certain texts and certain events together. Only now is feminist consciousness sufficiently widespread for us to distinguish between the many books on women (or on the eternal battle of the sexes) that have been written in France since the Middle Ages and the feminist inquiry. They are not, as our definition implies, the same.

Feminism owes its existence to the universality of misogyny, gynophobia, androcentrism, and heterosexism. Feminism exists because women are, and have been, everywhere oppressed at every level of exchange from the simplest social intercourse to the most elaborate discourse. Whatever the origins of this oppression—biological, economic, psychological, linguistic, ontological, political, or some combination of these—a polarity of opposites based on sexual analogy organizes our language and through it directs our manner of perceiving the world. Whether or not we can in fact escape from the structuring imposed by language is one of the major questions facing feminist and nonfeminist thinkers today.

Women have always been defined in relation to men. The categories within which men have elaborated the male/female opposition are quite simple: women are inferior or superior; or they are equal; or they are different; or they are complementary (different and equal). In any given culture certain traditions favor one and/or the other of these possibilities: the hierarchical structure of religious systems and aristocratic orders favors notions of superior and inferior but also favors complementary relationships among those women and men who belong to the same sect or caste; the demythifying orientation of revolutionary and anti-clerical movements *tends* toward equality (the famous French revolutionary slogan was "liberté, égalité, fraternité"). What is most peculiar to French culture and the history of that culture as it has been written are the extremes. The coexistence of *l'esprit gaulois* and *la galanterie* is a particularly strong blend, pervasive since the Middle Ages, of obscene humor and exalted idealization in which woman is simultaneously an insatiable cunt and the charming, gracious, virgin mother of God. There is no more constantly vilified object in French than the stupid, inert *con*, there is no more constantly adored object than the elegant, decorative woman. There is the coexistence, too, of a strong tradition of centralized government—Louis XIV, "the Sun King," Napoleon, "The Emperor," De Gaulle, "The Savior"—which reinforces the old Roman worship of the pater familias, and an equally strong revolutionary tradition which allows women to join in a common struggle for the civil and political rights of "mankind," and then represses them. Frenchmen, whatever their political affiliation, remain faithful to the old Salic Law and persist in excluding women from the exercise of power.

For centuries a specter has been haunting France, the specter of phallocratism; from the clerics of the Middle Ages who launched the *Querelle des femmes* by attacking women as lascivious corruptors of men, to the Napoleonic code that produced legislation confirming this dominant imagery, and beyond. Phallic criticism has steadily denigrated and ridiculed those women who moved outside the established parameters. For if, in anti-feminist discourse, women are often inferior to men, nothing in this same discourse is more ridiculous than a woman who imitates a male activity and is therefore no longer a woman.

There would be no reason to address ourselves to the French phenomenon if so many women had not conceived of moving beyond the bounds of custom. And if they were able to do so it is because they were often receiving double messages. There has always been in France one area in which performances by women and men were encouraged: language, both the spoken and the written word. Even though women's writing was immediately labeled feminine and denigrated because it was formless, subjective—because it had all the negative characteristics attributed to women by men (and usually desired in women by men)— nonetheless the prestige accorded those who could use the French language properly did on occasion overshadow assumptions of woman's fundamental imperfection. It was through this channel that women from the elite classes first began to gain a measure of respect and to voice their demand for a more systematic education. Until the French Revolution, when women from other segments of society began to protest and mobilize, the only women with any influence besides queens, courtesans, warriors like Joan of Arc, or murderesses like Jeanne Hachette and Charlotte Corday were those who became known for their conversation, their poetry, their diaries and letters, their essays, the reputation of their salons, or their protection of and friendship with great writers and thinkers of their time.

A complex line of French feminist descent begins with the salons of the sixteenth and seventeenth centuries, through the *précieuses* and the *femmes savantes*, to the women writers known as *Sappho 1900*, the all-women lycées, and the contemporary "politique et psychanalyse," and receives equally relevant genealogical support from Joan of Arc ("Hé, quel honneur au féminin/Sexe," wrote Christine de Pisan of Joan's victories), the *sorcières*, the aristocratic rebels of La Fronde, the *tricoteuses* of the French Revolution, the journalists and political organizers of the 1830s and '40s, the *pétroleuses* of the Commune, and the Resistance heroines of the Second World War. Although political action on the part of women predictably resulted in a strong anti-feminist backlash, it is still the combination of activism in language and politics that is most characteristic of French feminisms. Women writers and feminist activists also exist in the United States, and the issues of civil and legal rights, education, suffrage, divorce, abortion, contraception, prostitution, and rape are common to all feminist movements. But nowhere else have groups of women come together with the express purpose of criticizing and reshaping the official male language and, through it, male manners and male power.

The terms in which the official anti-feminist and feminist discourse have been carried on in France were established in the Middle Ages with the *Querelle des femmes*. Jean de Meung, author of the second part of the *Roman de la rose*, accused women of having numerous natural defects because they were inferior to men. Christine de Pisan in her *Épître au dieu d'amour* [Epistle to the god of love] and *Le livre de la cité des dames* [The book of the ladies' city] defended women against these charges by proposing lists of admirable women (what we would call today "token women"), enumerating their qualities, and suggesting that with comparable educational opportunities women would be, in some respects, man's intellectual equal. Faith in the liberating virtues of education—an education either equivalent to the one received by men or suitable to women's needs—has always been the most consistent assertion of the feminist argument. In French medieval theater the suggestion that a woman might be enrolled at a university was certain to provoke hilarity. Feminist discourse has always picked up the terms of anti-feminist discourse and been determined by it. Medieval phallocrats based their arguments on passages in the Bible: feminists answered with other passages from the Bible or with different interpretations of the same passages—the creation of Adam and Eve for example. Thus the feminists were always on the defensive, always pleading and, even if they affirmed the equality or superiority of women, never initiating the debate. This is true for the two outstanding feminist writers between Christine de Pisan and Simone de Beauvoir—Marie de Gournay, author of *Egalité des hommes et des femmes* [On the equality of men and women], 1622, and *Le grief des dames* [Complaints of the ladies], 1626; and Poulain de la Barre, author of *De l'égalité des deux sexes* [On the equality of both sexes], 1673; *De l'éducation des dames* [On the education of ladies], 1674; and *De l'excellence des hommes contre l'égalité des sexes* [On the excellence of men against the equality of the sexes], 1675. It is ironic that in the dialectic pro and con, women's reiterated affirmation contributes to the continuation of negativity.

This vicious circle that constitutes the model for written debate on the woman question in France was disrupted for the first time in 1949 with the publication of Simone de Beauvoir's *The Second Sex*. Because at the time she wrote the two volumes Simone de Beauvoir did not consider herself a feminist, she changed the terms of the discourse. Her text does not defend, does not answer previous attacks. Although she recapitulates them, the center of her study is elsewhere: how does a female baby become or not become a "feminine" woman? The focus of the argument is an analysis of process rather than an enumeration or realignment of categories. It took eight centuries for this shift to take place. The old model, of course, still continues: men are still attacking women as cunts, in the spirit of medieval *gauloiserie*; men and women are still defending the honor of women, in the spirit of *galanterie*. But *The Second Sex* made it possible to raise the woman question in relation to all domains and disciplines. The question was no longer relegated to an anti-feminist/feminist debate; it was fundamental to any discussion of human culture.

What happened between Jean de Meung's:

All you women
You are, you will be, you were
In reality or in intention, whores. . . .

Christine de Pisan's:

Thus are many women defamed
By many people and wrongly blamed
By word of mouth or written words
Yes, whether it be true or false that's what they say.
But I don't find this great evil
In any book or account
That speaks of Jesus and his life. . . .

and Simone de Beauvoir's: "One is not born a woman, one becomes a woman"? It seems plausible to assume that the difference could be explained by following the changes in ideology from the medieval scholastic categories to humanism, to rationalism, to utopian and scientific socialism, to existentialism. And indeed the major feminist texts that correspond to each of these ideologies all show a progression in the sense of arguments that liberate women from the constraints of the preceding ideology. The gradual secularization of French and Occidental thought involved a reworking of thought and of thinking. But if the laws of nature are different in origin from the laws of God, they are still laws and this similarity, at least in relation to the anti-feminist/feminist debate, is more significant than any difference. One set of laws was not substituted for another; instead the laws of nature were superimposed on the laws of God, natural law reinforcing God's law and consolidating the evidence. Even when scientific socialism, reiterating and concentrating on the cultural-relativist attitudes present in humanist and rationalist discourse (in Marie de Gournay and Poulain de la Barre), insisted on historical rather than divine or natural causality to explain the oppression (not the condition) of women, still the woman question was subordinate to a system. The anti-feminist/feminist debate was used to prove the validity of the system; the answers and questions proposed by scientific socialism were as sacred as those propounded by God or nature. Simone de Beauvoir was the first writer who was familiar with all the systems, a practitioner of the least systematic one (existentialism), but for whom systems were secondary to her inquiry. Indeed, one of the primary objectives of *The Second Sex* was to demonstrate the inadequacies of all existing systems of thought when they addressed themselves to the woman question. Simone de Beauvoir did not suggest that all the systems were biased because they had been devised by men—that argument was to be developed by others after 1968. She argued rather that all the systems were biased because they were limited, because from the beginning of history women had been left out.

Just how completely women were excluded from positions that required knowledge and conferred power can be demonstrated by charting their economic and legal status in France from Christine de Pisan to Simone de Beauvoir. The startling conclusion is that women were in a stronger position in society before the French Revolution and, indeed, before the French Renaissance. The great changes in the organization of feeling and of knowledge that we sometimes label progress and associate with different historical periods apply in fact to a relatively small group —almost exclusively male. The grandiose images of *l'homme* (the generic man or mankind) propagated within high culture had little or no effect on the quality of women's lives. The distance between discourse and "reality" is, in this instance, immeasurable.

Instead of presenting a historical narrative and placing women in a corner of the picture, we have moved feminism to a central position within a synoptic table. On the left-hand side, the briefest possible history of France, the traditional listing of wars, rulers, and regimes. On the right-hand side, the outline of a history of French feminism in which the juxtaposition of well-known and little-known names, texts, and events create their own and a new order.

Introduction II

Histories of France and of Feminism in France

History of France	History of feminism in France
496: Clovis, king of Franks, embraces Catholicism; a structured Church with laws and hierarchy reinforces social inferiority of women Early 6th century: Salic Law, the penal code, is first written down; declares that women cannot inherit land, and is eventually interpreted to mean that women could not accede to the throne of France	
771–814: Reign of Charlemagne; era of the great fiefs of France; feudalism takes root	
1096–1270: Crusades—series of wars undertaken by European Christians to recover the Holy Land from the Moslems; crusaders return with new images of luxurious living, new images of female elegance and refinement	10th and 11th centuries: Antifeminist currents propagated by churchmen who blame worldly evil on Eve. Roger de Caen writes in *Carmen de contemptu mundi* [Song about contempt for the world] that woman is the greatest danger in the world and that the duty of all Christians is to flee from her
Mid-13th to mid-18th centuries: Persecution of witches in Europe	12th and 13th centuries: Idealization of women in courtly love

feeds and is fed by cult of Virgin Mary; bourgeois *fabliaux* depict women as quick-witted, perverse, sensual, materialistic tormentors of husbands

c. 1275: Jean de Meung in the second part of *Le roman de la rose* [*The Romance of the Rose*] crystallizes medieval misogyny and revives the "querelle des femmes" which, since 11th century, had consisted of texts written by clerics and laymen attacking or defending women's "nature" as it related to the marriage/celibacy controversy

1317: Estates General invoke Salic Law to exclude female heirs or their sons from crown of France, claiming that "the kingdom of France is so noble that it cannot go to a female" (Froissart)

1337–1453: The Hundred Years' War

1399: Christine de Pisan responds to Jean de Meung's text and comes to the defense of women in *L'épître au dieu d'amour* [Epistle to the god of love]

Early 15th century: *Les quinze joyes de mariage* [*The Fifteen Joys of Marriage*], attributed to Antoine de la Sale, is a satirical description of the tribulations to which marriage exposes men

1429: Joan of Arc leads French army engaged in Hundred Years' War to victory and brings about coronation of Charles VII

1431: Joan of Arc tried for witchcraft and burned at the stake

1461–1483: Reign of Louis XI;
establishment of royal absolutism

1442: Martin le Franc in *Le
champion des dames* [Champion
of the ladies] recapitulates previous arguments pro and con and
passionately defends women

1486: *Malleus maleficarum* [*The
Hammer of Witchcraft*], by Jakob
Sprenger and Heinrich Kramer
Institoris, is a comprehensive legal
and theological textbook on
witches describing women as accomplices of Satan, and encouraging witch-burning

1491: Anne of Brittany, ruling
sovereign of independent duke-
dom of Brittany, loses her land to
France by marrying Charles VIII;
Brittany annexed to France

1515–1547: Reign of François I;
height of the French Renaissance

1526: Erasmus, whose ideas are
disseminated in France, writes in
Institutis Christiani Matrimonii
[*The Institution of Christian
Marriage*] that "a woman is always
a woman, that is, stupid"

1537: Translation into French of
Henry Cornelius Agrippa's *De
nobilitate et praecellentia feminei
sexus*, 1529 [*Of the Nobility and
Excellence of the Feminine Sex*]
in which he proclaims the superiority of the female sex

1541–42: Quarrel of "Les amyes,"
texts debating the perfect model
of Renaissance woman, and link-
ing her to the bourgeoisie or the
aristocracy; these are the first texts
to show that the woman question
concerns class as well as sexual
differences

1553: Guillaume Postel joins the
quarrel by publishing a treatise

containing utopic and mystical glorification of women

1555: Louise Labé, well-known poet, in dedication of her poems to Clémence de Bourges, strongly emphasizes the importance of study for women

1562–1598: The Religious Wars; persecution of Huguenots

1559: Marguerite de Navarre, most famous woman writer of the Renaissance, publishes the *Heptaméron* in which she defends women from continued misogynous attacks, claims that they are more capable of love than men, and advocates total reciprocity in marriage

1622: Marie de Gournay in *Egalité des hommes et des femmes* [On the equality of men and women] and in 1626 in *Le grief des dames* [Complaints of the ladies] opposes continuing argumentation on natural inferiority of women's minds, and rejects altogether the inferiority/superiority schema

1631–1648: French participation in Thirty Years' Wars

1637: Descartes, *Discours de la méthode* [*Discourse on Method*]

1643–1715: Reign of Louis XIV

1648–1653: La Fronde represents last attempt of French nobility to oppose the court by armed resistance

1650–1660: Height of *préciosité* movement; evolves into a rebellion against brutal male attitudes, which *précieuses* attempt to counter with feminine values in manners and language

1654: Madeleine de Scudéry, primary target of attacks on learned women, publishes *Clélie* [Clelia] under her brother's name

1660–1680: Apogee of Classical Age; France is a strong, bureaucratic, centralized state

1659: In *Les précieuses ridicules* [*The Ridiculous Précieuses*], Molière mocks the *préciosité* movement

1672–1678: War against Holland

1672: In *Les femmes savantes* [*The Learned Ladies*], Molière satirizes learned women

1673: Poulain de la Barre, in *De l'égalité des deux sexes* [On the equality of both sexes], applying the Cartesian method and presociological approach, opposes inferiority/superiority argument and discusses cultural conditioning as reason for sexual differentiation

1678: Publication of *La Princesse de Clèves* [*The Princess of Clèves*] by Madame de La Fayette

1685: Revocation of Edict of Nantes forces Protestant children to be educated in Catholic faith; 50,000 families emigrate

1687: Fénelon, in *Traité de l'éducation des filles* [*On the Education of Daughters*], offers a program of very limited subjects appropriate for young ladies

1694: Publication of Nicolas Boileau's *Satire X: Les femmes* [*Against Women*]; answered by Charles Perrault in *Apologie des femmes* [*The Vindication of Wives*]

1701–1714: War of the Spanish Succession

1750: Marivaux's play, *La colonie* [The colony], includes several themes of militant feminism: the mobilization of women and their solidarity despite class differences

1756–1763: Seven Years' War

1759: Publication of *Le journal des dames* [The ladies' magazine], first women's magazine devoted to health, education, fashion. Marriage is sometimes criticized

1762: Jean-Jacques Rousseau, in *Emile,* advocates respect of "natural" hierarchy which dictates woman's submission to men and the precedence of motherhood

1774–1792: Reign of Louis XVI

1777: Rétif de la Bretonne's *Les gynographes* is the most antifeminist pamphlet of the 18th century

1778–1783: France intervenes in war of American independence on side of colonists

1783: Choderlos de Laclos, in *De l'éducation des femmes* [On the education of women], advises study that will make women more graceful in spirit without excess of knowledge

1787: Condorcet's *Lettres d'un bourgeois de Newhaven à un citoyen de Virginie* [Letters from a bourgeois of Newhaven to a citizen of Virginia] is the first text to demand political rights for women, followed in 1790 by *Déclaration des droits et l'admission des femmes au droit de cité* [*On the Admission of Women to Citizens' Rights*]

1789: January: Women of the Third Estate address to king petitions containing numerous women's grievances

May 1789: Third Estate proclaims itself the General Assembly

May 1789–September 1791: Constitutional monarchy

August 1789: Proclamation of the *Droits de l'homme et du citoyen* [*Rights of Man and of the Citizen*]

—October: Market women lead 4,000 women on a march to National Assembly at Versailles to demand bread; although they are espousing the cause of their class this action shows their solidarity as women

1790: Women's political clubs are constituted to counter their exclusion from male revolutionary clubs, e.g., the Society for Revolutionary Republican Women Citizens led by Claire Lacombe and Pauline Léon

1791: Sade writes *Justine*

1791: The first "feminist" magazine, *Etrennes nationales des dames,* claims that "women are equal to men in rights and in pleasure"

October 1791–September 1792: Legislative Assembly

—September: Olympe de Gouges dedicates the *Déclaration des droits de la femme et de la citoyenne* [*Rights of Woman and of the Citizen*] to the queen

September 1792–October 1795: Height of the Revolution; Convention abolishes monarchy, condemns king to death and supports reign of terror

1792: Théroigne de Méricourt tries to organize groups of "Amazons" in the fight against Austria

1792–1797: War of First Coalition

1793: Marat assassinated by Charlotte Corday
—April: Convention declares that women, the demented, minors, and criminals are not citizens
—October: Women's political clubs are suppressed
—November: Olympe de Gouges is decapitated for "having forgotten the virtues which belong to her sex"

April 1795: Bread Riots in Paris

October 1795–November 1799: Directory; middle-class recovers its influence

1796–1797: Bonaparte's Italian campaigns

1795: Decree orders all women to return home, forbids them to attend political meetings or to gather in the street in numbers larger than five

1798–1799: Bonaparte's Egyptian expedition. War of Second Coalition

1799: Napoleon's coup d'état of Brumaire

1799–1804: Consulate, the civil and military rule of one man

1800: Renewal of campaign against Austria

1801: Concordat between France and Papacy

1804: Napoleon, proclaimed emperor, makes France the controlling power on the continent

1805–1807: War of Third Coalition

1800: Women forbidden to wear tricolor *cocarde* in order to keep this patriotic symbol respectable

1804: Napoleon's civil code consecrates inferiority of women and their total submission to marital authority

1808: Charles Fourier in *Théorie des quatre mouvements* [*Theory of the Four Movements*] states that social progress is relative to the progress of woman toward freedom

1812: French invasion of Russia

1815: Napoleon abdicates

1814–1830: Restoration monarchy; Louis XVIII grants constitution

1816: Divorce abolished in France

1822: Stendhal in *De l'éducation des femmes* [*The Education of Women*] and in *De l'amour* [*On Love*] shows how a woman can both study and retain her "femininity"

1829: Balzac's *La physiologie du mariage* [*The Physiology of Marriage*] states that the married woman "is a slave whom one must be able to set on a throne"

1830–1848: July Monarchy

July 1830: Establishment of rigid governmental control of the press; liberals turn to Louis-Philippe

1829–1834: Elaborations of feminist theories by Saint-Simon's followers deal with relations between sexes, the condition of women as proletarian and slave, the need to rehabilitate the flesh. L'Enfantin preaches his sexual mysticism

1832: Founding of *La tribune des femmes* [Women's tribune] directed by Suzanne Voilquin; it is a feminist paper run by proletarian women showing strong class consciousness (banned in 1834). George Sand's *Indiana* is a bitter attack against bourgeois marriage

1833: Claire Démar, an enthusiastic disciple of Saint-Simonian school, proclaims in *Ma loi d'avenir* [My law for the future] the abolition of the family, total sexual freedom for both sexes, and collective raising of children; commits suicide soon thereafter

1834: Charles Fourier, in his newspaper *Le phalanstère* [*Phalanx*] rejects Saint-Simonians' "cult of Woman" and advocates "concrete action"

1836–1838: Publication of *Gazette des femmes* [Women's gazette], a bourgeois magazine concentrating on women's right to petition government

1840–1848: Revival of radicalism and emergence of strong utopian socialism

1843: Flora Tristan, often referred to as the first French feminist, publishes *Union ouvière* [Workers' union]; a decade before Marx she analyzes workers' oppression and their need to unite, concentrates on the double oppression of working women ("la prolétaire du prolétaire"), and concludes with the inseparable nature of the liberation of women and of workers

1847: *Misère de la philosophie* [*Poverty of Philosophy*] is first work of Karl Marx to appear in France

1848: February: Demonstrations in Paris; Louis-Philippe abdicates and Second Republic is proclaimed
—June: Insurrection of June by Parisian workers leads to bloody street fights; suppression of the press, secret societies and political associations; in December 1848 Prince Louis Napoleon takes oath as President of Second Republic

1852: President becomes Emperor Napoleon III

1852–1860: Authoritarian period of Second Empire

1854–1856: Crimean War

1860–1870: Liberal phase of Empire

1848: First feminist daily, *La voix des femmes* [Women's voice], published by Eugénie Niboyet, Désirée Gay, Jeanne Deroin, and Suzanne Voilquin, advocates suffrage. Founding of numerous revolutionary clubs for women, which are closed down after June events

April 1848: Jeanne Deroin tries to run as candidate for legislative assembly but it is considered unconstitutional and she is stopped from speaking

1850: Primary school education extended to girls

1851: Socialist and feminist leaders including Pauline Roland, Suzanne Voilquin, and Jeanne Deroin are deported, imprisoned, or go into exile

1857: Parent-Duchâtel studies economic origins of prostitution and proves that practically all Parisian prostitutes are former factory workers

1858: Proudhon launches violent anti-feminist attack in *La justice dans la révolution et dans l'église* [*Justice in the Revolution and in the Church*]

1861–1867: Mexican Expedition

1861: Juliette Lamber responds to Proudhon in *Idées anti-Proudhoniennes* [Anti-Proudhonian ideas]

1862: Michelet, in *La sorcière* [*The Sorceress*], develops theory of witches as victims of and rebels against patriarchy

1864: First International in London

1869: *Le droit des femmes* [Women's rights], magazine published by Léon Richer and Maria Deraismes, emphasizes battle for legal rights. League for Women's Rights is created to integrate women into political life of the country

1870–1913: Third Republic

1870–1871: Siege of Paris (Franco-Prussian War)

March–May 1871: Paris Commune

1871: Women's Union constituted by Elisabeth Dimitrieff organizes women into syndicates. Louise Michel ("The Red Virgin") and other *pétroleuses* are active in defense of the Commune; they are condemned to death, to exile, or to prison

1878: First International Congress for Women's Rights organized by Maria Deraismes

1879–1885: Presidency of Jules Grévy: Conservative Republicans in power

1880: Enactment of the Camille Sée Law extends secondary school education (*lycées*) to girls. Creation of a Normal School for women at Fontenay-aux-Roses

1881: French occupation of Tunis

1881: Creation of a Normal School for women at Sèvres. Suffragist Hubertine Auclert refuses to pay her taxes claiming: "I don't vote, I don't pay"; a year later she begins a suffragist paper, *La citoyenne* [The Women-citizen]

1884: Effective French control over Indochina established	1884: Divorce reestablished; law favors men
	1892: First international women's congress to label itself "feminist"
1894–1906: The Dreyfus Affair	1893: Aline Valette in *Socialisme et sexualisme* [Socialism and sexualism] emphasizes woman's double oppression as producer and reproducer and exalts maternity
	1897: *La fronde* created by Marguerite Durand; first feminist daily administered, directed, written, and printed uniquely by women
	1904: Paul Lafargue, Marx's son-in-law, in *La question de la femme* [The question of woman] outlines Marxist theory of woman's oppression
1906–1911: Revival of French nationalism and royalism	1907: Married women acquire the right to dispose of their own salary. Lydia Pissarjevsky, in *Socialisme et féminisme* [Socialism and feminism], refutes Marxist analysis equating class and sex struggle, and emits strong doubts that the universal liberation promised by Marxists will change men's treatment of women
	1910: Marguerite Durand and Hubertine Auclert try, unsuccessfully, to run in legislative elections
1914–1918: World War I	1916: Hélène Brion in *La voie féministe: femme, ose être!* [The feminist way: woman, dare to be!] attacks Socialists and trade unions for their insensitivity to women's problems; tried in 1918 for pacifist propaganda and sentenced to prison

1917: Colette Reynaud starts *La voix des femmes* [Women's voice], paper which Nelly Roussel defines as "feminist, socialist, pacifist and internationalist"

1919: Nelly Roussel proclaims "strike of the wombs" against forced maternity and natalist propaganda of postwar government. Senate ignores proposal for women's suffrage; repeated in 1929, 1932, and 1935

1920: Law bans sale of contraceptives

1922: Victor Margueritte, in *La garçonne* [The bachelor girl], popularizes fears associated with postwar "masculinization" of women

1934: World Congress of Women against Fascism

1936–1939: Spanish Civil War

1936: Popular Front under the leadership of Léon Blum institutes many social and economic reforms including the 40-hour work week and vacations with pay

1937: Girls' and boys' lycées have identical programs

1938: Married women become legal majors

September 1939: Declaration of war against Germany

June 1940: Fall of France; Charles de Gaulle at the head of the Free French in London pledges continued French Resistance; Pétain signs armistice with Germans and becomes president of the Vichy government. "Liberté, Egalité, Fraternité" is replaced by "Travail, Famille, Patrie"

1942–1944: Large numbers of French women active in Resistance groups; many are imprisoned, deported, tortured

1944: Allies land on Normandy beaches

April 1944: French women obtain the vote

1946: Constitution recognizes equality of women in most domains

1949: Simone de Beauvoir publishes *Le deuxième sexe* [*The Second Sex*]

1954: Battle of Dien-Bien-Phu signals end of French control over Indochina

1954–1962: Algerian War

1956: Dr. Marie-Andrée Lagroua Weill-Hallé declares war on the 1920 law banning sale of contraceptives by founding the French Movement for Family Planning

1959: de Gaulle elected President of the Fifth Republic

1962: Independence of Algeria

1962: M. J. and P. H. Chombart de Lauwe publish *La femme dans la société* [Woman in society]

1964: Week of Marxist Thought organized around the theme of "Woman in Contemporary Society." Andrée Michel and Geneviève Texier publish *La condition de la française d'aujourd'hui* [Condition of the French woman today]

1965: Law revokes most anachronistic aspects of Napoleonic code

1966: Evelyne Sullerot publishes *Historie de la presse féminine en France des origines à 1848* [History of the feminine press in France from its beginnings to 1848]

1967: Neuwirth Law authorizes sale of contraceptives. Formation of feminist groups, "Féminin-Masculin-Futur" and "Féminisme-Marxisme"

May–June 1968: Mass student and worker strikes

1969: Resignation of de Gaulle after defeat in national referendum; Georges Pompidou becomes President

1968: Françoise Parturier publishes *Lettre ouverte aux hommes* [An open letter to men]. The group "psychanalyse et politique" is formed

1969: Monique Wittig publishes *Les guérillères*

1970: April–October: Fusion of smaller women's groups, consciousness of a movement
—August: Wittig, Rochefort, and others place on tomb of unknown soldier wreath dedicated to "the unknown wife of the soldier."
MLF, initials given by the press to radical women's groups, adopted by general public as name of women's liberation movement in France
—October: *Partisan, année zéro* puts out first full issue of a magazine devoted to women writing about women. Founding of "Féministes révolutionnaires," a group of radical feminists who stage disruptive activities with goal of destroying patriarchal order
—November: Estates General of *Elle* in Versailles, preoccupied with reformist issues; radical feminists try to disrupt the proceedings
1971: January: The law replaces "paternal" authority by "parental" authority within the family
—April: *Manifesto of the 343*
—Spring: "Féministes révolutionnaires" organize against Mother's Day

—Summer: Women's march from the Bastille to the Nation for contraception and free abortion on demand. "Choisir" is constituted. *Le torchon brûle*, radical feminist paper, is published

1972: Union of the Left; a political alliance between Communist and Socialist parties

1972: Founding of group "Spirale" by writer Catherine Valabrègue to study woman's culture and liberate "smothered creation." Françoise d'Eaubonne sets up "Ecologie-Féminisme"; maintains that destruction of the planet is due to the profit motive inherent in male power. The Bobigny trial draws attention to the abortion issue
—Spring: Founding of the "Cercle Dimitriev," which rejects the idea of general assemblies and tries to organize smaller neighborhood committees
May 13–14: Denunciation of crimes against women at the Mutualité

1973: Gisèle Halimi publishes *La cause des femmes* [In the cause of women]. MLAC is constituted [Movement for the freedom of abortion and contraception]
—June: Women's Fair in Vincennes (feminist happening on Father's Day)
—October: Founding of "Musidora," association of feminist actresses and film makers. Establishment of the des femmes bookstore, run by the group "politique et psychanalyse," sells and eventually publishes only women's works

1974: Giscard d'Estaing becomes President of the Fifth Republic

1974: Repeal of law forbidding abortions. Simone Veil, Minister of Health, plays an important role in this legislative decision. Julia Kristeva publishes *Des chinoises* [*About Chinese Women*]. Luce Irigaray publishes *Speculum de l'autre femme* [Speculum of the other woman]
—April: Feminist film festival in Paris
—April–May: Publication of *Les temps modernes*'s special issue, "Les femmes s'entêtent"
—June: Government creates Secretariat of State for the Status of Women, headed by Françoise Giroud. *Les pétroleuses*, feminist revolutionary communist paper, published
—July: Founding of the "Ligue du droit des femmes," presided by Simone de Beauvoir. *Le quotidien des femmes*, newspaper of "politique et psychanalyse" is begun

1975: Hélène Cixous publishes "Le rire de la méduse" ["The Laugh of the Medusa"] in *L'arc*. GLIFE is created as a center for feminist information
—June: Divorce by mutual consent adopted
—September: Feminists protest film, *Story of O*, claiming it encourages rape

1976: Prostitutes strike. Publication of the journal *Sorcières* [Sorceresses] edited by Xavière Gauthier
—Summer: Government replaces Secretariat of State for the Status

of Women by a less important office

1977: Publication of *Histoires du MLF* [Stories of the MLF] by Annie de Pisan and Anne Tristan. Publication of *Histoire du féminisme français* [History of French feminism] by Maïté Albistur and Daniel Armogathe. Publication of *Ce sexe qui n'en est pas un* [This sex which is not one] by Luce Irigaray. Publication of the journal *Histoires d'elles* [Story of her/s]. Publication of the journal *Questions féministes*, edited by Simone de Beauvoir

—June: International women's meeting organized by the "lutte des classes" (a Trotskyite group); 5,000 women from 20 countries attend

1978: Publication of the journal *des femmes en mouvements*, edited by the publishing house des femmes. Publication of *F Magazine* edited by Claude Servan-Schreiber. Publication of *Le fait féminin* [The feminine (matter of) fact] edited by Evelyne Sullerot. "Choisir" presents the *Programme commun des femmes* (Common program for women)

March 1978: Defeat of the Left in French elections

—May: the des femmes bookstore is twice vandalized

—September: Monique Pelletier, Minister for the Status of Women, becomes the third woman minister of the Barre government

1979: *Les écrits féministes de Simone de Beauvoir* is published

Introduction III

Contexts of the
New French Feminisms

The period between the end of the Second World War and the late 1960s had been propitious for the legal establishment of women's equality and women's rights. An increasing number of women had become visible outside their homes, in production. Many women had been active in the Resistance and had been killed in concentration camps. In recognition of their heroism and their suffering French women were given the right to vote in 1944 and the French Constitution of 1946 recognized the equality of women in most domains. This was followed in the early 1960s by a series of laws undoing the gynophobic strictures of the Napoleonic code. Women were no longer officially subordinate to men in marriage, in financial arrangements, or as parents.

Such reformist writers as Suzanne Lilar, Geneviève Gennari, Ménie Grégoire, and particularly Andrée Michel and Geneviève Texier, Evelyne Sullerot, M. J. and P. H. Chombart de Lauwe had, before May 1968, raised the level of debate around the woman question by providing sound historical information as well as sociological interpretations of the status, role, image, and condition of women in French society. The question was, at last, being treated with appropriate seriousness.

In 1962 an international colloquium was held in Prague on "The Woman in Contemporary Society." Two years later, in France, a "Week of Marxist Thought" was organized on the same theme. The French Communist party was eager to keep the growing restlessness of women workers within the confines of party thought; it feared an outbreak of feminism which would turn the analysis of oppression against male domination. Although socialist and Marxist thinkers of the nineteenth century had been in the vanguard of feminist theorizing (Fourier and Saint-Simon in France; Marx, Engels, and Bebel in Germany) and, indeed, had provided the only models for a theory of woman's oppression, the French Communist party was to become, on the woman question as on so many others, a bulwark against revolutionary manifestations. Its attitude was not fundamentally different from that of Françoise

Giroud who, when named to her governmental position, informed the journalists: "I am not a feminist because I am not a sexist."

The reports published by the Estates General of the magazine *Elle*, held at Versailles in 1970, coincide with the major preoccupations and positions of the reformists: how to be a wife, a mother, and a career woman; the condemnation of sexism in the media, in textbooks; the right to contraception, abortion, divorce, adequate medical care; the desire and the need to work with men for the construction of a better society.[1] The list of groups that would come under the reformist label is long. The most important include the oldest—"La Ligue pour le droit des femmes" [The league for women's rights]—whose goal is the integration of women into the political life of the country. One of the most recent and most active of the groups, "Choisir" [To choose] publishes a monthly newspaper also called *Choisir*. Its president, the activist lawyer Gisèle Halimi, had defended young Algerian women tortured by the French, and women condemned by the abortion laws of 1920. She founded "Choisir" in 1971 in order to protect the 343 women, including herself, who had signed a public manifesto admitting they had had illegal abortions. Simone de Beauvoir, who also signed, was, for a time, co-president. Dissension between Gisèle Halimi and certain members of the more radical groups erupted in 1972 and obliged "Choisir" to clarify its objectives: "neither to make a revolution, nor to change the means of production, nor to question the status of medicine as a liberal profession." Gisèle Halimi, in the best reformist tradition, chose a precise and limited fight. Without the reformists, without "Choisir" and the Minister of Health, Simone Veil, the 1974 laws on contraception and abortion would never have been passed.[2]

But if the 1960s were a period of steady reformist feminist activity, they were years of increasing radicalism among the alienated youth of the middle classes in France and elsewhere in Western industrial and corporate societies. France did not have a black movement or Vietnam, but it had the Algerian rebellion and war, it had the unrest among university students for whom the system was providing neither bread nor

---

[1] For some of the information in this chapter we thank the diligent efforts of Maïté Albistur and Daniel Armogathe, the authors of *Histoire du féminisme français*.

[2] "Choisir" has continued its commitment to women's issues, focusing on rape, legally defending women who have been raped, and forcing the public, through the media, to become aware of the frequency and the implications of rape and of the legal difficulties in prosecuting rapists. During the legislative elections of March 1978, "Choisir" had to combat not only the established machinery of French political parties on the Right, in the Center and on the Left, but also the voices of radical feminism in France urging women not to participate in this phallic display of power. Although none of "Choisir's" candidates was elected, women's issues received considerable attention. (See "Actions-Manifestoes.")

roses. And it received the echoes of the American black, hippie, yippie, and draft-resister manifestations, and of the Chinese cultural revolution of 1966. This new radicalism, sometimes labeled "Existential Marxism," with its emphasis on making all the necessary connections between apparently isolated cultural facts, encouraged rigorous analysis both of existing institutions (the government, the church, the university, the family) and of hitherto unexamined assumptions about history, science, sexuality, language, and the kinds of human relationships these institutions and these assumptions fostered or suppressed. May 1968 and the demand by students and workers for self-management was predictable; so was the radical women's liberation movement that followed.

The new French feminisms cannot be understood diachronically as part of the history of feminism in France. The significant differences between the old and the new feminisms are best perceived by situating the new feminisms synchronically in relation to the profound changes in the orientation of French intellectual life. These changes reflect, in a complex manner, the shifts in economic and demographic conditions, the multiple defeats of French "power" at home, since June 1940, and abroad, in Indochina and Algeria, a sense of impotency and of closure, and a growing belief in the triumph of an agentless, bureaucratic, and technological order. The structuralist assault on the existentialist "I" behaving as if it were independent of the structures imposed by language or desire, myth or kinship, is indicative of this same sense of impotency and closure. It is as if Ferdinand de Saussure's description of language as "a closed system in which all parts are interrelated" had been extrapolated from the realm of linguistic theory to serve as a model for all aspects of the human adventure. Within the structuralist vision (as this model has become known), there is no liberation from oppression, but there is an immense energy released by the attempts to analyze and demystify the structures that determine and oppress us. It is this energy, derived from the analytic techniques of structuralism and semiotics and combined with the revolutionary fervor of May 1968, that has given its particular impetus to the new French feminisms.

The "Mouvement de Libération des Femmes" [Women's liberation movement], commonly referred to as the MLF, is not an organization. It is the name invented by the French press during the summer of 1970 to identify the diverse radical women's groups that had been visible in Paris, Lyon, and Toulouse since the fall of 1968. The original groups were composed of women students who had participated in the May revolution and who were dismayed to discover that the vast majority of their male comrades were as deeply phallocratic as the bourgeois enemy.

These groups, often unaware of each other's existence, were revitalized in 1970. Their contacts with English feminists during the English National Conference at Oxford, the experience of a group of women at Vincennes in April, who were subjected to the jeers of young men shouting "Power is at the tip of the phallus," and the women's general strike on August 26 in the United States all played a crucial and structuring role. The English contacts reinforced the feasibility of solidarity between different ideologies; the Vincennes events confirmed the suspicion that radical feminists would have to work, indeed must work, without men; the American manifestation suggested the possibility of a mass movement. The first subversive act in France to receive widespread publicity involved a small group of women (including, significantly, the writers Christiane Rochefort and Monique Wittig) who, immediately following the strike in the United States, tried to place a wreath on the tomb of the unknown soldier in Paris. On the wreath were inscribed the words: "to the unknown wife of the soldier." The official press reacted as if a sacrilege had been committed. And so, in a sense, it had. The tomb of the unknown soldier occupies a sacred place within the French symbolic order and within Western mythology. Located in the center of Paris it signifies patriotism, nationalism, and the masculine virtues of heroism and courage. The Arc de Triomphe is one of the most explicit signs of a French, and, by extension, of a victorious, universal, male order. It is the shrine of shrines that glorifies war and the cult of the dead. Under it the flag hangs on commemorative occasions, around it victorious armies march, to it admiring tourists flock. The wreath not only challenged these values and these rites. The wreath raised the possibility of another series of values, those, unknown, that might have come, that might now come into being through the absent women. The French women's liberation movement, with its emphasis on silence and absence as the major form of women's oppression, was born.

The fundamental intuition that directs the policies and passions of the radical feminist groups is that the order of the universe is not a natural order; it is an order imposed by men. But if there is a consensus in relation to the fact of oppression there is none on the theory of either oppression or liberation. The group now known as "politique et psychanalyse," one of the earliest to be formed (1968), has become the cultural and intellectual center of the MLF. "Politique et psychanalyse" controls the successful publishing house éditions des femmes and exercises, in Paris at least, a kind of intellectual terrorism. Its goal from the beginning has been to study and to draw all the inevitable conclusions from psychoanalysis and historical materialism; to see how these theories can be used dialectically by women. The spokeswoman of the group, a psychoanalyst, Antoinette Fouque (she rarely uses her family name), considers the other feminist groups bourgeois, insufficiently committed to the exploration of woman's unconscious and the radical subversion of society. "Politique et psychanalyse" often refuses to participate in "feminist" manifestations because it views these manifestations as imitations of male power within the male establishment, because it views the women who call themselves "feminists" as imitators of male models. There is, to date, no full, acknowledged statement of the group's position. We can only deduce it from remarks made by Antoinette and published in the *Nouvel Observateur* (August 27, 1973), from descriptions of Antoinette's interventions and behavior at meetings described in *Histoires du MLF* (1977), from the questions put to Julia Kristeva by "Psych et Po" during an interview included in this volume, and from the unsigned editorials in the journal *des femmes en mouvements*. The books that the éditions des femmes publish do not necessarily represent the specific ideology of the group. If the notice printed at the end of *Histoire du féminisme français* is exemplary, their own discourse, in imitation of the prose of Jacques Lacan, is premeditatedly hermetic:

in a deliberate political gesture we refused to be included in this history of Feminism; however necessary and useful the publication of this debt to the past may be.

a history of Feminism which thus, here, is compelled to acknowledge on its reverse side the other-counter side of the old order, Humanism, that side which originating from the discourse of the narcissistic son (the female son) only acts as writing in order to deny, repress, censure—but in order to exploit it, the mortgaged place, henceforth an unavoidable obstacle, of the mother's body.

in this movement our social-political, our theoretical practices will never be the same although these misunderstandings try so hard and at any cost not to see the truth.

our grounds are to question by analysis; our position is impregnable.

the women of the éditions des femmes
the group politics and psychoanalysis
the women's liberation movement

"Politique et psychanalyse," like other avant-garde intellectual groups in France—"Tel Quel" for example—is convinced that there can be no revolution without the disruption of the symbolic order[3]—bourgeois lan-

[3] The symbolic order, in Lacanian terminology, is the order instituted within the individual by language. The carrier of this order is the father figure. (See Xavière Gauthier, "Is There Such a Thing As Women's Writing?" note 4.)

guage, the language of the old humanisms with their belief in a coherent subject—and that only by dislocating syntax, playing with the signifier, punning outrageously and constantly can the old language and the old order be subverted. "Politique et psychanalyse" is the most original of the women's liberation groups in France and perhaps in the Western world. It is also, ironically, the most dependent on male psychoanalytic and linguistic theoretical models. The writer whose texts sometimes correspond to what appear to be their ideological preferences and verbal praxis is Hélène Cixous.

Another important and antagonistic radical association, the "Féministes révolutionnaires," was formed in October 1970. For a time at least, Monique Wittig was spokeswoman for the group. The "Féministes révolutionnaires" were devoted to the total destruction of the patriarchal order. They adopted the American model of consciousness-raising groups, each group having no more than six or seven members. Their intentions were obvious: to allow each person to speak, to eliminate the possibility of the most skilled speaker taking over (which was what was happening at the general assemblies of the MLF), and to change the relationships between women. The "Féministes révolutionnaires" had, from the beginning, separatist tendencies. The notion of working without, of doing without, men is more scandalous in France than in the United States where there is the precedent of the black separatists and a less excessive need for male approval. The lesbians among the members of the "Féministes révolutionnaires" were convinced that only a lesbian position could withstand appropriation by a patriarchal, capitalist society. Like most American feminists they considered Freud, in particular, the enemy. They were not averse to spectacular public actions: interruption of a Right to Life meeting during which they distributed pieces of veal lung; manifestations against Mother's Day and Father's Day; the organization of "Days for Denouncing Crimes against Women"; sit-ins to help unwed mothers; disruptions of reformist and of government meetings. What was important was to receive attention from the press, to be talked about, to be visible. But the "Féministes révolutionnaires" could not withstand the pressure from without (the attacks originating from "politique et psychanalyse": the denigration of the word "feminist," the accusation of adherence to the male libidinal economy, the charge of anti-intellectualism) and from within (the conflicts between lesbian separatists and heterosexual radicals).

Dissensions, which must be recognized, are not necessarily indications of weakness. Indeed it has often been stated that radical feminism is the only revolutionary force that has maintained the exuberance of May 1968; it is the only movement in France today that combines the conviction of a cause with a serious theoretical quest and unlimited occasions to test the relation between theory and practice. In *Histoire du féminisme français* Albistur and Armogathe conclude:

> When we examine both radical feminist literature and films, we are struck by the many domains that are mentioned and also by the extraordinary will to create something new while avoiding references to traditional analysis, to the archetypes of patriarchal culture. In the July–October 1970 issue of *Partisans*, in the special issue of *Les temps modernes*, "Les femmes s'entêtent" [4] (April–May 1974) we find the entire range of radical feminist preoccupations. In *Partisans* there is an invaluable documentation on the condition of women in the Soviet Union; in *Les temps modernes* [5] there are analyses of the condition of peasant women, sexual segregation in the schools, the relationship between the structures of urban life and the reclusion of women. [6]

We might add to this list still another publication that will remain as an important marker in the directions of new French feminisms: *L'arc*, no. 61 (1975), entitled "Simone de Beauvoir et la lutte des femmes" [Simone de Beauvoir and the women's struggle]. This issue brings together a variety of interesting points of view, including Sartre's relation to women, poetic manifestoes by Hélène Cixous and Catherine Clément, an analysis of materialist feminism by C.D. (Christine Delphy), an analysis of feminist consciousness by the sociologist Andrée Michel, reports on feminisms in America, and a round table discussion with Simone de Beauvoir and a group of younger women. The range of theoretical and practical concerns is impressive. There is no corner of culture into which French radical feminism will not eventually delve and about which it will not comment.

It would be possible to trace the diverse ideologies and activities of radical women's groups in France through the pronouncements in interviews and prefaces of Simone de Beauvoir. She does not, of course, represent all the tendencies, but she refers to them all, refutes some, defends others in her constant attempt to refine and redefine her own position.

---

[4] "Les femmes s'entêtent" contains an untranslatable quadruple pun: *s'entêter* ("to be stubborn"); *entêter* ("to be self-intoxicated"); *sans tête* ("headless, decapitated"); *cent têtes* ("one hundred heads"). There are also significant fragments in *téter* ("to nurse"). The title oscillates between women as survivors and as victims.

[5] Jean Paul Sartre's journal *Les temps modernes* has, since 1974, been one of the liveliest centers of feminist debate. The women who write the column "Le sexisme ordinaire" [Everyday sexism] are a kind of vigilante committee watching French cultural manifestations. They have been particularly vigorous in their diatribes against Lacanian psychoanalytic theories.

[6] Albistur and Armogathe, *Histoire du féminisme français*, p. 461.

In 1949 Simone de Beauvoir was not a feminist. We might add that in 1949 there was no radical feminism. She strongly believed that a change in woman's oppression would occur only through a socialist revolution and that class struggle always had priority over the woman question. This position has changed since 1968. Although Simone de Beauvoir rejects the notion of a distinct woman's language corresponding to woman's desire, she admits the necessity for feminist action independent of any other political action. She signified this acceptance by becoming the president of the "Ligue du droit des femmes" [League of women's rights], founded in early 1974 by a group of militant feminists dissatisfied with both "politique et psychanalyse" and the "Féministes révolutionnaires." The "Ligue" had a newspaper, the *Nouvelles féministes* (1974–1977), and a subsidiary group, "SOS Femmes-alternatives," is actively involved in establishing places of refuge for women victimized by male violence. The "Ligue" is concerned with three forms of action: the denunciation of sexism; the defense of women and their legal education; the establishment of new rights for women. Its strength is in its ability to cope with problems as they occur and to sustain an exacting relationship between theory and practice, between revolution and reform.

In 1977 still another journal, *Questions féministes*, was launched under the editorship of Simone de Beauvoir. *Questions féministes*, which includes among its contributors Monique Wittig and Christine Delphy, proposes in an opening editorial (see "Manifestoes-Actions") to be a radical feminist journal devoted to theoretical texts on women's oppression. It is consciously hostile, in its own language of analysis, to the punning and *préciosité* of other theoreticians. The inclusion in the second issue (February 1978) of both Simone de Beauvoir and Monique Wittig marks a significant political and literary event in the history of the new French feminisms.

In a culture as self-consciously critical and sophisticated as twentieth-century France, radical feminism plays a privileged role. Freud spoke of the three revolutions that had severely wounded man's narcissistic image of himself: the Copernican, the Darwinian, and his own. We might add a fourth: radical feminism. It has stolen the intellectual tools of patriarchy and, in many cases, has turned them against their inventors. The fundamental concerns with the proper relationship between sex and class, with understanding sexuality and with exploring feminine creativity all tend toward the destruction of androcentric and heterosexist regimes, toward a challenging of the word "human" as applied to man's inventions. In general, French feminists, whether radical or reformist, attack male systems, male values, the pervasiveness of misogyny, more vigorously than do American feminists (with the exception of radical lesbian writers).

Calmly, lucidly I repeat it (and I scream, I shout, I pronounce and express it until the very end and with my voice and my pen): I believe in the generality, the depth, the universality of misogyny: yes, always and everywhere, on the part of the capitalist and the proletariat, in the European-American camp and in the socialist camp, and in the third world, and in sub-cultures, in the Vatican as in Cuba; I believe it exists in the young man who can get it up and in the old man who can't. I believe in the phallocentrism of every second, of every male, in every class and every country. . . .[7]

The French feminists are more convinced than their American counterparts of the difference between male and female; they are more imbued with notions of sexual specificity. These French feminists attack where it hurts most. They poke fun at the male erection, the male preoccupation with getting it up, keeping it up, and the ways in which the life and death of the penis are projected into other aspects of culture: in the need for immortality and posterity, in the fear of death, in the centralized organization of political systems, in the impossibility of living in the here and now. This is particularly true of the more popular writers: Françoise Parturier, Annie Leclerc, Benoîte Groult. But Hélène Cixous, in a less direct but no less vigorous manner, also ridicules "the little pocket signifier." Those who follow the psychoanalytic tradition speak not of the penis but of the phallus. Their attempts to find a discourse that is not governed by a prime signifier—a discourse compatible with rigorous atheism, a discourse that is not God centered—are in fact attempts at decentering the reigning phallus from its dominant position in the symbolic order. They refuse ritual acts of obedience to the phallus, they refuse to accept the inevitable oppression of women described by Freud and Lévi-Strauss as the sine qua non of human culture: the obligatory journey from clitoris to vagina; the inevitable exchange of women. In both cases what is being massively repressed, as Julia Kristeva has ingeniously pointed out in Des chinoises, is the figure of la mère qui jouit ("the mother who has sexual pleasure").[8] It is therefore not surprising

---

[7] Françoise d'Eaubonne, Le féminisme ou la mort, pp. 18–19.

[8] The verb jouir ("to enjoy, to experience sexual pleasure") and the substantive la jouissance ("sexual pleasure, bliss, rapture") occur frequently in the texts of the new French feminisms. We have constantly used the English words "sexual pleasure" in our translations. This pleasure, when attributed to a woman, is considered to be of a different order from the pleasure that is represented within the male libidinal economy often described in terms of the capitalist gain and profit motive. Women's jouissance carries with it the notion of fluidity, diffusion, duration. It is a kind of

that one of the areas of greatest verbal concentration among French feminists is the description of woman's pleasure: from Annie Leclerc's deification of woman's body to Monique Wittig's deconstruction and reconstruction of the lesbian body, from the post-Lacanian analyses of Luce Irigaray to the revised imagery of Hélène Cixous. Because these texts exist and are circulated a change has already taken place. In spite of the very serious problem of reconciling language disruption which leads to esoteric writing, and the desire to reach the masses of women, radical feminism has engendered at least two texts that seem destined, perhaps ironically, for a measure of immortality: Monique Wittig's *Les guérillères*, 1969 and Hélène Cixous's "Le rire de la méduse," 1975 ["The Laugh of the Medusa"]. Both texts are innovative combinations of fiction and manifesto. Although neither conforms to traditional genre semiotics, each has already reached a wider audience than the more restricted feminist tracts which tend to appeal by virtue of content alone. It is fitting, too, that *Les guérillères* should have been published in 1969 before the French women's liberation movement was officially launched. It announces and marks with apocalyptic urgency the initial elan and solidarity of the movement. "The Laugh of the Medusa" marks a second moment. The storytelling *guérillères* have been replaced, at least temporarily, by the poet-intellectual no less determined to change heads and hearts. Contextual differences are less important than textual similarities. On the level of a new imagery of woman, the explicit ideological disagreements between Monique Wittig and Hélène Cixous fade. The reader reacts to the representation of the female triumphant.

It is too early to say whether or not the new French feminisms will eventually have as strong an impact on the consciousness and the behavior of French women as the new American feminisms have had on American women. It may well be that specific cultural influences will continue to dominate in certain areas, withstanding all feminist critiques —fashion in France, which dictates not only styles of elegance, but reinforces male images of female attractiveness; religion in the United States, which impedes certain forms of Marxist and psychoanalytic analysis, thus strengthening an essentialist, nontheoretical position. But it is clear, despite these local resistances, that the new feminisms have produced, within each culture, modes of thought and of conduct which, while intimately linked to the particular culture, nonetheless add to it a pre-

---

potlatch in the world of orgasms, a giving, expending, dispensing of pleasure without concern about ends or closure. One can easily see how the same imagery could be used to describe women's writing.

For further discussion of the representation of the virgin mother as opposed to the mother who knows sexual pleasure, see Luce Irigaray, "This Sex Which is Not One," in "Demystifications."

viously unknown dimension. Feminist theory and feminist action in France and in the United States are among the few encouraging signs of an attempt to rethink, in depth, the human adventure and, whatever the despair, to move on toward what is yet to be.

Because the prestige of the French word in French culture is far greater than the ridicule that impedes the feminist initiative, the future of French feminisms and of the writing that engenders them and is engendered by them lies open.

Beginnings

This section contains Simone de Beauvoir's Introduction to The Second Sex, *a text that occupies a central position in the history of discourse on women and feminism.*

Simone de Beauvoir

For a long time I have hesitated to write a book on woman. The subject is irritating, especially to women; and it is not new. Enough ink has been spilled in the quarreling over feminism, now practically over, and perhaps we should say no more about it. It is still talked about, however, for the voluminous nonsense uttered during the last century seems to have done little to illuminate the problem. After all, is there a problem? And if so, what is it? Are there women, really? Most assuredly the theory of the eternal feminine still has its adherents who will whisper in your ear: "Even in Russia women still are *women*"; and other erudite persons—sometimes the very same—say with a sigh: "Woman is losing her way, woman is lost." One wonders if women still exist, if they will always exist, whether or not it is desirable that they should, what place they occupy in this world, what their place should be. "What has become of women?" was asked recently in an ephemeral magazine.[1]

But first we must ask: what is a woman? "*Tota mulier in utero*," says one, "Woman is a womb." But in speaking of certain women, connoisseurs declare that they are not women, although they are equipped with a uterus like the rest. All agree in recognizing the fact that females exist in the human species; today as always they make up about one half of humanity. And yet we are told that femininity is in danger; we are exhorted to be women, remain women, become women. It would appear, then, that every female human being is not necessarily a woman; to be so considered she must share in that mysterious and threatened reality known as femininity. Is this attribute something secreted by the ovaries? Or is it a Platonic essence, a product of the philosophic imagination?

Introduction to *The Second Sex* [*Le deuxième sexe*] (Vintage, 1974)
[1] *Franchise*, now defunct. There are three kinds of footnotes accompanying the translations: those made by the author of the text; those made by the translator which explain French references (indicated by Tr.); and those made by the editors which point out recurrent features of new French feminist writing (indicated by Ed.).
—Ed.

Is a rustling petticoat enough to bring it down to earth? Although some women try zealously to incarnate this essence, it is hardly patentable. It is frequently described in vague and dazzling terms that seem to have been borrowed from the vocabulary of the seers, and indeed in the times of St. Thomas it was considered an essence as certainly defined as the somniferous virtue of the poppy.

But conceptualism has lost ground. The biological and social sciences no longer admit the existence of unchangeably fixed entities that determine given characteristics, such as those ascribed to woman, the Jew, or the Negro. Science regards any characteristic as a reaction dependent in part upon a *situation*. If today femininity no longer exists, then it never existed. But does the word *woman*, then, have no specific content? This is stoutly affirmed by those who hold to the philosophy of the enlightenment, of rationalism, of nominalism; women, to them, are merely the human beings arbitrarily designated by the word "woman." Many American women particularly are prepared to think that there is no longer any place for woman as such; if a backward individual still takes herself for a woman, her friends advise her to be psychoanalyzed and thus get rid of this obsession. In regard to a work, *Modern Woman: The Lost Sex*, which in other respects has its irritating features, Dorothy Parker has written: "I cannot be just to books which treat of woman as woman. ... My idea is that all of us, men as well as women, should be regarded as human beings." But nominalism is a rather inadequate doctrine, and the antifeminists have had no trouble in showing that women simply *are not* men. Surely woman is, like man, a human being; but such a declaration is abstract. The fact is that every concrete human being is always a singular, separate individual. To decline to accept such notions as the eternal feminine, the black soul, the Jewish character, is not to deny that Jews, Negroes, women exist today—this denial does not represent a liberation for those concerned, but rather a flight from reality. Some years ago a well-known woman writer refused to permit her portrait to appear in a series of photographs especially devoted to women writers; she wished to be counted among the men. But in order to gain this privilege she made use of her husband's influence! Women who assert that they are men lay claim none the less to masculine consideration and respect. I recall also a young Trotskyite standing on a platform at a boisterous meeting and getting ready to use her fists, in spite of her evident fragility. She was denying her feminine weakness; but it was for love of a militant male whose equal she wished to be. The attitude of defiance of many American women proves that they are haunted by a sense of their femininity. In truth, to go for a walk with one's eyes open is enough to demonstrate that humanity is divided into two classes of individuals whose clothes, faces, bodies, smiles, gaits, interests, and occupations are manifestly different. Perhaps these differences are superficial, perhaps they are destined to disappear. What is certain is that right now they do most obviously exist.

If her functioning as a female is not enough to define woman, if we decline also to explain her through "the eternal feminine," and if nevertheless we admit, provisionally, that women do exist, then we must face the question: what is a woman?

To state the question is, to me, to suggest, at once, a preliminary answer. The fact that I ask it is in itself significant. A man would never get the notion of writing a book on the peculiar situation of the human male.[2] But if I wish to define myself, I must first of all say: "I am a woman"; on this truth must be based all further discussion. A man never begins by presenting himself as an individual of a certain sex; it goes without saying that he is a man. The terms *masculine* and *feminine* are used symmetrically only as a matter of form, as on legal papers. In actuality the relation of the two sexes is not quite like that of two electrical poles, for man represents both the positive and the neutral, as is indicated by the common use of *man* to designate human beings in general; whereas woman represents only the negative, defined by limiting criteria, without reciprocity. In the midst of an abstract discussion it is vexing to hear a man say: "You think thus and so because you are a woman"; but I know that my only defense is to reply: "I think thus and so because it is true," thereby removing my subjective self from the argument. It would be out of the question to reply: "And you think the contrary because you are a man," [3] for it is understood that the fact of being a man is no peculiarity. A man is in the right in being a man; it is the woman who is in the wrong. It amounts to this: just as for the ancients there was an absolute vertical with reference to which the oblique was defined, so there is an absolute human type, the masculine. Woman has ovaries, a uterus; these peculiarities imprison her in her subjectivity, circumscribe her within the limits of her own nature. It is often said that she thinks with her glands. Man superbly ignores the fact that his anatomy also includes glands, such as the testicles, and that they secrete hormones. He thinks of his body as a direct and normal connection with the world, which he believes he apprehends objectively, whereas he regards the body of woman as a hindrance, a prison, weighed down by everything peculiar to it. "The female is a female by virtue of a certain lack of qualities," said Aristotle; "we should regard the female

[2] The Kinsey Report [Alfred C. Kinsey and others: *Sexual Behavior in the Human Male* (W. B. Saunders Co., 1948)] is no exception, for it is limited to describing the sexual characteristics of American men, which is quite a different matter.
[3] This is no longer true. Many new French feminists criticize the way men—as opposed to women—think.—Ed.

nature as afflicted with a natural defectiveness." And St. Thomas for his part pronounced woman to be an "imperfect man," an "incidental" being. This is symbolized in Genesis where Eve is depicted as made from what Bossuet called "a supernumerary bone" of Adam.

Thus humanity is male and man defines woman not in herself but as relative to him; she is not regarded as an autonomous being. Michelet writes: "Woman, the relative being. . . ." And Benda is most positive in his *Rapport d'Uriel*: "The body of man makes sense in itself quite apart from that of woman, whereas the latter seems wanting in significance by itself. . . . Man can think of himself without woman. She cannot think of herself without man." And she is simply what man decrees; thus she is called "the sex," by which is meant that she appears essentially to the male as a sexual being. For him she is sex—absolute sex, no less. She is defined and differentiated with reference to man and not he with reference to her; she is the incidental, the inessential as opposed to the essential. He is the Subject, he is the Absolute—she is the Other.[4]

The category of the *Other* is as primordial as consciousness itself. In the most primitive societies, in the most ancient mythologies, one finds the expression of a duality—that of the Self and the Other. This duality was not originally attached to the division of the sexes; it was not dependent upon any empirical facts. It is revealed in such works as that of Granet on Chinese thought and those of Dumézil on the East Indies and Rome. The feminine element was at first no more involved in such pairs as Varuna-Mitra, Uranus-Zeus, Sun-Moon, and Day-Night than it was in the contrasts between Good and Evil, lucky and unlucky auspices, right and left, God and Lucifer. Otherness is a fundamental category of human thought.

Thus it is that no group ever sets itself up as the One without at once setting up the Other over against itself. If three travelers chance to

---

[4] E. Lévinas expresses this idea most explicitly in his essay *Le temps et l'autre*. "Is there not a case in which otherness, alterity (*altérité*) unquestionably marks the nature of a being, as its essence, an instance of otherness not consisting purely and simply in the opposition of two species of the same genus? I think that the feminine represents the contrary in its absolute sense, this contrariness being in no wise affected by any relation between it and its correlative and thus remaining absolutely other. Sex is not a certain specific difference . . . no more is the sexual difference a mere contradiction. . . . Nor does this difference lie in the duality of two complementary terms, for two complementary terms imply a pre-existing whole. . . . Otherness reaches its full flowering in the feminine, a term of the same rank as consciousness but of opposite meaning."

I suppose that Lévinas does not forget that woman, too, is aware of her own consciousness, or ego. But it is striking that he deliberately takes a man's point of view, disregarding the reciprocity of subject and object. When he writes that woman is mystery, he implies that she is mystery for man. Thus his description, which is intended to be objective, is in fact an assertion of masculine privilege.

occupy the same compartment, that is enough to make vaguely hostile "others" out of all the rest of the passengers on the train. In small-town eyes all persons not belonging to the village are "strangers" and suspect; to the native of a country all who inhabit other countries are "foreigners"; Jews are "different" for the anti-Semite, Negroes are "inferior" for American racists, aborigines are "natives" for colonists, proletarians are the "lower class" for the privileged.

Lévi-Strauss, at the end of a profound work on the various forms of primitive societies, reaches the following conclusion: "Passage from the state of Nature to the state of Culture is marked by man's ability to view biological relations as a series of contrasts; duality, alternation, opposition, and symmetry, whether under definite or vague forms, constitute not so much phenomena to be explained as fundamental and immediately given data of social reality." [5] These phenomena would be incomprehensible if in fact human society were simply a *Mitsein* or fellowship based on solidarity and friendliness. Things become clear, on the contrary, if, following Hegel, we find in consciousness itself a fundamental hostility toward every other consciousness; the subject can be posed only in being opposed—he sets himself up as the essential, as opposed to the other, the inessential, the object.

But the other consciousness, the other ego, sets up a reciprocal claim. The native traveling abroad is shocked to find himself in turn regarded as a "stranger" by the natives of neighboring countries. As a matter of fact, wars, festivals, trading, treaties, and contests among tribes, nations, and classes tend to deprive the concept *Other* of its absolute sense and to make manifest its relativity; willy-nilly, individuals and groups are forced to realize the reciprocity of their relations. How is it, then, that this reciprocity has not been recognized between the sexes, that one of the contrasting terms is set up as the sole essential, denying any relativity in regard to its correlative and defining the latter as pure otherness? Why is it that women do not dispute male sovereignty? No subject will readily volunteer to become the object, the inessential; it is not the Other who, in defining himself as the Other, establishes the One. The Other is posed as such by the One in defining himself as the One. But if the Other is not to regain the status of being the One, he must be submissive enough to accept this alien point of view. Whence comes this submission in the case of woman?

There are, to be sure, other cases in which a certain category has been able to dominate another completely for a time. Very often this privilege depends upon inequality of numbers—the majority imposes its rule

[5] See C. Lévi-Strauss: *Les structures élémentaires de la parenté*. My thanks are due to C. Lévi-Strauss for his kindness in furnishing me with the proofs of his work, which, among others, I have used liberally in Part II.

upon the minority or persecutes it. But women are not a minority, like the American Negroes or the Jews; there are as many women as men on earth. Again, the two groups concerned have often been originally independent; they may have been formerly unaware of each other's existence, or perhaps they recognized each other's autonomy. But a historical event has resulted in the subjugation of the weaker by the stronger. The scattering of the Jews, the introduction of slavery into America, the conquests of imperialism are examples in point. In these cases the oppressed retained at least the memory of former days; they possessed in common a past, a tradition, sometimes a religion or a culture.

The parallel drawn by Bebel between women and the proletariat is valid in that neither ever formed a minority or a separate collective unit of mankind. And instead of a single historical event it is in both cases a historical development that explains their status as a class and accounts for the membership of *particular individuals* in that class. But proletarians have not always existed, whereas there have always been women. They are women in virtue of their anatomy and physiology. Throughout history they have always been subordinated to men,[6] and hence their dependency is not the result of a historical event or a social change—it was not something that *occurred*. The reason why otherness in this case seems to be an absolute is in part that it lacks the contingent or incidental nature of historical facts. A condition brought about at a certain time can be abolished at some other time, as the Negroes of Haiti and others have proved; but it might seem that a natural condition is beyond the possibility of change. In truth, however, the nature of things is no more immutably given, once for all, than is historical reality. If woman seems to be the inessential which never becomes the essential, it is because she herself fails to bring about this change. Proletarians say "We"; Negroes also. Regarding themselves as subjects, they transform the bourgeois, the whites, into "others." But women do not say "We," except at some congress of feminists or similar formal demonstration; men say "women," and women use the same word in referring to themselves. They do not authentically assume a subjective attitude. The proletarians have accomplished the revolution in Russia, the Negroes in Haiti, the Indo-Chinese are battling for it in Indo-China; but the women's effort has never been anything more than a symbolic agitation. They have gained only what men have been willing to grant; they have taken nothing, they have only received.

---

[6] With rare exceptions, perhaps, like certain matriarchal rulers, queens, and the like.—Tr.

The reason for this is that women lack concrete means for organizing themselves into a unit which can stand face to face with the correlative unit. They have no past, no history, no religion of their own; and they have no such solidarity of work and interest as that of the proletariat. They are not even promiscuously herded together in the way that creates community feeling among the American Negroes, the ghetto Jews, the workers of Saint-Denis, or the factory hands of Renault. They live dispersed among the males, attached through residence, housework, economic condition, and social standing to certain men—fathers or husbands—more firmly than they are to other women. If they belong to the bourgeoisie, they feel solidarity with men of that class, not with proletarian women; if they are white, their allegiance is to white men, not to Negro women. The proletariat can propose to massacre the ruling class, and a sufficiently fanatical Jew or Negro might dream of getting sole possession of the atomic bomb and making humanity wholly Jewish or black; but woman cannot even dream of exterminating the males. The bond that unites her to her oppressors is not comparable to any other. The division of the sexes is a biological fact, not an event in human history. Male and female stand opposed within a *primordial Mitsein*, and woman has not broken it. The couple is a fundamental unity with its two halves riveted together, and the cleavage of society along the line of sex is impossible. Here is to be found the basic trait of woman: she is the Other in a totality of which the two components are necessary to one another.

One could suppose that this reciprocity might have facilitated the liberation of woman. When Hercules sat at the feet of Omphale and helped with her spinning, his desire for her held him captive; but why did she fail to gain a lasting power? To revenge herself on Jason, Medea killed their children; and this grim legend would seem to suggest that she might have obtained a formidable influence over him through his love for his offspring. In *Lysistrata* Aristophanes gaily depicts a band of women who joined forces to gain social ends through the sexual needs of their men; but this is only a play. In the legend of the Sabine women, the latter soon abandoned their plan of remaining sterile to punish their ravishers. In truth woman has not been socially emancipated through man's need—sexual desire and the desire for offspring—which makes the male dependent for satisfaction upon the female.

Master and slave, also, are united by a reciprocal need, in this case economic, which does not liberate the slave. In the relation of master to slave the master does not make a point of the need that he has for the other; he has in his grasp the power of satisfying this need through his own action; whereas the slave, in his dependent condition, his hope and fear, is quite conscious of the need he has for his master. Even if the need is at bottom equally urgent for both, it always works in favor of the oppressor and against the oppressed. That is why the liberation of the working class, for example, has been slow.

Now, woman has always been man's dependent, if not his slave; the two sexes have never shared the world in equality. And even today woman is heavily handicapped, though her situation is beginning to change. Almost nowhere is her legal status the same as man's,[7] and frequently it is much to her disadvantage. Even when her rights are legally recognized in the abstract, long-standing custom prevents their full expression in the mores. In the economic sphere men and women can almost be said to make up two castes; other things being equal, the former hold the better jobs, get higher wages, and have more opportunity for success than their new competitors. In industry and politics men have a great many more positions and they monopolize the most important posts. In addition to all this, they enjoy a traditional prestige that the education of children tends in every way to support, for the present enshrines the past—and in the past all history has been made by men. At the present time, when women are beginning to take part in the affairs of the world, it is still a world that belongs to men—they have no doubt of it at all and women have scarcely any. To decline to be the Other, to refuse to be a party to the deal—this would be for women to renounce all the advantages conferred upon them by their alliance with the superior caste. Man-the-sovereign will provide woman-the-liege with material protection and will undertake the moral justification of her existence; thus she can evade at once both economic risk and the metaphysical risk of a liberty in which ends and aims must be contrived without assistance. Indeed, along with the ethical urge of each individual to affirm his subjective existence, there is also the temptation to forgo liberty and become a thing. This is an inauspicious road, for he who takes it—passive, lost, ruined—becomes henceforth the creature of another's will, frustrated in his transcendence and deprived of every value. But it is an easy road; on it one avoids the strain involved in undertaking an authentic existence. When man makes of woman the *Other*, he may, then, expect her to manifest deep-seated tendencies toward complicity. Thus, woman may fail to lay claim to the status of subject because she lacks definite resources, because she feels the necessary bond that ties her to man regardless of reciprocity, and because she is often very well pleased with her role as the *Other*.

---

[7] At the moment an "equal rights" amendment to the Constitution of the United States is before Congress.—Tr. The Equal Rights Amendment was passed by Congress in 1972. It had in 1978 been ratified by thirty-five states.—Ed.

But it will be asked at once: how did all this begin? It is easy to see that the duality of the sexes, like any duality, gives rise to conflict. And doubtless the winner will assume the status of absolute. But why should man have won from the start? It seems possible that women could have won the victory; or that the outcome of the conflict might never have been decided. How is it that this world has always belonged to the men and that things have begun to change only recently? Is this change a good thing? Will it bring an equal sharing of the world between men and women?

These questions are not new, and they have often been answered. But the very fact that woman is the Other tends to cast suspicion upon all the justifications that men have ever been able to provide for it. These have all too evidently been dictated by men's interest. A little-known feminist of the seventeenth century, Poulain de la Barre, put it this way: "All that has been written about women by men should be suspect, for the men are at once judge and party to the lawsuit." Everywhere, at all times, the males have displayed their satisfaction in feeling that they are the lords of creation. "Blessed be God . . . that He did not make me a woman," say the Jews in their morning prayers, while their wives pray on a note of resignation: "Blessed be the Lord, who created me according to His will." The first among the blessings for which Plato thanked the gods was that he had been created free, not enslaved; the second, a man, not a woman. But the males could not enjoy this privilege fully unless they believed it to be founded on the absolute and the eternal; they sought to make the fact of their supremacy into a right. "Being men, those who have made and compiled the laws have favored their own sex, and jurists have elevated these laws into principles," to quote Poulain de la Barre once more.

Legislators, priests, philosophers, writers, and scientists have striven to show that the subordinate position of woman is willed in heaven and advantageous on earth. The religions invented by men reflect this wish for domination. In the legends of Eve and Pandora men have taken up arms against women. They have made use of philosophy and theology, as the quotations from Aristotle and St. Thomas have shown. Since ancient times satirists and moralists have delighted in showing up the weaknesses of women. We are familiar with the savage indictments hurled against women throughout French literature. Montherlant,[8] for example, follows the tradition of Jean de Meung, though with less gusto. This hostility may at times be well founded, often it is gratuitous; but in truth it more or less successfully conceals a desire for self-justification.

[8] French writer attacked by Simone de Beauvoir for his blatant misogyny and his suspicious inactivity during the German occupation.—Ed.

As Montaigne says, "It is easier to accuse one sex than to excuse the other." Sometimes what is going on is clear enough. For instance, the Roman law limiting the rights of woman cited "the imbecility, the instability of the sex" just when the weakening of family ties seemed to threaten the interests of male heirs. And in the effort to keep the married woman under guardianship, appeal was made in the sixteenth century to the authority of St. Augustine, who declared that "woman is a creature neither decisive nor constant," at a time when the single woman was thought capable of managing her property. Montaigne understood clearly how arbitrary and unjust was woman's appointed lot: "Women are not in the wrong when they decline to accept the rules laid down for them, since the men make these rules without consulting them. No wonder intrigue and strife abound." But he did not go so far as to champion their cause.

It was only later, in the eighteenth century, that genuinely democratic men began to view the matter objectively. Diderot, among others, strove to show that woman is, like man, a human being. Later, John Stuart Mill came fervently to her defense. But these philosophers displayed unusual impartiality. In the nineteenth century the feminist quarrel became again a quarrel of partisans. One of the consequences of the industrial revolution was the entrance of women into productive labor, and it was just here that the claims of the feminists emerged from the realm of theory and acquired an economic basis, while their opponents became the more aggressive. Although landed property lost power to some extent, the bourgeoisie clung to the old morality that found the guarantee of private property in the solidity of the family. Woman was ordered back into the home the more harshly as her emancipation became a real menace. Even within the working class the men endeavored to restrain woman's liberation, because they began to see the women as dangerous competitors—the more so because they were accustomed to work for lower wages.

In proving woman's inferiority, the antifeminists then began to draw not only upon religion, philosophy, and theology, as before, but also upon science—biology, experimental psychology, etc. At most they were willing to grant "equality in difference" to the *other* sex. That profitable formula is most significant; it is precisely like the "equal but separate" formula of the Jim Crow laws aimed at the North American Negroes. As is well known, this so-called equalitarian segregation has resulted only in the most extreme discrimination. The similarity just noted is in no way due to chance, for whether it is a race, a caste, a class, or a sex that is reduced to a position of inferiority, the methods of justification are the same. "The eternal feminine" corresponds to "the black soul" and to "the Jewish character." True, the Jewish problem is on the whole very different from the other two—to the anti-Semite the Jew is not so much an inferior as he is an enemy for whom there is to be granted no place on earth, for whom annihilation is the fate desired. But there are deep similarities between the situation of woman and that of the Negro. Both are being emancipated today from a like paternalism, and the former master class wishes to "keep them in their place"—that is, the place chosen for them. In both cases the former masters lavish more or less sincere eulogies, either on the virtues of "the good Negro" with his dormant, childish, merry soul—the submissive Negro—or on the merits of the woman who is "truly feminine"—that is, frivolous, infantile, irresponsible—the submissive woman. In both cases the dominant class bases its argument on a state of affairs that it has itself created. As George Bernard Shaw puts it, in substance, "The American white relegates the black to the rank of shoeshine boy; and he concludes from this that the black is good for nothing but shining shoes." This vicious circle is met with in all analogous circumstances; when an individual (or a group of individuals) is kept in a situation of inferiority, the fact is that he *is* inferior. But the significance of the verb *to be* must be rightly understood here; it is in bad faith to give it a static value when it really has the dynamic Hegelian sense of "to have become." Yes, women on the whole *are* today inferior to men; that is, their situation affords them fewer possibilities. The question is: should that state of affairs continue?

Many men hope that it will continue; not all have given up the battle. The conservative bourgeoisie still see in the emancipation of women a menace to their morality and their interests. Some men dread feminine[9] competition. Recently a male student wrote in the *Hebdo-Latin*: "Every woman student who goes into medicine or law robs us of a job." He never questioned his rights in this world. And economic interests are not the only ones concerned. One of the benefits that oppression confers upon the oppressors is that the most humble among them is made to *feel* superior; thus, a "poor white" in the South can console himself with the thought that he is not a "dirty nigger"—and the more prosperous whites cleverly exploit this pride.

Similarly, the most mediocre of males feels himself a demigod as compared with women. It was much easier for M. de Montherlant to think himself a hero when he faced women (and women chosen for his purpose) than when he was obliged to act the man among men—something many women have done better than he, for that matter. And in September 1948, in one of his articles in the *Figaro littéraire*, Claude

[9] The adjective "féminin(e)" is often used in French as a synonym for woman, pertaining to woman. Unlike its English equivalent it is a classificatory, not a judgmental, term, i.e., "la concurrence féminine" does not mean that the competition is feminine (soft, tender, delicate) but that women are competing.—Ed.

Mauriac—whose great originality is admired by all—could [10] write regarding woman: "*We* listen on a tone [*sic!*] of polite indifference . . . to the most brilliant among them, well knowing that her wit reflects more or less luminously ideas that come from *us.*" Evidently the speaker referred to is not reflecting the ideas of Mauriac himself, for no one knows of his having any. It may be that she reflects ideas originating with men, but then, even among men there are those who have been known to appropriate ideas not their own; and one can well ask whether Claude Mauriac might not find more interesting a conversation reflecting Descartes, Marx, or Gide rather than himself. What is really remarkable is that by using the questionable *we* he identifies himself with St. Paul, Hegel, Lenin, and Nietzsche, and from the lofty eminence of their grandeur looks down disdainfully upon the bevy of women who make bold to converse with him on a footing of equality. In truth, I know of more than one woman who would refuse to suffer with patience Mauriac's "tone of polite indifference."

I have lingered on this example because the masculine attitude is here displayed with disarming ingenuousness. But men profit in many more subtle ways from the otherness, the alterity of woman. Here is miraculous balm for those afflicted with an inferiority complex, and indeed no one is more arrogant toward women, more aggressive or scornful, than the man who is anxious about his virility. Those who are not fear-ridden in the presence of their fellow men are much more disposed to recognize a fellow creature in woman; but even to these the myth of Woman, the Other, is precious for many reasons.[11] They cannot be blamed for not cheerfully relinquishing all the benefits they derive from the myth, for they realize what they would lose in relinquishing woman as they fancy her to be, while they fail to realize what they have to gain from the woman of tomorrow. Refusal to pose oneself as the Subject, unique and absolute, requires great self-denial. Furthermore, the vast majority of men make no such claim explicitly. They do not *postulate* woman as inferior, for today they are too thoroughly imbued with the ideal of democracy not to recognize all human beings as equals.

In the bosom of the family, woman seems in the eyes of childhood and youth to be clothed in the same social dignity as the adult males.

[10] Or at least he thought he could.

[11] A significant article on this theme by Michel Carrouges appeared in no. 292 of the *Cahiers du sud*. He writes indignantly: "Would that there were no woman-myth at all but only a cohort of cooks, matrons, prostitutes, and blue-stockings serving functions of pleasure or usefulness!" That is to say, in his view woman has no existence in and for herself; he thinks only of her *function* in the male world. Her reason for existence lies in man. But then, in fact, her poetic "function" as a myth might be more valued than any other. The real problem is precisely to find out why woman should be defined with relation to man.

Later on, the young man, desiring and loving, experiences the resistance, the independence of the woman desired and loved; in marriage, he respects woman as wife and mother, and in the concrete events of conjugal life she stands there before him as a free being. He can therefore feel that social subordination as between the sexes no longer exists and that on the whole, in spite of differences, woman is an equal. As, however, he observes some points of inferiority—the most important being unfitness for the professions—he attributes these to natural causes. When he is in a co-operative and benevolent relation with woman, his theme is the principle of abstract equality, and he does not base his attitude upon such inequality as may exist. But when he is in conflict with her, the situation is reversed: his theme will be the existing inequality, and he will even take it as justification for denying abstract equality.[12]

So it is that many men will affirm as if in good faith that women *are* the equals of man and that they have nothing to clamor for, while *at the same time* they will say that women can never be the equals of man and that their demands are in vain. It is, in point of fact, a difficult matter for man to realize the extreme importance of social discriminations which seem outwardly insignificant but which produce in woman moral and intellectual effects so profound that they appear to spring from her original nature.[13] The most sympathetic of men never fully comprehend woman's concrete situation. And there is no reason to put much trust in the men when they rush to the defense of privileges whose full extent they can hardly measure. We shall not, then, permit ourselves to be intimidated by the number and violence of the attacks launched against women, nor to be entrapped by the self-seeking eulogies bestowed on the "true woman," nor to profit by the enthusiasm for woman's destiny manifested by men who would not for the world have any part of it.

We should consider the arguments of the feminists with no less suspicion, however, for very often their controversial aim deprives them of all real value. If the "woman question" seems trivial, it is because masculine arrogance has made of it a "quarrel"; and when quarreling one no longer reasons well. People have tirelessly sought to prove that woman is superior, inferior, or equal to man. Some say that, having been created after Adam, she is evidently a secondary being; others say, on the contrary, that Adam was only a rough draft and that God succeeded in

---

12 For example, a man will say that he considers his wife in no wise degraded because she has no gainful occupation. The profession of housewife is just as lofty, and so on. But when the first quarrel comes, he will exclaim: "Why you couldn't make your living without me!"
13 The specific purpose of Book II of this study is to describe this process.

producing the human being in perfection when He created Eve. Woman's brain is smaller; yes, but it is relatively larger. Christ was made a man; yes, but perhaps for his greater humility. Each argument at once suggests its opposite, and both are often fallacious. If we are to gain understanding, we must get out of these ruts; we must discard the vague notions of superiority, inferiority, equality which have hitherto corrupted every discussion of the subject and start afresh.

Very well, but just how shall we pose the question? And, to begin with, who are we to propound it at all? Man is at once judge and party to the case; but so is woman. What we need is an angel—neither man nor woman—but where shall we find one? Still, the angel would be poorly qualified to speak, for an angel is ignorant of all the basic facts involved in the problem. With a hermaphrodite we should be no better off, for here the situation is most peculiar; the hermaphrodite is not really the combination of a whole man and a whole woman, but consists of parts of each and thus is neither. It looks to me as if there are, after all, certain women who are best qualified to elucidate the situation of woman. Let us not be misled by the sophism that because Epimenides was a Cretan he was necessarily a liar; it is not a mysterious essence that compels men and women to act in good or in bad faith, it is their situation that inclines them more or less toward the search for truth. Many of today's women, fortunate in the restoration of all the privileges pertaining to the estate of the human being, can afford the luxury of impartiality—we even recognize its necessity. We are no longer like our partisan elders; by and large we have won the game. In recent debates on the status of women, the United Nations has persistently maintained that the equality of the sexes is now becoming a reality, and already some of us have never had to sense in our femininity an inconvenience or an obstacle. Many problems appear to us to be more pressing than those which concern us in particular, and this detachment even allows us to hope that our attitude will be objective. Still, we know the feminine world more intimately than do the men because we have our roots in it, we grasp more immediately than do men what it means to a human being to be feminine; and we are more concerned with such knowledge. I have said that there are more pressing problems, but this does not prevent us from seeing some importance in asking how the fact of being women will affect our lives. What opportunities precisely have been given us and what withheld? What fate awaits our younger sisters, and what directions should they take? It is significant that books by women on women are in general animated in our day less by a wish to demand our rights than by an effort toward clarity and understanding. As we emerge from an era of excessive controversy, this book is offered as one attempt among others to confirm that statement.

But it is doubtless impossible to approach any human problem with a mind free from bias. The way in which questions are put, the points of view assumed, presuppose a relativity of interest; all characteristics imply values, and every objective description, so called, implies an ethical background. Rather than attempt to conceal principles more or less definitely implied, it is better to state them openly at the beginning. This will make it unnecessary to specify on every page in just what sense one uses such words as *superior, inferior, better, worse, progress, reaction,* and the like. If we survey some of the works on woman, we note that one of the points of view most frequently adopted is that of the public good, the general interest; and one always means by this the benefit of society as one wishes it to be maintained or established. For our part, we hold that the only public good is that which assures the private good of the citizens; we shall pass judgment on institutions according to their effectiveness in giving concrete opportunities to individuals. But we do not confuse the idea of private interest with that of happiness, although that is another common point of view. Are not women of the harem more happy than women voters? Is not the housekeeper happier than the working-woman? It is not too clear just what the word *happy* really means and still less what true values it may mask. There is no possibility of measuring the happiness of others, and it is always easy to describe as happy the situation in which one wishes to place them.

In particular those who are condemned to stagnation are often pronounced happy on the pretext that happiness consists in being at rest. This notion we reject, for our perspective is that of existentialist ethics. Every subject plays his part as such specifically through exploits or projects that serve as a mode of transcendence; he achieves liberty only through a continual reaching out toward other liberties. There is no justification for present existence other than its expansion into an indefinitely open future. Every time transcendence falls back into immanence, stagnation, there is a degradation of existence into the *"en-soi"*—the brutish life of subjection to given conditions—and of liberty into constraint and contingence. This downfall represents a moral fault if the subject consents to it; if it is inflicted upon him, it spells frustration and oppression. In both cases it is an absolute evil. Every individual concerned to justify his existence feels that his existence involves an undefined need to transcend himself, to engage in freely chosen projects.

Now, what peculiarly signalizes the situation of woman is that she—a free and autonomous being like all human creatures—nevertheless finds herself living in a world where men compel her to assume the status of the Other. They propose to stabilize her as object and to doom her to immanence since her transcendence is to be overshadowed and forever transcended by another ego (*conscience*) which is essential and sovereign. The drama of woman lies in this conflict between the fundamental aspirations of every subject (ego)—who always regards the self as the essential—and the compulsions of a situation in which she is the inessential. How can a human being in woman's situation attain fulfillment? What roads are open to her? Which are blocked? How can independence be recovered in a state of dependency? What circumstances limit woman's liberty and how can they be overcome? These are the fundamental questions on which I would fain throw some light. This means that I am interested in the fortunes of the individual as defined not in terms of happiness but in terms of liberty.

Quite evidently this problem would be without significance if we were to believe that woman's destiny is inevitably determined by physiological, psychological, or economic forces. Hence I shall discuss first of all the light in which woman is viewed by biology, psychoanalysis, and historical materialism. Next I shall try to show exactly how the concept of the "truly feminine" has been fashioned—why woman has been defined as the Other—and what have been the consequences from man's point of view. Then from woman's point of view I shall describe the world in which women must live; and thus we shall be able to envisage the difficulties in their way as, endeavoring to make their escape from the sphere hitherto assigned them, they aspire to full membership in the human race.

Translated by H. M. Parshley

Demystifications

This section presents critical analyses of certain official male models and categories such as phallocentrism, logocentrism, misogyny, pornography, and heroism.

Françoise Parturier

Explain to me why the most intelligent man whose mind is the most scientifically advanced about the laws of procreation can turn around and start thinking like a rabbit. "Woman's destiny is inscribed in her anatomy—" "Woman's alienation is a law of the species—" Yet you navigate the cosmos, you know the temperature of Venus, you can graft live cats onto live rats and live rats onto live birds, you can change the color of a fly's eyes, you can impregnate virgin tree frogs, you can freeze sperm cells, you can split the atom; nothing stops you when you do experiments, no scruple, no risk; bombs explode everywhere and your laboratories are full of monsters invented by your mad need for knowledge; you don't shy from any act of cruelty, you make life scream beneath your scalpels and your flame throwers, you plunge past all limits but suddenly, at the ovary's edge, you become cautious, timid, respectful, even pious. You no longer dare to touch nature. To be sure, you always felt pity for "this delightful, adorable thing" whenever she exhausted herself making man's offspring, but you could only pity her in private— and adorn her in public. And you, who are usually so eager to display your skill, so proud of your discoveries, you have hidden away in your drawers for half a century those inventions which would have allowed woman herself biologically to triumph over woman's destiny. You have sacrificed two generations and have preferred to let millions of women abort in order not to clash, you said, with the principles of a religion which you no longer obey, even while claiming to believe in it. And when you were reproached for your silence, you answered that you agreed, that it was all too bad, but that unfortunately you couldn't have said anything since it was against the law— Well, on the contrary, sir, you *could* have done something: you could have changed the laws; the proof is that you

---

From *Lettre ouverte aux hommes* [*An open letter to men*] (Albin Michel, 1968). This text is in the form of a letter to an imaginary male interlocutor who sometimes responds to the narrator's accusations.

have just done that. But as for the famous decree of December 1967[1] which frees women from their biological servitude and which is as important for them as the laws of 1789 are for you (since the condom is the key to the active world and, in its own way, a sexual version of the night of August 4, 1789)[2]—the truth of it is, they say, that it was self-interest alone that made you propose it and self-interest alone that made you vote for it. There had to be an electoral struggle of unprecedented violence for the male opposition to hold up the Pill like a candy, and there had to be a brush with the shadow of defeat for the male majority to finally agree to swallow that pill. And they did this not joyfully, but in order to take the candy from their opponent's hand and to try to reap from under their noses the next electoral harvest. The only ones to be congratulated are the few women, mostly doctors and lawyers, who dared put themselves on the wrong side of the law (therefore it *was* possible to do so) in order to make public opinion more informed and more sensitive.

By finding the right words to anesthetize your pride, like "happy motherhood," or to flatter the organizational and technocratic maniac in you, like the term "planning"—with the two combined in the expression "family planning"—by allowing you to appear responsible for the victory and progress, these women displayed tact and skill which I admire all the more knowing their true impatient natures and how they must have suffered because of the subtle and always intentional and masculine inertia, the famous "we'll see."

But really, sir, what frightens you so about the Pill? Could you be afraid that we are no longer afraid? . . .

—Let's assume, madam, that many middle-aged men, in a conservative milieu, think this way, and even do so unconsciously; but don't you think that paternalism, I mean misogyny, is really a thing of the past? What do you think?

[1] Law no. 67-1176, December 28, 1967: a timid law, full of restrictions, which brought contraception out of the clandestineness imposed by the July 1920 law. It authorizes "the manufacture and importation of contraceptive products," but the latter "can be sold only in drugstores and with the authorization of the Minister of Social Affairs." There are even further restrictions for minors and generally heavy penalties for those who disobey the law. (Pierrette Sartin, *Aujourd'hui la femme* [Stock, 1974], pp. 95–119.)—Tr.

[2] August 4, 1789: during this famous night session of the National Constituent Assembly, described as a "sacrificial frenzy" of "indescribable emotionalism," one deputy after another spoke and gave up his traditional rights and privileges. By the session's end, "the exhausted but happy deputies had legislated the Old Regime out of existence," making way for the Declaration of the Rights of Man. (Leo Gershoy, *The Era of the French Revolution* [D. Van Nostrand, 1957] pp. 34–36.)—Tr.

—Paternalistic misogyny and the misogyny of past generations are not the same thing. You can be paternalistic at the age of ten, as are so many little boys toward their mothers and sisters. Paternalism is an affectionate despotism which consists in proclaiming as good for women things that serve masculine interests and that allow one sex to exploit the other in good conscience. It would be amusing to list what is "good" for women: in addition to what Dr. Soubiran recommended [3]—that is, doing the laundry, making jam, being submissive, and living like Polish peasant women—some classic themes remain: being pregnant (wonderful for the complexion); being taken savagely by some Cossack; accepting a good punishment from time to time (women love that); always needing something to desire (something women, who are so impatient, find hard to understand), etc.

Be that as it may, the misogyny of the past, paternalistic or not, is flourishing today, and old man Chrysale[4] is not dead, but rather undergoing a revival. Some twelve-year-old boys who had been taken to see *Les femmes savantes* screamed with joy at the famous line: "The hen must not crow before the rooster."

And in a recent film, a boy said to his friends: "You should never talk with a chick before sundown," which is more realistic, but comes down to the same thing.

You were thinking, weren't you, sir, that my correspondents were old dotards who are hardened in their prejudices, but that the young boys of today— on the contrary, I think that young boys are even more misogynous than their fathers.

Here is a letter from a student which may shock you, sir, as it shocked me, but which is a document of sufficient interest for me to pass it on to you:

Dear Madam,

... Another attitude which is prevalent since woman has been "liberated from sexual prejudices" is reflected in these painful words which I heard spoken one day by a boy who had a girl in his arms: "A woman is a piece of ass." I'll bet this kind of boy has never responded to the sight of female nudity without a mouthful of obscene jibes. . . .

[3] Dr. Soubiran: writer of a medical column for the "woman's magazine" *Jours de France*. This simplified, paternalistic, "Ann Landers"-type of advice column reveals the author's support for the "happy housewife" and his sympathy for the unfortunate, sick women of today, "so little suited to their new condition that they become ill because of it" (Parturier, *Lettre ouverte aux hommes* [Albin Michel, 1974] p. 46.)—Tr.

[4] Chrysale: character in Molière's *Les femmes savantes:* a prosaic, pedantic bourgeois whose daughters' happiness is less important than his ideas on the danger of educated women.—Tr.

I showed this letter to young people who told me, "It's true, many boys talk like that," and sometimes worse: "A woman is a hole, a receptacle. Let them open their legs and shut up, that's all we ask of them." "But you see," they added, "it's often the girl's fault, and after all, they only get what they deserve. Since they act like whores, why be surprised that they are treated like whores?"

There you have them, your modern boys, all Turks: a harem for them and virtue for women. The contradiction doesn't bother them any more than it did their fathers, who in the end will have demystified feelings, but without also having reconciled their sons to the human body. And here we are back again at the scandal of female flesh, which you cannot forgive for being open to your needs. In all cases, outside of love which is a special grace, the woman who satisfies these needs finds herself denatured and degraded in your eyes. With certain exceptions, you respect only women you don't sleep with, your mother, your sister—Inaccessible women remain your loved ones: dead women, exiled women, women prisoners, women saints, fiancées, angels, queens, heroines, stars, infidels, fugitives. It's not women you love, sir, but Woman; that is, an invention which "real presence" doesn't live up to. You have in you a secret preference for imaginary pleasures. You fight for Isolde when it is forbidden to approach her, but as soon as she belongs to you, you place a sword between the two of you so you can sleep in peace.

The difference between you and your ancestors is that they exalted "woman" while belittling *women*, whereas today, with the demystification of love, you continue to denigrate women while no longer honoring the female principle. The twentieth century is all the more misogynous since physical love is freer, which proves that it is not prostitution you despise, but copulation in general. Another paradox of our time is that not until women were able to love you freely have they been so badly loved by you. But I see you are laughing—

—Not at all, not at all. I was only thinking like the young people you mentioned: whose fault is it? Personally, I don't despise women, but to listen to you, one could wonder if there isn't really something base in them that would explain why everywhere, in the whole world, at all times—

—You see, sir, you can't help despising women as soon as they do not scrupulously conform to the moral and social laws which you have decreed. You are an incontinent puritan, if I may say so. Modesty and feminine virtue are postulates you cling to. You go on living with your old ideas, and if morals change, it's because women refuse to be confined by the difficult qualities to which you have so generously given them exclusive rights.

For you there were two domains into which women were not supposed to venture, at the risk of losing their natural virtues: sexuality and intellectuality. You left them the heart, which is surely no bargain. For centuries you have carefully kept sex, the heart, and the mind separate, which gave you a pleasant triple life. Now that women have conquered the intellectual domain, you lead the offensive to hold on at least to the imprescriptible male rights over the physical domain; and since you seem to think that women want to play around for their own enjoyment and not yours, well, you will doubtless treat them like generous whores and take advantage of this great and wonderful freedom to catch them again when they round the corner and enslave them even better. In this way, by using the new morality, you are trying to renew your former rights, and you are taking advantage of this morality now to despise and molest not just whores, but all women. You want to be free, young ladies, well you'll see which games we boys like and enjoy.

The young men who reason this way are just the good pupils of a ferociously misogynous century. Never has the disdain for women, which is denied in laws and official remarks, gone so far as in our time, an era that has seen the triumph of thought and sex at the expense of the heart. Never has physical love been so coldly surrendered to the philosophers. With sex now subject to the exercises of thought, sexuality can no longer be sublimated in love, but rather in eroticism, which in the West is much more a philosophy, a cerebral enterprise, than an art of pleasure. Because it is founded on the theorem that woman is an object, that love and pleasure are two distinct realities which are mutually harmful, eroticism can only be misogynous.

And eroticism has established itself as master of contemporary artistic life: it's not by chance that we are now witnessing the triumph of the Marquis de Sade, who has been reedited, rehabilitated, finally admitted into the bosom of society, put forth as a modern, bold mind, a precursor whose imprisonment paid for the hypocrisy of his contemporaries, almost a martyr who was guilty of just whipping a few whores for his entertainment, nothing more!

Translated by Elissa Gelfand

Françoise d'Eaubonne

Patriarchal man is therefore above all responsible for the demographic madness, just as he is for the destruction of the environment and for the accelerated pollution which accompanies this madness, bequeathing an uninhabitable planet to posterity.

"The feminist movement is not international, it is planetary," says Carla Lonzi in *Spit on Hegel*.[1]

Thus a transfer of power is urgently needed, *then*, as soon as possible, a destruction of power.

The transfer must be made from phallocratic man, responsible for this sexist civilization, into the hands of the awakened women.

For we have seen that we can without hesitation hold man directly responsible for today's deplorable demographic situation, and not only male power: man at every level. For each Catholic housewife who persists in using the rhythm method,[2] there are ten other women who, no matter how reactionary in sexual matters, demand at least increased access to therapeutic abortions and contraceptive devices. We even read in *Elle*,[3] which is not an extremely progressive magazine, after the papal pronouncements on the issue: "I am Catholic and I don't agree." As dogged as is the resistance on this point of the Catholic Church, which in France has a considerable female clientele, when it is a question of their bodies and their control over the future, the most timid women tend to inform themselves, and even protest on occasion, if they enjoy a minimum of social status.

From *Le féminisme ou la mort* [Feminism or death] (Horay, 1974).

[1] An Italian feminist text to which Françoise d'Eaubonne often refers.—Tr.

[2] One must not exaggerate however. Fanatical about virginity and conjugal fidelity, the practicing Catholic becomes skeptical in the face of the prohibition of contraception. "Many *Catholic mothers* have only two or three children," observes Simone de Beauvoir (*The Second Sex*).

[3] A weekly women's magazine which includes, along with traditional "feminine" preoccupations, occasional controversial feminist questions.—Tr.

We are speaking here about French women. The picture would change for other countries. American and English women are much more determined in their demands for total sexual freedom; but American women in addition are outraged over discriminatory employment practices. Spanish and South American women remain silent in countries where, even in order to save the mother's life, abortion is often impossible; the number of illegal abortions in these countries is not known, but judging by Italy's example, it must be astonishingly high. But in general, the opinion of women in Europe and America is extremely sensitized on the issue of contraception and abortion. Birth control has *always* been women's obsession. Whatever the burden of excess births represents either for a father or for a nation, their experience never comes close to that experienced by the female Atlas, this weak body that carries the entire weight of the world.

That the Catholic Church, which excludes women from the priesthood, remains the principal obstacle to reevaluation of the question of abortion effectively illustrates that it is a man's problem. That those who officially have neither sexual relations nor children be charged with controlling and directing not only the sexual relations but even the reproductive life of run-of-the-mill people is hardly a scandal in our modern, our millennial culture; it is enough that these people are men. The Pope decides *ex cathedra*; the priests carry out his will; aside from this segment of the Catholic world, the rest of us will deal with people who are either among the faithful, or are not, who have sexual relations, children. But be they legislators, judges, doctors, —they are always men.[4] Men only became concerned with the problem of birth rate, as with that of the destruction of the environment, when the situation became catastrophic, even hopeless.

You will perhaps disagree with me here on the grounds that all society's evils therefore have a masculine origin. Since masculinity is the very essence of this society, why emphasize one aspect rather than another? This is largely true; but it warrants distinctions, important ones. On the one hand, the most negative attitudes and behavior of women are due to the men who formed and fashioned them as they are for men's own purposes, without a doubt; on the other hand, women preserve certain of these negative behaviors—just as in the oppressed groups, as the culture evolves, we find the worst reactionaries accomplices of the oppressor— even in spite of the evolution of male attitudes. Take an example: in modern attempts to emancipate women, however modest they may have been (since total emancipation can only be achieved with the revolution), the most resolute adversaries of this change are the masses of women.

---

[4] The proportion of women in these professions is still so small as to be negligible.

(Just as not so long ago the most spirited protests against government subsidies of large families came from the old proletarians who had raised their families themselves without help from the state.) The slackening of progress in sexual enlightenment and in giving minors access to the Pill, the strongest approval of the repression of homosexuals—these negative dispositions come from a majority of women. Women continue to defend the morality of the oppressor at a time when he is beginning to have doubts about its validity. On the other hand, if a woman's consciousness is raised, even just once in her life, nothing will stand in her way.

At the present moment, women are the only group that can lead the minorities in opposition, since women are the only majority to be treated as a minority.

The new advent of women has provided the young with the opportunity to live marginally and to manifest in every possible way, destructively but peacefully, their desire to start from scratch.—Spit on Hegel!

It is essential today that the spirit of the revolution to be accomplished go beyond what has been called until now the "revolutionary spirit," just as the latter went beyond reformism. Ultimately, it is no longer a revolution that we need, but a mutation, in order to solve the global problem of which the demographic threat is but one extreme aspect, undoubtedly the most severe. . . .

Practically everybody knows that today the two most immediate threats to survival are overpopulation and the destruction of our resources; fewer recognize the complete responsibility of the male System, in so far as it is male (and not capitalist or socialist) in these two dangers; but even fewer still have discovered that each of the *two* threats is the logical outcome of one of the *two* parallel discoveries which gave men their power over fifty centuries ago: their ability to plant the seed in the earth as in women, and their participation in the act of reproduction.

Up until then, women alone held the monopoly on agriculture, and the male believed them impregnated by the gods. From the moment he discovered at once his two capacities as farmer and procreator, he instituted what Lederer[5] calls "the great reversal" to his own advantage. Having taken possession of the land, thus of *productivity* (later of industry) and of woman's body (thus of *reproduction*), it was natural that

[5] Wolfgang Lederer, author of *The Fear of Women* (Harcourt Brace Jovanovich, Inc., 1968). The book is well known in France.—Tr.

the overexploitation of both of these would end in this threatening and parallel menace: overpopulation, surplus births, and destruction of the environment, surplus production.

The only change capable of saving the world today is that of the "great reversal" of male power which is represented, after agricultural overproductivity, by this mortal industrial expansion. Not "matriarchy," to be sure, nor "power-to-the-women," but destruction of power by women. And finally, the end of the tunnel: egalitarian management of a world to be *reborn* (and no longer "protected" as is still believed by the first wave of timid ecologists).

Translated by Betty Schmitz

Benoîte Groult

Ah! That dear old image of woman! Many people cannot watch it fade without feeling nostalgic, worried, or angry. This newly begun and irreversible change—woman's new-born indifference toward the various kinds of blackmail that have worked so well until now and her newly acquired taste for love that does not mean a fall from grace into sin, a love that does not mean the obligation to give herself completely—these are the things that are overthrowing the glorious tradition of feminine humiliation which has been the basis for masculine pride, the things that are setting off a hysterical/sadistic rage in all those who cannot accept giving up the fascinating and degrading relationship between hangman and victim.

Having exhausted many different methods, these unresigned people came up with an ingenious idea: coopting below the belt. Under the guise of exalting the freedom brought by the sexual revolution, they in fact treated all women like potential whores, thus counterbalancing the rights women had just obtained with debasement, defilement, and torture, all artistically packaged and presented as eroticism and pornography. Since virtue had been obligatory, promiscuity had to become a duty: this is the theory whose sordid echo can be found today in certain kinds of male behavior:

—You're not a virgin? So why are you making such a fuss? This is a common line of reasoning, in this case used by a male militant leftist on a female militant in order, in a sense, to limit her political independence by playing up her sexual dependence (case cited by *Les temps modernes*, 1974).

The huge wave of nude and chained adolescents, lustful and unchained old women, and ravenous female "deep throats" that is unfolding on film screens, and the complacent descriptions of so many despised,

From "Les portiers de nuit" [Night porters] in *Ainsi soit-elle* [Amen/Awomen] (Grasset, 1975).

stinking, tortured, ripped, pissed on, and pistol-raped cunts in specialized literature is only a more commercialized aspect of this same cooptation.

Ever eager to find illustrious supporting authorities (even if it involves deforming them for their own needs), the commercialized sex movement's theoreticians have unearthed the Marquis de Sade and undertaken to deify him; and since it would be impossible today to do without psychoanalytical references, they have also appropriated Freud who, in spite of his puritanical and rather bland sex life, provided some grist for their sinister mill. Reassured by the snobbism surrounding the Sade cult and by the reverential fear aroused by the name Freud, they had the temerity to claim that cruelty was the highest form of love since it conformed to both partners' deepest natures, satisfying both the female's passive masochism and the male's natural aggressiveness.

The truth is that this violent and death-associated sexuality is just a so-called new avatar of a morality which is as old as sin.

"The unique and supreme sensual pleasure of love lies in the certainty of causing pain," wrote Baudelaire, as could have Sade, Lautréamont, Masoch, Bataille, Leiris,[1] and a thousand others as well. "The essence of eroticism is defilement. . . . Sex makes me feel nothing but a sense of dread and repulsion. . . . I would say that that repulsion, horror are the very principle of my desire. . . . I often tend to think of the female organ as a dirty thing or as a wound, though no less attractive because of that, yet dangerous in itself like all bloody, mucous, contaminated things. . . . Woman, that obscene and infected horror." It doesn't matter who wrote this monotonous litany: the authors are all worthy spiritual sons of the Church Fathers; all feel the same fascinated horror for the female sexual organs. For them, the slit is the Devil: a hairy thing lying underneath a dress, a thing which lies open to filth and brings down the menstrual blood, the latter being the "formless horror of violence." This is very old language which even an occasionally admirable style cannot justify. Desire is reduced to the taste for that which is dirty, degrading, and destructive, which is to say, for death. This idea moves us onto familiar ground, the one ruled by the "Divine Marquis" who, to his credit, at least openly displayed "the most monstrous disdain for woman upon which a philosophy has ever been built."

We ought to be wary of his rehabilitation today. The truth is, "it is because of excessive imprisonment and vindictive and cowardly censorship that Sade has been put on a pedestal and consecrated a martyr, great philosopher, major writer and specialist in eroticism," writes dear Gérard

---

[1] Writers whose texts are part of the avant-garde canon. Benoîte Groult's attack on pornography is also an attack on those contemporary writers who analyze pornography in terms of its revolutionary potential. This list also includes Roland Barthes and Philippe Sollers, whom she mentions later.—Ed.

Zwang.[2] Suddenly his neurosis, whose shit- and blood-smeared portrait he tirelessly paints, has been colorfully embellished: "his neurosis has been made to become the erotic—" But once the characters have finished ejaculating, Zwang continues (and it's really good to see such lines come from a masculine pen), their "only desire is to take the floor and give endless sermons, in a style which is as lifeless as it is bombastic" and which even Georges Bataille admits must be read with patience and resignation.

A point common to all these authors—the way women are used:

"The owners of cunts are not worthy of attention."

"The state her heart and mind might be in absolutely doesn't matter."

"Do you feel pity for the chicken you eat? No, you don't even think about it. So do the same with women."

"I use a woman out of necessity as one uses a round and hollow receptacle for a different need."

"During coitus, it all flowed out of me as if I were dumping garbage into a sewer."

"It isn't at all necessary to give them pleasure in order to receive pleasure. Men should view them the way nature prescribes and the way the wisest peoples do—as nothing more than individuals created for man's pleasure, subject to man's whims, individuals whose weakness and wickedness deserve nothing but men's scorn."

"You will never again open your mouth here in the presence of a man except to scream or to caress."

It is by the style, not the themes, that we can recognize the authors. There is not the slightest trace of a kiss in the words of these morticians, not the slightest tenderness, not a gesture of complicity, no exchange of any kind: all the passages bear the mark of monstrous selfishness, morbid scatology, and the most classic of sado-anal regressions. There is virtually no mention of the clitoris in these works, since the "heroes" give no thought to wasting their time by arousing female pleasure. This organ is never mentioned in the works of Georges Bataille, who nonetheless is considered the great theoretician of eroticism. These writers' fantasms and pleasures are based solely on the ignominy of the cunt. Is the following sexual fantasy Sade's, Miller's or Bataille's? "I'd like a very lewd whore, I'd like her to spring off the toilet seat, I'd like her ass to really smell like shit and her cunt to smell like beached fish."

And is this anti-clerical ejaculation taken from Bataille, Miller, or Sade?

2 Dr. Gérard Zwang: author of *La fonction érotique* and *Le sexe de la femme*, whom Groult quotes frequently for his speaking "of sexuality with humor and of the female body with love" (*Ainsi soit-elle*, p. 99 n).—Tr.

Simone sucked off [the priest] again and brought him to the climax of sensory rage; then,
—That's not all, she said, now you must piss.
She slapped him on the face a second time, then stripped naked before him, and I stimulated her sex. Don Aminado noisily filled with urine the chalice which Simone was holding beneath his penis.
—And now drink, said Sir Edmund.
The poor creature drank in unspeakably vile ecstasy.

The heroine of *The Story of O* [3] has the same alluring program to follow:[4] "Your hands are not your own, nor are your breasts, and especially none of your body's orifices which we can explore and plunge into as we wish."

No matter what book it is, we always find the same male hero who, with the same arrogance, takes his pleasure in some creature who for him is reduced to two holes in the bottom of her body, plus a third on the bottom of her face; and he insists upon calling this creature "woman," even though she is nothing more than a doll that wets and cries, but can't even say "mama" any more.

Even now it still seems that the only true act of subversion and the best way to free society from its bourgeois morality is to rewrite *Justine*, *Sexus*, or *The Story of O*, only seasoned with that little extra violence and hate that are so widely sanctioned and appreciated today. Stylistic marvels or an occasionally brilliant talent may turn these books into works of art or aphrodisiacs; but it is staggering for Roland Barthes, Philippe Sollers, or Michel Leiris to speak of these books as revolutionary acts when in fact they join the tradition of the most banal sadism. Both Madeleine Chapsal's remark about Tony Duvert's *Paysage de fantaisie*— "The difficulty of reading it brings back the often-lost dimension of *subversive* activity"— and Poirot-Delpech's comment that the same book evokes "the only true *subversiveness* that can lead to a *liberated* [5] world" seem all the more surprising since these authors, far from seeming liberated, instead show all signs of being slaves to long-standing obsessions and phobias. In fact, beneath their pseudo-revolutionary and pseudo-modern themes, they faithfully perpetuate the old curse of original sin

[3] Originally published in 1954, under the pseudonym Pauline Réage, *L'histoire d'O* has for more than twenty years been the center of a literary and political controversy. Feminists in France reacted violently to the first showing of the film in 1975. —Ed.
[4] As do Miller's, Mailer's, Lawrence's, and Michel Bernard's obedient heroines. —Tr.
[5] Groult's italics.—Tr.

and all the superstitious taboos of that society they claim they are destroying.

It's along these lines that Pierre Guyotat's *Eden, Eden, Eden* (which would more appropriately be called "Gehenna, Gehenna, Gehenna"—) has been put forth as a free or liberated text: free of all objects and symbols. "One has the impression the text is writing itself in that empty space in which the traditional elements of discourse would be "de trop'—." [6] It seems to me—and admittedly I am not a critic—that Guyotat's works, as well as Tony Duvert's, contain, if not the traditional components of discourse, at least all the components of the most classic pornographic literature.

"The old man the old woman are naked—I have brought several whips there we are the strongest men we each have a whip we whip them bloody and they obey—The old lady lying crosswise chains on all four limbs that are stretched by winches her legs move further and further apart her hips make a horrible cracking noise her cunt opens we plunge in a spike-covered club whose points have been soaked in a madness-inducing solution...."

There are 270 pages of this style of "free text."

Dammit, no! I'm sick and tired of these same old obsessions that never change, even in "modern style" without punctuation; I'm sick and tired of the way eminent philosophers and sociologists put forth as "free," "new," and "revolutionary" those same old perverse scripts which do nothing but try, unsuccessfully, to stage the little sadist's timeless repertory in a new way: the same old shit, pus, blood, sperm (oh! come on!), whips, and chains are dressed in smart new clothes; but the works they are in are regressive in that they continue to present women as imprisoned and taunted by men who spring from megalo-sexist dreams, men who discharge torrents of sperm upon creatures who just can't get enough of it.

That's revolution? That's subversion? To be precise, it's an extension of the bourgeois world, that world in which a few males obsessed with virile violence and convinced they are prophets shit on women, rip apart their vaginas, and kill them while fucking them—all because they hate women so for being desirable. It's a completely falsified world in which sex is artificially separated from life and served in nauseating doses until you can't stomach them any more. Once your first hunger is blunted, you could almost be overcome by reinvigorating laughter if it weren't all so full of deadly hatred and sadness.

Of course these texts, like any others, must have the right to be published, read, on occasion relished, and acted out by two, three, ten, as

---

[6] Groult quotes Roland Barthes's preface to Guyotat's book.—Tr.

many people as you wish. They speak to a nostalgia for violence and domination felt by more men than one would think. These texts can have a therapeutic importance and be of cathartic value since it's not easy today to find the setting and actors for such psychodramas. The concentration camp described by Lilianna Cavanni in her film *Night Porter* comes closest ultimately to those nightmarish castles, to that closed universe where the very depths of the human soul can overflow in complete peace.

But we mustn't allow ourselves to be impressed by prophesies, even when written by the most intelligent men. Sometimes, these books are wonderfully written. Often, they are titillating—stimulating, even. But they are irremediably old, slaves to old fantasms, defenders of a very old imagery of woman, and written by old children who never left the pee-pee-doodoo stage, all of which does not, of course, exclude poetic or literary genius.

He would keep her prisoner in the shack, she would always be tied up, nude, and given no water, no food, he goes there secretly after school he fucks her he never speaks to her she is dying slowly he bites her pussy until it bleeds he smashes in her ass too at right angles to the wall behind her he has nailed a piece of wood which cuts into her anus and he tears her on top of it while fucking her he pisses on her stomach before leaving he comes back in the evening he punches her dying face he spreads apart her vulva with his fingers he plunges in his hand he closes his fist while inside he unties the girl he throws her on the ground gets on his knees lifts her onto him by pulling her by her feet rocks her on his penis and comes once, twice while rocking—[7]

An apotheosis of the male in climax. That's not revolutionary—that's the sexual version of the "great binge." [8]

"In order to accomplish this undermining (of bourgeois morality), the author, Tony Duvert, relies in particular on pornography, which is considered less bourgeois and less coopting than eroticism" (Poirot-Delpech).

But aren't we precisely that—coopted—in this text by Tony Duvert? "Nothing like it has been tried since Sade," claims Roland Barthes in the preface. My eye,[9] as Bataille would say! Pornography has always existed and has never undermined anything. It has always given pleasure to the same men and the same women and shocked the same others. It

[7] Tony Duvert, *Sur un paysage de fantaisie* [A fantasy landscape].
[8] Groult uses the expression "grande bouffe," which brings to mind Marco Ferreri's film of the same name.—Tr.
[9] The reference is to George Bataille's *The Story of the Eye* [*Histoire de l'oeil*]—Tr.

has always shown contempt for the same jerks who, instead of simply admitting that these books help get them off, hold forth learnedly about these virile manifestations of violence and disdain, which they claim are "sometimes unbearable." (That's when it's best of all!)

The readers who are eaten up with Christianity feel the divine excitation of having transgressed while savoring "books that morality condemns, society disapproves, justice punishes, and the conscious represses" (M. Chapsal). In point of fact editors do not repress them, justice rarely punishes them, and society either could not be happier—or is completely unaware.

With his usual lucidity, Zwang points up the real motives behind censorship, whose advocates in essence agree with the Baudelairean or Sadean vision of love-as-defilement, though they don't dare express it in the same obscene terms: "The greatest artist can describe, paint, design, or film the most beautiful, most moving, most happy erotic scenes: he risks getting into trouble. If, however, he inserts misfortune, violence, ugliness, horror into these scenes, the fetid sauce will suit the consumer's palate— The poor adolescent who is tormented by eroticism (the real kind) has no chance of forming a pleasant, and therefore harmful image of the subject."

There is *no* danger whatsoever—except that of losing a little money— in writing books like these, and they have *no* revolutionary value whatsoever—they are even extraordinarily colonialist.

Moreover, this view of sexuality, which keeps sex cut off and guarded from life, is responsible for the astonishing visible change that takes place in so many of our contemporaries when they undress in sacrificial offering to what they consider the dark, animalistic part of their lives.

Who has not seen—and I am speaking of free women for whom marriage is not the secular equivalent of Mount Carmel and for whom youth is not a chaste wait for Prince Charming—the timid, bespectacled student, the learned exegetist of Plato or quantum theory, transformed himself, the moment he takes off his glasses and undershorts, into a brutal and driven ram who, while urging himself on with locker-room obscenities, arouses himself by acting out the rape of a captive?

Who has not met a distinguished leader, a politician, an elegant aristocrat, who was suddenly compelled by some kind of atavistic urge, some mass-produced imagery of sex, to talk like a gangster, to insult his partner and describe his sperm like celestial manna that has come to fertilize the desert? Why is it so often impossible to make love with the man you like, the whole man, rather than the beast which he believes is consigned for this purpose and which he carefully hides in his suit jacket after the bullfight—and before washing his hands—when he assumes his true personality once again and, with uncongested balls and a sigh of relief, thinks about something else? It is better yet if he doesn't feel obliged to ask his vanquished prey, "Well—are you happy?" and confuse contentment with happiness.

It is very possible to like that approach—women are so easily moved! But sometimes their surprise is a stinging one. "Oh no! not him too—" Generally speaking, what estrangement they feel!

If one day, miraculously, educational, familial, religious, and cultural censorship stopped relegating sex and pleasure to the domain of the unspeakable, if we could approach the "erotic function" in its entirety and with both a legitimate appetite and, when the opportunity arises, a little humor, what sudden relief that would bring to all those who suffer in love: the impotent, the frigid, the timid, the premature ejaculators, the overdue ejaculators, the men who are very scared of women, and the women who are very scared of men, and all the others too—

Erotic-pornographic books—at least those written by men—have the serious drawback of being sad. They wind up making an impression on the reader by dint of grandiose cruelty and lofty seriousness. I hold your thingy, you hold my thingy— The first one who laughs—

You just wish you could give these morticians a transfusion of Rabelaisian ribaldry—but they just might die of it.

At least our children wriggle with laughter when they play "touch me." But our writers take themselves seriously and prefer to writhe in pain. They would no doubt consider it blasphemous to set out on life's paths exclaiming joyously, as do the Polynesians: "May your penis penetrate" to which the polite response is a kindly, "And may your clitoris climax!"

Translated by Elissa Gelfand

Dominique Poggi

It is commonplace to say that pornography arises entirely from male fantasies and that it is a staging of male imaginings (if it is possible to use this term to designate this mediocre display of repetitive couplings, this lamentable redundancy of rapes, all of which, with the exception of a few details, are the same). In the following discussion, I shall analyze pornography from a slightly different point of view: one that will show the relationship between, on the one hand, the "discourse" that pornography produces and, on the other, the social relationships between men and women.

What pornography says

What does pornography "say," what images of women, their "nature," their pleasure does it purvey? As pornography presents them, women supposedly love to be forced, humiliated, whipped, and above all, raped. When the *Story of O* came out, *L'Express* wrote, "A woman has finally decided to admit: 'I like being beaten,'" as if the magazine had been privy to her personal confession. The conclusion to be drawn from this, once again in *L'Express*: "The *Story of O* is woman's future." What then is this future which awaits us and in which our bodies will bloom? A world of chains, whips, violent coitus; a world in which we will belong not to just one man, but to *all* men, who will pass us around to one another like pieces of merchandise;[1] a world in which we will be happy complying with rules established by our masters, who love us passion-

---

"Une apologie des rapports de domination" [A defense of the master-slave relationship] in *La quinzaine littéraire*, August 1976.

[1] The notion that the exchange of women is fundamental to social organization was proposed originally in 1949 by Claude Lévi-Strauss in his *Elementary Structures of Kinship* (*Les structures élémentaires de la parenté*). See Simone de Beauvoir, Introduction to *The Second Sex*, n. 5.)—Ed.

ately for our docility. The logic behind the *Story of O* is that men desire women and women desire to belong to men. Women are never represented as active subjects with their own desires. Their only wish is to be enslaved.

Pornography defends the coercive master-slave relationship that controls the sexual act. The supreme act, and the only acknowledged one, is coitus by brutal penetration, which coitus is performed either in the missionary position or via rear entry, but in all cases in a situation that reduces women to mere inflatable dolls. The "success" of the "love-" making is measured according to the volume of tears shed by the woman.

In point of fact, the sex act, as it appears in porn films, *is* a rape, and women who show any resistance, any signs of refusal or suffering, are always presented after the act as pleased, fulfilled, and entirely happy. From this, we can clearly see one of the principal functions of pornography: the purveying of an ideology of pleasure and enjoyment which urges rapelike relations, exalts rapists, and persuades the victims that they are in fact consenting and satisfied because they (and they alone) fully bloom only under masochistic conditions.

Women are raped every day and the threat of rape weighs on all women constantly; society, common sense, and the law believe that a woman who hitchhikes, walks alone at night, or travels alone (that is, without a protector) is taking a risk and that if she is raped, she has gotten, as it were, just what she deserved. We can see how rape and the fear of rape become deterrents to women who try to adopt autonomous modes of behaving and living.

This deterrent is not abstract: it takes the form of predators, rapists, and all those who interrogate, aggress, insult, and rape women in the street, in the woods, or on the road. These men hold the objective position of inspectors of women and guardians of the patriarchal order, since their attitude serves to punish women who aren't "hooked up" with a man. In order to ensure that men perform this function, patriarchal society conditions, enlists, drugs, and reassures them by means of numerous ideological mechanisms, among which pornographic productions occupy a special place.

Pornography is therefore a tool of propaganda which serves the patriarchy and which reinforces the myth of a passive and masochistic feminine sexuality, even while it glorifies images of male predators and sadists. But it is a propaganda tool that adapts to societal evolution. When confronted with feminist demonstrations which questioned the norms and ethics of the dominant view of sexuality, pornography was made fashionable: the women's movement denounced the opposing yet complementary images of the mother and the whore and demystified women's so-called frigidity; and pornography cheerfully picked up on some of these themes in order to undercut them that much more effectively. Thus, Emmanuelle[2] is a young woman who is in love with her husband and wishes to remain faithful to him; *he* encourages her to offer herself to other men (in the language of pornography, women "give themselves," or "want to belong to, be at the service of"; there is no trace of any active desire expressing a choice). But Emmanuelle refuses and does not understand that her romantic and petit-bourgeois prejudices make her laughable and old-fashioned. However, thanks to the influence of a "liberated" milieu, she gradually learns the laws (made by whom?) of pleasure and allows herself to be placed in the hands of a master-initiator by her husband. The initiator hands her over to some drunken soldier and then takes her around to places of ill-repute where she is pursued, forcibly undressed, and finally raped. Thus initiated, she affirms that she is all through with her old prejudices and that she finally feels like "a real woman." So that means that any woman who refuses to be circulated among men in this way is therefore not genuine? Whereas the feminist movements are demanding that women be allowed to control their own bodies, pornography proposes women's bodies be put at the disposal of all men.

The sexual liberation preached by pornography is actually a channeling of sexuality toward a heterosexual world in which men are still the sole masters of the game; in this way, pornography militates in favor of maintaining men's appropriation of women.

Translated by Elissa Gelfand

2 Heroine of a novel and of a widely distributed film.—Ed.

Annie Leclerc

Men have principles, and they insist upon them.
And at the heart of these principles, engraved, in the cold splendor of an
    eternal and almost super-human law, the value of woman and the
    value of man:
Woman is valuable in so far as she permits man to fulfill his being as
    man.
But man is valuable in and of himself.
For out of him cometh forth all value, as the sperm out of his penis.

If like him I were able to say: the highest, the best, is man-directed
and he alone is able to aspire to it, then, yes, if I were able to say that, I
would willingly attune my value to his.

But there's the rub, I cannot say it. That which he imposes upon my
judgment as humanity's supreme subtlety seems to me twisted with
weakness and misery.

Therefore I say (nothing will stop me): man's value has no value. My
best proof: the laughter that takes hold of me when I observe him in
those very areas where he wishes to be distinguished. And that is also
my best weapon.

One must not wage war on man. That is his way of attaining value.
Deny in order to affirm. Kill to love. One must simply deflate his values
with the needle of ridicule.

For years I rebelled against men because of their demands and their
contempt, because of the monopoly on their glory. But I have noticed
that men happily accepted women's rebellion and delicately savored
their bites: they perceived in our anger the expression of a supreme and
sad devotion to those values of theirs to which we could never accede.

It was then that I started to question their right to demand and despise, their source of self-glorification. And I encountered their values
inscribed in the firmament of greatness and human dignity.

From *Parole de femme* [Woman's word] (Grasset, 1974).

It was indeed on that occasion that laughter began to tickle me— I took to observing the men around me, Tom, Dick, and Harry, in the light of greatness and human dignity and, honestly, those men who could pass for the best in the business were simply not up to standard. Weaklings in the light of Strength. Cowards in the light of Courage. Blinkered in the light of Genius. Short-winded in the light of Inspiration. Stingy in the light of Generosity. It was pitiful to see them falling so far short—

But whereas this was rather entertaining, I did not linger over it. I generously granted them what they grant each other every time they come to grief and sigh: "I am only a man after all"— and I told myself, don't let's haggle over this "they're only men after all"— A minor diversion which already, almost imperceptibly, taught me something important. Man is Great, but careful, men are only men. Which proves that if man makes my life for me, and if he lays down the law to me it is not by right of what he is but by right of some abstract and virile virtues.

And I said to myself, those particular men are closer to my heart than to their beautiful and oppressive virtues. They offer no great field of observation, let's take a look at the men who inspire men.

And I went off to take a look at the heroes of my time who are charged with the burden of assuming men's values.

Where are these heroes? Condemned by literature to certain death, they have, in the nick of time, changed camp: they have gone over to the cinema. Fortunate move! For them. And for the movies.

Heroes have flourished in this century of mine, more effective in their malolatry than all the Jean Valjeans[1] of literature. And the cinema prospers; nothing is more profitable than the display of male virtues in the fight for valor.

They are sheriff, cowboy or settler, policeman or outlaw, Dr. Schweitzer or contented father. A highly colored, somewhat repetitive iconography of real-life men.

Just one look at that great face is generally enough to identify the hero. No subtle, no delicate features. The hero owes it to himself to appear carved out of solid rock, with a knife, or an axe. A few well-placed lines at the corner of the mouth, contempt and superiority, near the temples, round the eyes, which are preferably clear and blue to show nobility of race, the kind of eyes that have seen it all before, have seen all there is to see and that still go right on looking.

The hero prefers silence. Eloquent silence. For he is on the trail of all human villainy, treachery, ferocity, and baseness. No one's going to put anything over on him.

[1] Hero of Victor Hugo's famous novel *Les misérables.*—Tr.

The hero has stature, volume. Burdened with silent sorrow and the weight of years, the hero is never old but inevitably tall. In the United States, he gets up around six feet six. John Wayne, Gregory Peck, Henry Fonda, Burt Lancaster, all pretty much on the tall side. If the American hero put his inches into height, our French hero sends his out sideways. Here we prefer the big, strapping kind. Broad face, nose bashed in in some old manly fist fight, thick, solid body. Ham-fisted, heavy, almost peasant features, a massive voice, scratched with sympathy, streaked with popular idioms.

In the United States, then, the hero lays down the law by dint of an aristocratic and silent superiority. Over here, the law emanates directly from the hero and imposes itself as the effect, the spontaneous prolongation of his very nature. Because we want our he-men to be the real thing, all of a piece, strong-voiced and full volume. Like Danton.[2] Tribune of the people type. Which produces the highly appreciated faces of a Gabin or a Leno Ventura[3]. . . .

Master, master: there is the master word of all our submissions to the greatness of man. There is the most pernicious and most obscure of our facts: the best is master and the master is the best. Will we ever be able to break our ideas free of that tyrannical law of the master?

If I open up my little notebook and find the word "master," I learn that the master is "one who commands, either de jure or de facto." As if that were not precisely the same thing! As if the law were not recognized through the fact, as if the fact could do without the law! The master is only master when he has snatched the right to be so—

So the master is one who commands. Fine. But as you only command those who obey, it was first necessary to win obedience of those who might seek to act and speak for themselves. It was necessary to conquer them, to take away their acts and their words. It was necessary to possess them.

There is no de facto master, there are only master thieves, rapists, and usurpers. Master of life and death, schoolmaster and lord and master, master of arts and letters, master of law, master of self and master chef (cock),[4] there is only one master, he who possesses. The master is nothing but a proprietor.

The master is free to use and enjoy his goods, lands, Negroes, houses, women, disciples, Arabs, and himself when he has nothing better to sink his teeth into.

[2] A leader during the French Revolution of 1789.—Tr.
[3] Two well-known French film stars.—Tr.
[4] A *maître queux* is a chef or a cook. Annie Leclerc has used *queue* ("tail") suggesting a penis.—Tr.

Thus, I know that what a man likes about himself and what he's made the object of his respect are the virtues of the conqueror and the proprietor. He needs the strength to conquer and the bulk to possess with impunity.

The virtue of virtues, the *virtus*, is force.

But force cannot be extracted from its favorite image: force is always the muscle flexed, the blow received by the blow given, the fist triumphant over the hand.

There is courage also, but that's the same. The force of force going beyond peril. And the man uncertain of his strength plumbs with manic rage the force of the force of his force. Finally, it's always death that he must brave; death obsesses him. But if the death which finally catches up with him can teach him nothing, the triumph of life, which he is unsure whether to attribute to destiny, to chance, or to himself, always leaves him in uncertainty.

His courage, his strength of mind, his generosity, as they used to say, can only be experienced when he puts them to the test, but for him there is never any real proof, either in death or in life. For lack of proof, he must rest content with that dominance over the weak conferred upon him by his glorious exploits.

To tell the truth, the courage the hero seeks within himself is unlimited, elusive, equal to his rage for possession. If he doesn't die at the end of the film, he rides away from the scene of his triumphs, prefiguring his death, haloed in pathos. His tall mare carries him away to impossible climes, for never will his thirst be quenched. Or else, lonely, intangible, he plunges into the derisory night of the city as if never to emerge.

Once you understand what the hero wants, you also understand why he can never be happy. He knows he will die one day and for him this idea is intolerable. Because after his death the world will go on turning. A world rich and pregnant with all the things the hero was unable to possess but also, o cruel fate! with all the things he had succeeded in possessing.

Death will relentlessly steal from him all that he considers his own, real or potential, and death is his greatest torment.

It is death that raises the hero's temperature. Not life; that leaves him cold.

Heroism is played out in the face of death.

Once outside the fatal aura, no life conjoins with virile greatness.

If no bird of doom circles above, no greatness can be here accomplished.

This is the basic thread, unperceived when successful, out of which is woven the Western, the war film, the detective movie. And the film catches our imagination if it has the colored vigor of myth. The story is fascinating in that it silently insinuates in the heart of each spectator these words: it is in the region of death and in the fight against death that life wins its spurs.

A constant, unchanging point of view but one that comes to us, often attractively packaged, in the peripeteia of manly exploits.

That said, it is not only in the cinema that heroism pays off. The fortune of a Saint-Exupéry, even better the indestructible fortune of a Malraux,[5] owe everything to it.

Our wordy Malraux (discretion is not his strong point) has simply managed to make his own the ancient truth of the necessary link between heroism and death and has made it the much vaunted, guaranteed, grandiose theme of his prose. He claims it, declaims it, proclaims it, declines it, and conjugates it as if finally he, Malraux, had discovered what little heroes were made of.

But at least with him you run no risk of getting lost in the by-ways of interpretation. Everything is signposted. Black on white. It is stated at the beginning of his work and repeated word for word for hundreds and hundreds of pages.

Nothing in the world of values is less inventive, nothing more repetitive than Malraux's ideas.

What sterile complacence and sad enthusiasm, that of those young people bowled over by an extreme display of the most conventional of values.

Here are a few happy phrases, picked at random almost in that *Royal Way* (the way of heroes) that all of Malraux's characters will stubbornly continue to walk.

First a phrase to define that royal way called adventure.

"Adventure is not an escape but a hunt." Pascal would have said that there is no better way of escaping than by hunting. That the prize at the end of the hunt mattered little. But Malraux is far from such subtleties.

And if his hero declares: "To be king is foolish: what counts is making a kingdom," this is not to despise power itself but only a power that would not be the outcome of a conquest.

Take, conquer, vanquish, *have*. That's what hunting is about. A hunt for treasure, for women, a man-hunt. To possess makes up the program of adventure.

"To possess more than himself, to escape the moth-ball lives of the men he saw each day."

---

[5] Saint-Exupéry and André Malraux, French writers of the twentieth century who, in different ways, exalted heroism.—Tr.

"Each body one has not *had* is an enemy."

" 'No, these women are not bodies: they are—possibilities, that's it. And I desire them—' He made a gesture that Claude simply conjectured in the darkness, like a hand crushing—'As I have desired to conquer men.' "

Alongside this statement of intent we find laid out and annotated the deep significance of adventure, designed to reveal the amplitude and ultimately to justify the cruelty of the intent itself. It is the significance of "the austere dominance of death."

"Since I must wager against my death, I prefer to gamble with twenty tribes than with one child." And the hero then explains that what he wants—that is, to win in the face of death—he wants "just as my father wanted the property of his neighbor, just as I want women."

A country, women, conquered men, they all amount to the same, especially when it's a question of facing *his* death and possessing it too —the rebel bitch—like everything else.

And the hero commits himself to death by reason of the obsessional gaze he casts upon death that has only one face, his own.

Death: "That monstrous defeat."

For the hero the world has only one metaphysical dimension: the future dissolution of his I-me, the end of possessions.

So it's useless to wonder whether it's because he loves possessing things above all else that makes him try to possess what escapes him or if it's because his death escapes him that he is seized with the rage for possessions that might survive him. It is all the same in the end. I-me can exist only in possession.

And the best phrase the hero can use to define his quest: "I want to leave a scar on this map."

The hero is I-me, for as long as possible. My brand, my distraint, my possession, now and forever.

So what now? Must we indefinitely acquiesce to this watchword of human greatness: to possess, in the face of all comers?

Will it always be necessary to look on life solely with the eyes of hatred turned upon death, that implacable, that ironic sneak-thief?

Death, a defeat? And monstrous to boot?

But who has set himself up as judge of the monstrousness of death? How and in the name of what can we, who are mortal, qualify death as monstrous? And this is where greatness is meant to lie?

It is life itself that seems to them a monstrosity, they hate it and forge for themselves a truly monstrous image of life, a sort of fabulous empire where there would be no death. But those heroes are just profaners of life, miserable puppets, the grotesque clowns of their monstrous imaginings.

That's what a hero is, a failure in life, an impotent in life, and one who takes his revenge by stealing, enslaving, pillaging, and insulting everything alive. For him courage is the complete kit required to flout life. Monsters are never just monsters; they are alive. Only the hero is a monster who wagers life against life.

But whence comes this monster? Who provides grist to his mill, who sustains him, who robes him and ennobles him? Always the same, the thinker, the logomachinist.

Listen to him for once with a sound ear. He says that life is absurd. Life absurd! And all because his reason cannot manage to account for it. And he submits life to examination and to the judgment of his imbecile reason. And it simply never occurs to him that there is something unhinged, something *monstrous* in a reason that enunciates such absurdities!

Hence the question: "Is life worth living or not worth living?" is not the most basic of human questions; it is the most profoundly stupid expression and as it were ultimate image of a thinking corrupted by reason.

As if anything could be worthwhile outside of life or allow anything to be appreciated outside of life—

As if thought, that life alone makes possible, could have any other task than serving life.

There is only one just form of thought, the living thought that can revive the smothered fire of life and sow revolt against the poisoners, the pillagers, the profaners of life.

To revolt: that's the right word. Yet it's still not quite strong enough. Let the bell toll the end not only of those eminent possessors but also of their carrion-eating values that have polluted the whole world.

And, in fact, do we yet have any idea of what the word revolutionary may mean outside the normal dimension of the hero?

When the cinema portrays a revolutionary (or Malraux portrays one in his novels) it immediately changes him into a hero. And indeed that's how he wins the unanimous approbation of the bourgeois spectators, stimulated in their unchanging feeling of greatness. The hero is only secondarily, even accidentally, a revolutionary. What counts and what is presented in close-up is the theme of someone who fights to give *his* life meaning and for whom revolution is only a means.

What matters in the revolutionary hero, therefore, is not what he's fighting against, but his personal fight, his personal value, his personal strength.

The screen is flooded with the hero's courage, its failings and triumphs.

Be he crusader, nazi, highwayman, cop, or revolutionary, it's always the same mixture. The courage of the hero. And courage is worthless in itself. Less than worthless. Courage is not beautiful. Courage is not great. It is wretched, hateful, swollen, puffy, deathly, since its mission is to subdue, oppress, and repress all living things. And courage is nothing but that pain, that harsh violence wrought upon the self when one must pass through it into the fight against oppression.

No, it's over, finished. I pity the masquerades of the hero. And I laugh at him, with his important airs, his tragic antics. He may count on me no longer to help him in the way he asks, in the way he demands, to establish his rule. The rule of human greatness. Because I don't give a damn.

Translated by Gillian C. Gill

Claudine Herrmann

If feminine thought has always been hidden, masculine thought in all of its forms has, on the contrary, left its mark on the world as we see it. It is inscribed in things, forms, art, thought, in different social systems, with the tireless persistence of a child sure of its mother's approval.

But then, is that not a woman's primary duty: approval?

There is not a murderer, a concentration camp torturer, a degenerate monarch, who could not find a wife, usually totally devoted to him, and no court has ever asked the question: "Why didn't you leave that man?"

When woman penetrates at last—always through a side door—into this mysterious masculine world from which she was for so long excluded (this center of so many marvelous adventures recounted in song and story, surrounded by the aura of a long-forbidden culture), she is struck by the fact that abstraction dominates in two ways: system and hierarchy.

It is possible that man's thought reflects the order of structures outside of himself, but judging by the malaise she experiences contemplating these structures, woman knows very well that they are totally alien to her.

It is noteworthy, for example, that the first definition of the word "system" in the *dictionnaire Robert* is: "An organized ensemble of intellectual elements." It is only in the second definition that one finds: "An ensemble possessing a structure or constituting an organic whole."

From "Le système viril" [The virile system] in *Les voleuses de langue* [The tongue snatchers] (des femmes, 1976). This is a series of essays that comes closer to feminist literary criticism as Americans understand it than other texts produced in France. Through the analysis of texts by women and men writers, Claudine Herrmann relentlessly illustrates her thesis that women and men are fundamentally different and write differently. The title contains a play on the verb *voler* ("to fly and to steal") that is frequently used by the new French feminists.

The first meaning is mental and abstract, it is only the second one that impinges on objective reality as it functions *outside* of man's vision.

Man prefers himself over all that surrounds him to such a degree that he imposes his mental categories *first, before* those of objective reality.

One will be quick to point out that if the structures of matter and mind are homologous, little harm is done: to put one before the other comes down to a simple question of priority. But this *priority*, this way of putting himself *first* is precisely what characterizes—not only Christian humanist thought—but all masculine thought.

From this first act there follows a world view that distinguishes man from woman.

Woman, who is always obliged to take others *into account*, and also to consider a material reality from which she escapes less easily than man, can only conceptualize a cosmos of which she is not the center.

This is at the root of many failures, when with only a technical or scientific preparation, she penetrates the world of men. Everything stuns her: there is the proliferation of systems—economic, political, juridical, intellectual—and each considers itself determinant; only life is excluded from them, in order to maintain a model which eliminates everything that does not conform to it.

Men move about within this swarming mass, and frequently one wonders why they occupy one place rather than another, except that they were thrust there by that pathological force that resembles men in that it is deaf to all reason and concerned only with itself: society.

In this world where everyone wears an invisible mask, woman imagines that she will at last be able to remove her veil, but she should beware: here she will lose her last illusions.

Masculine mystery had intrigued her so: she had learned to dream about it and she had been raised to please it. Until now masculine mystery was disguised by desire or familial conformity, but it is nothing other than the absolute inability to love anything other than oneself or one's possessions (women and children being occasionally among them).

Work that appears to be the most disinterested is nothing but an empire being created with a new master, and to construct his new pyramids each man must find his own slaves.

So women will often be welcome. They will be laughed at behind their backs because of their eagerness to pursue a goal that will bring them nothing, and because of their ability to love those who exploit them. They will be mocked because of their belief in the immense social superstructure that gives a useful, virtuous façade to the most brazen schemes.

If woman remains true to herself, and continues to think in terms of harmony rather than struggle, of giving rather than exchange, she will be ruthlessly crushed.

If she adopts masculine values along the way, like coldness and imperialism, she will succeed only by destroying herself, and she will surely be the object of ridicule.

What she gains in the social arena she will lose on a personal level.

It means nothing to allow women to participate in society if it robs them of everything that makes them different. But men cannot conceive without scorn anything that is not exactly like them. . . .

Translated by Marilyn R. Schuster

Hélène Cixous

Where is she?

Activity/passivity,
Sun/Moon,
Culture/Nature,
Day/Night,

Father/Mother,
Head/heart,
Intelligible/sensitive,
Logos/Pathos.

Form, convex, step, advance, seed, progress.
Matter, concave, ground—which supports the step, receptacle.

Man
———
Woman

Always the same metaphor: we follow it, it transports us, in all of its forms, wherever a discourse is organized. The same thread, or double tress leads us, whether we are reading or speaking, through literature, philosophy, criticism, centuries of representation, of reflection.

Thought has always worked by opposition,
Speech/Writing
High/Low

From "Sorties" in *La jeune née* [The newly born woman] (Union Générale d'Editions, 10/18, 1975). This is a text that combines essay, autobiography, and poetic-prophetic prose. In this extract, Hélène Cixous suggests ways of deconstructing classical philosophical and psychoanalytic thought. The first part of *La jeune née*, "The Guilty One," is an essay by Catherine Clément on the witch and the hysteric, seduction and guilt.

By dual, *hierarchized* [1] oppositions. Superior/Inferior. Myths, legends, books. Philosophical systems. Wherever an ordering intervenes, a law organizes the thinkable by (dual, irreconcilable; or mitigable, dialectical) oppositions. And all the couples of oppositions are *couples*. Does this mean something? Is the fact that logocentrism subjects thought—all of the concepts, the codes, the values—to a two-term system, related to "the" couple man/woman?
Nature/History,
Nature/Art,
Nature/Mind,
Passion/Action.

Theory of culture, theory of society, the ensemble of symbolic systems —art, religion, family, language, —everything elaborates the same systems. And the movement by which each opposition is set up to produce meaning is the movement by which the couple is destroyed. A universal battlefield. Each time a war breaks out. Death is always at work.

Father/son   Relationships of authority, of privilege, of force.
Logos/writing Relationships: opposition, conflict, relief, reversion.
Master/slave   Violence. Repression.

And we perceive that the "victory" always amounts to the same thing: it is hierarchized. The hierarchization subjects the entire conceptual organization to man. A male privilege, which can be seen in the opposition by which it sustains itself, between *activity* and *passivity*. Traditionally, the question of sexual difference is coupled with the same opposition: activity/passivity.

That goes a long way. If we examine the history of philosophy—in so far as philosophical discourse orders and reproduces all thought—we perceive[2] that: it is marked by an absolute constant, the orchestrator of values, which is precisely the opposition activity/passivity.

In philosophy, woman is always on the side of passivity. Every time the question comes up; when we examine kinship structures; whenever a family model is brought into play; in fact as soon as the ontological question is raised; as soon as you ask yourself what is meant by the question "What is it?"; as soon as there is a will to say something. A will: desire, authority, you examine that, and you are led right back— to the father. You can even fail to notice that there's no place at all

1 The translation is faithful to Hélène Cixous's many neologisms.—Tr.
2 This is what all of Derrida's work traversing—investigating the history of philosophy—seeks to make apparent. In Plato, Hegel, Nietzsche, the same process goes on, repression, exclusion, distancing of woman. Murder which intermingles with history as a manifestation and representation of masculine power.

for women in the operation! In the extreme the world of "being" can function to the exclusion of the mother. No need for mother—provided that there is something of the maternal: and it is the father then who acts as—is—the mother. Either the woman is passive; or she doesn't exist. What is left is unthinkable, unthought of. She does not enter into the oppositions, she is not coupled with the father (who is coupled with the son).

There is Mallarmé's[3] tragic dream, a father lamenting the mystery of paternity, which mourning tears out of the poet, the mourning of mournings, the death of the beloved son: this dream of a union between the father and the son—and no mother then. Man's dream is the face of death. Which always threatens him differently than it threatens woman.

"an alliance
a union, superb
—and the life
remaining in me
I shall use it
to—
so no mother then?"

And dream of masculine
filiation, dream of God the father
emerging from himself
in his son, —and
no mother then

She does not exist, she may be nonexistent; but there must be something of her. Of woman, upon whom he no longer depends, he retains only this space, always virginal, matter subjected to the desire that he wishes to imprint.

And if you examine literary history, it's the same story. It all refers back to man to *his* torment, his desire to be (at) the origin. Back to the father. There is an intrinsic bond between the philosophical and the literary (to the extent that it signifies, literature is commanded by the philosophical) and phallocentrism. The philosophical constructs itself starting with the abasement of woman. Subordination of the feminine to the masculine order which appears to be the condition for the functioning of the machine.

The challenging of this solidarity of logocentrism and phallocentrism has today become insistent enough—the bringing to light of the fate which has been imposed upon woman, of her burial—to threaten the stability of the masculine edifice which passed itself off as eternal-natural; by bringing forth from the world of femininity reflections, hypotheses which are necessarily ruinous for the bastion which still holds the authority. What would become of logocentrism, of the great philo-

[3] *Pour un tombeau d'Anatole* (Editions du Seuil, 1961, p. 138) tomb in which Mallarmé preserves his son, guards him, he himself the mother, from death.

sophical systems, of world order in general if the rock upon which they founded their church were to crumble?

If it were to come out in a new day that the logocentric project had always been, undeniably, to *found* (fund)[4] phallocentrism, to insure for masculine order a rationale equal to history itself?

Then all the stories would have to be told differently, the future would be incalculable, the historical forces would, will, change hands, bodies; another thinking as yet not thinkable will transform the functioning of all society. Well, we are living through this very period when the conceptual foundation of a millenial culture is in process of being undermined by millions of a species of mole as yet not recognized.

When they awaken from among the dead, from among the words, from among the laws. . . .

What does one give?

The specific difference that has determined the movement of history as a movement of property is articulated between two economies that define themselves in relation to the problematics of giving.

The (political) economy of the masculine and of the feminine is organized by different requirements and constraints, which, when socialized and metaphorized, produce signs, relationships of power, relationships of production and of reproduction, an entire immense system of cultural inscription readable as masculine or feminine.

I am careful here to use the *qualifiers* of sexual difference, in order to avoid the confusion man/masculine, woman/feminine: for there are men who do not repress their femininity, women who more or less forcefully inscribe their masculinity. The difference is not, of course, distributed according to socially determined "sexes." Furthermore, when I speak of political economy and of libidinal economy, in putting the two together, I am not bringing into play the false question of origin, that tall tale sustained by male privilege. We must guard against falling complacently or blindly into the essentialist ideological interpretation, as, for example, Freud and Jones, in different ways, ventured to do; in their quarrel over the subject of feminine sexuality, both of them, starting from opposite points of view, came to support the awesome thesis of a "natural," anatomical determination of sexual difference-opposition. And from there on, both implicitly support phallocentrism's position of power.

Let us review the main points of the opposing positions: [Ernest] Jones (in *Early Feminine Sexuality*), using an ambiguous approach, attacks the Freudian theses that make of woman an imperfect man.

---

4 *Fonder* in French means both "to found" and "to fund."—Tr.

For Freud:

(1) the "fatality" of the feminine situation is a result of an anatomical "defectiveness."

(2) there is only one libido, and its essence is male; the inscription of sexual difference begins only with a phallic phase which both boys and girls go through. Until then, the girl has been a sort of little boy: the genital organization of the infantile libido is articulated by the equivalence activity/masculinity; the vagina has not as yet been "discovered."

(3) the first love object being, for both sexes, the mother, it is only for the boy that love of the opposite sex is "natural."

For Jones: femininity is an autonomous "essence."

From the outset (starting from the age of six months) the girl has a *feminine* desire for her father; an analysis of the little girl's earliest fantasms would in fact show that, in place of the breast which is perceived as disappointing, it is the penis that is desired, or an object of the same form (by an analogical displacement). It follows, since we are already into the chain of substitutions, that in the series of partial objects, in place of the penis, would come the child—for in order to counter Freud, Jones docilely returns to the Freudian terrain. And then some. From the equation breast-penis-child, he concludes that the little girl experiences with regard to the father a primary desire. (And this would include the desire to have a child by the father as well.) And, of course, the girl also has a primary love for the opposite sex. She too, then, has a right to her Oedipal complex as a primary formation, and to the threat of mutilation by the mother. At last she is a woman, anatomically, without defect: her clitoris is not a minipenis. Clitoral masturbation is not, as Freud claims, a masculine practice. And it would seem in light of precocious fantasms that the vagina is discovered very early.

In fact, in affirming that there is a specific femininity (while in other respects preserving the theses of an orthodoxy) it is still phallocentrism that Jones reinforces, on the pretext of taking the part of femininity (and of God, who he recalls created them male and female—!). And bisexuality vanishes into the unbridged abyss that separates the opponents here.

As for Freud, if we subscribe to what he sets forth when he identifies with Napoleon in his article of 1933 on *The Disappearance of the Oedipus Complex*: "anatomy is destiny," then we participate in the sentencing to death of woman. And in the completion of all History.

That the difference between the sexes may have psychic consequences is undeniable. But they are surely not reducible to those designated by a Freudian analysis. Starting with the relationship of the two sexes to the Oedipal complex, the boy and the girl are oriented toward a division of social roles so that women "inescapably" have a lesser productivity, because they "sublimate" less than men and because symbolic activity, hence the production of culture, is men's doing.[5]

Freud moreover starts from what he calls the *anatomical* difference between the sexes. And we know how that is pictured in his eyes: as the difference between having/not having the phallus. With reference to these precious parts. Starting from what will be specified, by Lacan, as the transcendental signifier.

But *sexual difference* is not determined merely by the fantasized relationship to anatomy, which is based, to a great extent, upon the point of *view*, therefore upon a strange importance accorded [by Freud and Lacan] to exteriority and to the specular in the elaboration of sexuality. A voyeur's theory, of course.

No, it is at the level of sexual pleasure [*jouissance*] [6] in my opinion that the difference makes itself most clearly apparent in as far as woman's libidinal economy is neither identifiable by a man nor referable to the masculine economy.

For me, the question "What does she want?" that they ask of woman, a question that in fact woman asks herself because they ask it of her, because precisely there is so little place in society for her desire that she ends up by dint of not knowing what to do with it, no longer knowing where to put it, or if she has any, conceals the most immediate and the most urgent question: "How do I experience sexual pleasure?" What is feminine *sexual pleasure*, where does it take place, how is it inscribed at the level of her body, of her unconscious? And then how is it put into writing?

[5] Freud's thesis is the following: when the Oedipal complex disappears the superego becomes its heir. At the moment when the boy begins to feel the threat of castration, he begins to overcome the Oedipus complex, with the help of a very severe superego. The Oedipus complex for the boy is a primary process: his first love object, as for the girl, is the mother. But the girl's development is inevitably controlled by the pressure of a less severe superego: the discovery of her castration results in a less vigorous superego. She never completely overcomes the Oedipus complex. The feminine Oedipus complex is not a primary process: the pre-Oedipal attachment to the mother entails for the girl a difficulty from which, says Freud, she never recovers: the necessity of changing objects (to love the father), in mid-stream is a painful conversion, which is accompanied by an additional renunciation: the passage from pre-Oedipal sexuality to "normal" sexuality implies the abandonment of the clitoris in order to move on to the vagina. When this "destiny" is fulfilled, women have a reduced symbolic activity: they have nothing to lose, to gain, to defend.

[6] *Jouissance*: see the introductory essay, "Contexts of the New French Feminisms," n. 8. It is a word used by Hélène Cixous to refer to that intense, rapturous pleasure which women know and which men fear.—Ed.

We can go on at length about a hypothetical prehistory and about a matriarchal era. Or we can, as did Bachofen,[7] attempt to reconstitute a gynecocratic society, and to deduce from it poetic and mythical effects that have a powerfully subversive import with regard to the family and to male power.

All the other ways of depicting the history of power, property, masculine domination, the constitution of the State, the ideological apparatus have their effectiveness. But the change taking place has nothing to do with question of "origin." Phallocentrism is. History has never produced, recorded anything but that. Which does not mean that this form is inevitable or natural. Phallocentrism is the enemy. Of *everyone*. Men stand to lose by it, differently but as seriously as women. And it is time to transform. To invent the other history.

There is no such thing as "destiny," "nature," or essence, but living structures, caught up, sometimes frozen within historicocultural limits which intermingle with the historical scene to such a degree that it has long been impossible and is still difficult to think or even to imagine something else. At present, we are living through a transitional period —where the classical structure appears as if it might crack.

To predict what will happen to sexual difference—in another time (in two or three hundred years?) is impossible. But there should be no misunderstanding: men and women are caught up in a network of millenial cultural determinations of a complexity that is practically unanalyzable: we can no more talk about "woman" than about "man" without getting caught up in an ideological theater where the multiplication of representations, images, reflections, myths, identifications constantly transforms, deforms, alters each person's imaginary order and in advance, renders all conceptualization null and void.[8]

There is no reason to exclude the possibility of radical transformations of behavior, mentalities, roles, and political economy. The effects of these transformations on the libidinal economy are unthinkable today. Let us imagine simultaneously a *general* change in all of the structures of for-

---

[7] J.-J. Bachofen (1815–1887) Swiss historian of "gynecocracy," "historian" of a nonhistory. His project is to demonstrate that the nations (Greek, Roman, Hebrew) went through an age of "gynecocracy," the reign of the Mother, before arriving at a patriarchy. This epoch can only be deduced, as it has no history. Bachofen advances that this state of affairs, humiliating for men, must have been repressed, covered over by historical forgetfulness. And he attempts to create (in *Das Mutterrecht* in particular, 1861) an archeology of the matriarchal system, of great beauty, starting with a reading of the first historical texts, at the level of the symptom, of their unsaid. Gynecocracy, he says, is well-ordered materialism.

[8] There are coded paradigms, symptomatic of a repeated consensus, which project the man/woman robot couple as seen by contemporary societies. See the 1975 issue of UNESCO consecrated to the International Year of Woman.

mation, education, framework, hence of reproduction, of ideological effects, and let us imagine a real liberation of sexuality, that is, a transformation of our relationship to our body (—and to another body), an approximation of the immense material organic sensual universe that we are, this not being possible, of course, without equally radical political transformations (imagine!). Then "femininity," "masculinity," would inscribe their effects of difference, their economy, their relationships to expenditure, to deficit, to giving, quite differently. That which appears as "feminine" or "masculine" today would no longer amount to the same thing. The general logic of difference would no longer fit into the opposition that still dominates. The difference would be a crowning display of new differences.

But we are still floundering about—with certain exceptions—in the Old order.

The masculine future:

There are exceptions. There always have been those uncertain, poetic beings, who have not let themselves be reduced to the state of coded mannequins by the relentless repression of the homosexual component. Men or women, complex, mobile, open beings. Admitting the component of the other sex makes them at once much richer, plural, strong, and to the extent of this mobility, very fragile. We invent only on this condition: thinkers, artists, creators of new values, "philosophers" of the mad Nietzschean sort, inventors and destroyers of concepts, of forms, the changers of life cannot but be agitated by singularities—complementary or contradictory. This does not mean that in order to create you must be homosexual. But there is no *invention* possible, whether it be philosophical or poetic, without the presence in the inventing subject of an abundance of the other, of the diverse: persons-detached, persons-thought, peoples born of the unconscious, and in each desert, suddenly animated, a springing forth of self that we did not know about—our women, our monsters, our jackals, our Arabs, our fellow-creatures, our fears.[9] But there is no invention of other I's, no poetry, no fiction without a certain homosexuality (interplay therefore of bisexuality) making in me a crystallized work of my ultrasubjectivities.[10] I is this matter, personal, exuberant, lively masculine, feminine, or other in which I delights me and distresses me. And in the concert of personalizations called I, at

[9] The French here, *nos semblables, nos frayeurs*, plays on and with the last line of Baudelaire's famous poem "Au lecteur" [To the reader]: "Hypocrite lecteur,—mon semblable,—mon frère."—Tr.

[10] Hélène Cixous, *Prénoms de personne* (Editions du Seuil, 1974) "Tales of Hoffman," p. 112 passim.

the same time that you repress a certain homosexuality, symbolically, substitutively, it comes out through various signs—traits, comportments, manners, gestures—and it is seen still more clearly in writing.

Thus, under the name of Jean Genet,[11] what is inscribed in the movement of a text which divides itself, breaks itself into bits, regroups itself, is an abundant, maternal, pederastic femininity. A phantasmatical mingling of men, of males, of messieurs, of monarchs, princes, orphans, flowers, mothers, breasts, gravitates around a marvelous "sun of energy" love, which bombards and disintegrates these ephemeral amorous singularities so that they may recompose themselves in other bodies for new passions. . . .

Translated by Ann Liddle

[11] Jean Genet, French novelist and playwright, to whose writing Hélène Cixous refers when she gives examples of the inscription of pederastic femininity.—Tr.

Luce Irigaray

Female sexuality has always been theorized within masculine parameters. Thus, the opposition "viril" clitoral activity/"feminine" vaginal passivity which Freud—and many others—claims are alternative behaviors or steps in the process of becoming a sexually normal woman, seems prescribed more by the practice of masculine sexuality than by anything else. For the clitoris is thought of as a little penis which is pleasurable to masturbate, as long as the anxiety of castration does not exist (for the little boy), while the vagina derives its value from the "home" it offers the male penis when the now forbidden hand must find a substitute to take its place in giving pleasure.

According to these theorists, woman's erogenous zones are no more than a clitoris-sex, which cannot stand up in comparison with the valued phallic organ; or a hole-envelope, a sheath which surrounds and rubs the penis during coition; a nonsex organ or a masculine sex organ turned inside out in order to caress itself.

Woman and her pleasure are not mentioned in this conception of the sexual relationship. Her fate is one of "lack," "atrophy" (of her genitals), and "penis envy," since the penis is the only recognized sex organ of any worth. Therefore she tries to appropriate it for herself, by all the means at her disposal: by her somewhat servile love of the father-husband capable of giving it to her; by her desire of a penis-child, preferably male; by gaining access to those cultural values which are still "by right" reserved for males alone and are therefore always masculine, etc. Woman lives her desire only as an attempt to possess at long last the equivalent of the male sex organ.

All of that seems rather foreign to her pleasure however, unless she

---

"Ce sexe qui n'en est pas un" [This sex which is not one] in *Ce sexe qui n'en est pas un* (Minuit, 1977). This and the following essay by Luce Irigaray are from the same volume. The title is, of course, a pun: woman's sex is not a sex within the Freudian paradigm and within Irigaray's paradigm it is not one but multiple, plural.

remains within the dominant phallic economy. Thus, for example, woman's autoeroticism is very different from man's. He needs an instrument in order to touch himself: his hand, woman's genitals, language— And this self-stimulation requires a minimum of activity. But a woman touches herself by and within herself directly, without mediation, and before any distinction between activity and passivity is possible. A woman "touches herself" constantly without anyone being able to forbid her to do so, for her sex is composed of two lips which embrace continually. Thus, within herself she is already two—but not divisible into ones—who stimulate each other.

This autoeroticism, which she needs in order not to risk the disappearance of her pleasure in the sex act, is interrupted by a violent intrusion: the brutal spreading of these two lips by a violating penis. If, in order to assure an articulation between autoeroticism and heteroeroticism in coition (the encounter with the absolute other which always signifies death), the vagina must also, but not only, substitute for the little boy's hand, how can woman's autoeroticism possibly be perpetuated in the classic representation of sexuality? Will she not indeed be left the impossible choice between defensive virginity, fiercely turned back upon itself, or a body open for penetration, which no longer recognizes in its "hole" of a sex organ the pleasure of retouching itself? The almost exclusive, and ever so anxious, attention accorded the erection in Occidental sexuality proves to what extent the imaginary that commands it is foreign to everything female. For the most part, one finds in Occidental sexuality nothing more than imperatives dictated by rivalry among males: the "strongest" being the one who "gets it up the most," who has the longest, thickest, hardest penis or indeed the one who "pisses the farthest" (cf. little boys' games). These imperatives can also be dictated by sado-masochist fantasies, which in turn are ordered by the relationship between man and mother: his desire to force open, to penetrate, to appropriate for himself the mystery of the stomach in which he was conceived, the secret of his conception, of his "origin." Desire-need, also, once again, to make blood flow in order to revive a very ancient—intrauterine, undoubtedly, but also prehistoric—relation to the maternal.

Woman, in this sexual imaginary, is only a more or less complacent facilitator for the working out of man's fantasies. It is possible, and even certain, that she experiences vicarious pleasure there, but this pleasure is above all a masochistic prostitution of her body to a desire that is not her own and that leaves her in her well-known state of dependency. Not knowing what she wants, ready for anything, even asking for more, if only he will "take" her as the "object" of *his* pleasure, she will not say what *she* wants. Moreover, she does not know, or no longer knows, what she wants. As Freud admits, the beginnings of the sexual life of the little girl are so "obscure," so "faded by the years," that one would have to dig very deep in order to find, behind the traces of this civilization, this history, the vestiges of a more archaic civilization which could give some indication as to what woman's sexuality is all about. This very ancient civilization undoubtedly would not have the same language, the same alphabet— Woman's desire most likely does not speak the same language as man's desire, and it probably has been covered over by the logic that has dominated the West since the Greeks.

In this logic, the prevalence of the gaze, discrimination of form, and individualization of form is particularly foreign to female eroticism. Woman finds pleasure more in touch than in sight and her entrance into a dominant scopic economy signifies, once again, her relegation to passivity: she will be the beautiful object. Although her body is in this way eroticized and solicited to a double movement between exhibition and pudic retreat in order to excite the instincts of the "subject," her sex organ represents the horror of having nothing to see. In this system of representation and desire, the vagina is a flaw, a hole in the representation's scoptophilic objective. It was admitted already in Greek statuary that this "nothing to be seen" must be excluded, rejected, from such a scene of representation. Woman's sexual organs are simply absent from this scene: they are masked and her "slit" is sewn up.

In addition, this sex organ which offers nothing to the view has no distinctive form of its own. Although woman finds pleasure precisely in this incompleteness of the form of her sex organ, which is why it retouches itself indefinitely, her pleasure is denied by a civilization that privileges phallomorphism. The value accorded to the only definable form excludes the form involved in female autoeroticism. The *one* of form, the individual sex, proper name, literal meaning—supersedes, by spreading apart and dividing, this touching of *at least two* (lips) which keeps woman in contact with herself, although it would be impossible to distinguish exactly what "parts" are touching each other.

Whence the mystery that she represents in a culture that claims to enumerate everything, cipher everything by units, inventory everything by individualities. *She is neither one nor two.* She cannot, strictly speaking, be determined either as one person or as two. She renders any definition inadequate. Moreover she has no "proper" name. And her sex organ, which is not *a* sex organ, is counted as *no* sex organ. It is the negative, the opposite, the reverse, the counterpart, of the only visible and morphologically designatable sex organ (even if it does pose a few problems in its passage from erection to detumescence): the penis.

But woman holds the secret of the "thickness" of this "form," its many-layered volume, its metamorphosis from smaller to larger and vice versa, and even the intervals at which this change takes place. Without even knowing it. When she is asked to maintain, to revive, man's desire, what this means in terms of the value of her own desire is neglected. Moreover, she is not aware of her desire, at least not explicitly. But the force and continuity of her desire are capable of nurturing all the "feminine" masquerades that are expected of her for a long time.

It is true that she still has the child, with whom her appetite for touching, for contact, is given free reign, unless this appetite is already lost, or alienated by the taboo placed upon touching in a largely obsessional civilization. In her relation to the child she finds compensatory pleasure for the frustrations she encounters all too often in sexual relations proper. Thus maternity supplants the deficiencies of repressed female sexuality. Is it possible that man and woman no longer even caress each other except indirectly through the mediation between them represented by the child? Preferably male. Man, identified with his son, rediscovers the pleasure of maternal coddling; woman retouches herself in fondling that part of her body: her baby-penis-clitoris.

What that entails for the amorous trio has been clearly spelled out. The Oedipal interdict seems, however, a rather artificial and imprecise law—even though it is the very means of perpetuating the authoritarian discourse of fathers—when it is decreed in a culture where sexual relations are impracticable, since the desire of man and the desire of woman are so foreign to each other. Each of them is forced to search for some common meeting ground by indirect means: either an archaic, sensory relation to the mother's body, or a current, active or passive prolongation of the law of the father. Their attempts are characterized by regressive emotional behavior and the exchange of words so far from the realm of the sexual that they are completely exiled from it. "Mother" and "father" dominate the couple's functioning, but only as social roles. The division of labor prevents them from making love. They produce or reproduce. Not knowing too well how to use their leisure. If indeed they have any, if moreover they want to have any leisure. For what can be done with leisure? What substitute for amorous invention can be created?

We could go on and on—but perhaps we should return to the repressed female imaginary? Thus woman does not have a sex. She has at least two of them, but they cannot be identified as ones. Indeed she has many more of them than that. Her sexuality, always at least double, is in fact *plural*. Plural as culture now wishes to be plural? Plural as the manner in which current texts are written, with very little knowledge of the censorship from which they arise? Indeed, woman's pleasure does not have to choose between clitoral activity and vaginal passivity, for example. The pleasure of the vaginal caress does not have to substitute itself for the pleasure of the clitoral caress. Both contribute irreplaceably to woman's pleasure but they are only two caresses among many to do so.

Caressing the breasts, touching the vulva, opening the lips, gently stroking the posterior wall of the vagina, lightly massaging the cervix, etc., evoke a few of the most specifically female pleasures. They remain rather unfamiliar pleasures in the sexual difference as it is currently imagined, or rather as it is currently ignored: the other sex being only the indispensable complement of the only sex.

But *woman has sex organs just about everywhere*. She experiences pleasure almost everywhere. Even without speaking of the hysterization of her entire body, one can say that the geography of her pleasure is much more diversified, more multiple in its differences, more complex, more subtle, than is imagined—in an imaginary centered a bit too much on one and the same.

"She" is indefinitely other in herself. That is undoubtedly the reason she is called temperamental, incomprehensible, perturbed, capricious— not to mention her language in which "she" goes off in all directions and in which "he" is unable to discern the coherence of any meaning. Contradictory words seem a little crazy to the logic of reason, and inaudible for him who listens with ready-made grids, a code prepared in advance. In her statements—at least when she dares to speak out— woman retouches herself constantly. She just barely separates from herself some chatter, an exclamation, a half-secret, a sentence left in suspense— When she returns to it, it is only to set out again from another point of pleasure or pain. One must listen to her differently in order to hear an *"other meaning" which is constantly in the process of weaving itself, at the same time ceaselessly embracing words and yet casting them off to avoid becoming fixed, immobilized*. For when "she" says something, it is already no longer identical to what she means. Moreover, her statements are never identical to anything. Their distinguishing feature is one of contiguity. They touch (*upon*). And when they wander too far from this nearness, she stops and begins again from "zero": her body-sex organ.

It is therefore useless to trap women into giving an exact definition of what they mean, to make them repeat (themselves) so the meaning will be clear. They are already elsewhere than in this discursive machinery where you claim to take them by surprise. They have turned back within themselves, which does not mean the same thing as "within yourself." They do not experience the same interiority that you do and which perhaps you mistakenly presume they share. "Within themselves" means *in the privacy of this silent, multiple, diffuse tact*. If you ask them insistently what they are thinking about, they can only reply: nothing. Everything.

Thus they desire at the same time nothing and everything. It is always more and other than this *one*—of sex, for example—that you give them, that you attribute to them and which is often interpreted, and feared, as a sort of insatiable hunger, a voracity which will engulf you entirely. While in fact it is really a question of another economy which diverts the linearity of a project, undermines the target-object of a desire, explodes the polarization of desire on only one pleasure, and disconcerts fidelity to only one discourse—

Must the multiple nature of female desire and language be understood as the fragmentary, scattered remains of a raped or denied sexuality? This is not an easy question to answer. The rejection, the exclusion of a female imaginary undoubtedly places woman in a position where she can experience herself only fragmentarily as waste or as excess in the little structured margins of a dominant ideology, this mirror entrusted by the (masculine) "subject" with the task of reflecting and redoubling himself. The role of "femininity" is prescribed moreover by this masculine specula(riza)tion and corresponds only slightly to woman's desire, which is recuperated only secretly, in hiding, and in a disturbing and unpardonable manner.

But if the female imaginary happened to unfold, if it happened to come into play other than as pieces, scraps, deprived of their assemblage, would it present itself for all that as *a* universe? Would it indeed be volume rather than surface? No. Unless female imaginary is taken to mean, once again, the prerogative of the maternal over the female. This maternal would be phallic in nature however, closed in upon the jealous possession of its valuable product, and competing with man in his esteem for surplus. In this race for power, woman loses the uniqueness of her pleasure. By diminishing herself in volume, she renounces the pleasure derived from the nonsuture of her lips: she is a mother certainly, but she is a virgin mother. Mythology long ago assigned this role to her in which she is allowed a certain social power as long as she is reduced, with her own complicity, to sexual impotence.

Thus a woman's (re)discovery of herself can only signify the possibility of not sacrificing any of her pleasures to another, of not identifying with anyone in particular, of never being simply one. It is a sort of universe in expansion for which no limits could be fixed and which, for all that, would not be incoherency. Nor would it be the polymorphic perversion of the infant during which its erogenous zones await their consolidation under the primacy of the phallus.

Woman would always remain multiple, but she would be protected from dispersion because the other is a part of her, and is autoerotically familiar to her. That does not mean that she would appropriate the other for herself, that she would make it her property. Property and propriety are undoubtedly rather foreign to all that is female. At least sexually. *Nearness*, however, is not foreign to woman, a nearness so close that any identification of one or the other, and therefore any form of property, is impossible. Woman enjoys a closeness with the other that is *so near she cannot possess it, any more than she can possess herself.* She constantly trades herself for the other without any possible identification of either one of them. Woman's pleasure, which grows indefinitely from its passage in/through the other, poses a problem for any current economy in that all computations that attempt to account for woman's incalculable pleasure are irremediably destined to fail.

However, in order for woman to arrive at the point where she can enjoy her pleasure as a woman, a long detour by the analysis of the various systems of oppression which affect her is certainly necessary. By claiming to resort to pleasure alone as the solution to her problem, she runs the risk of missing the reconsideration of a social practice upon which *her* pleasure depends.

For woman is traditionally use-value for man, exchange-value among men. Merchandise, then. This makes her the guardian of matter whose price will be determined by "subjects": workers, tradesmen, consumers, according to the standard of their work and their need-desire. Women are marked phallically by their fathers, husbands, procurers. This stamp-(ing) determines their value in sexual commerce. Woman is never anything more than the scene of more or less rival exchange between two men, even when they are competing for the possession of mother-earth.

How can this object of transaction assert a right to pleasure without extricating itself from the established commercial system? How can this merchandise relate to other goods on the market other than with aggressive jealousy? How can raw materials possess themselves without provoking in the consumer fear of the disappearance of his nourishing soil? How can this exchange in nothingness that can be defined in "proper" terms of woman's desire not seem to be pure enticement, folly, all too quickly covered over by a more sensible discourse and an apparently more tangible system of values?

A woman's evolution, however radical it might seek to be, would not suffice then to liberate woman's desire. Neither political theory nor political practice have yet resolved nor sufficiently taken into account this historical problem, although Marxism has announced its importance. But women are not, strictly speaking, a class and their dispersion in several classes makes their political struggle complex and their demands sometimes contradictory.

Their underdeveloped condition stemming from their submission by/to a culture which oppresses them, uses them, cashes in on them, still remains. Women reap no advantage from this situation except that of their quasi-monopoly of masochistic pleasure, housework, and reproduction. The power of slaves? It is considerable since the master is not necessarily well served in matters of pleasure. Therefore, the inversion of the relationship, especially in sexual economy, does not seem to be an enviable objective.

But if women are to preserve their auto-eroticism, their homo-sexuality, and let it flourish, would not the renunciation of heterosexual pleasure simply be another form of this amputation of power that is traditionally associated with women? Would this renunciation not be a new incarceration, a new cloister that women would willingly build? Let women tacitly go on strike, avoid men long enough to learn to defend their desire notably by their speech, let them discover the love of other women protected from that imperious choice of men which puts them in a position of rival goods, let them forge a social status which demands recognition, let them earn their living in order to leave behind their condition of prostitute— These are certainly indispensable steps in their effort to escape their proletarization on the trade market. But, if their goal is to reverse the existing order—even if that were possible— history would simply repeat itself and return to phallocratism, where neither women's sex, their imaginary, nor their language can exist.

Translated by Claudia Reeder

Luce Irigaray

The trade that organizes patriarchal societies takes place exclusively among men. Women, signs, goods, currency, all pass from one man to another or—so it is said—suffer the penalty of relapsing into the incestuous and exclusively endogamous ties that would paralyze all commerce. The work force, products, even those of mother-earth, would thus be the object of transactions among men only. This signifies that the *very possibility of the socio-cultural order would necessitate homosexuality*. Homosexuality is the law that regulates the socio-cultural order. Heterosexuality amounts to the assignment of roles in the economy: some are given the role of producing and exchanging subjects, while others are assigned the role of productive earth and goods.

Culture, at least patriarchal culture, would prohibit then the return to *red blood*, and even sex. *The result is the sovereign authority of pretense which does not yet recognize its endogamies.* For sex, and different sexes, would exist only as prescribed by the successful conduct of (business) relations among men.

Why then consider masculine homosexuality as an exception, while in fact it is the very basis of the general economy? Why exclude homosexuals, when society postulates homosexuality? Unless it is because the "incest" at work in homosexuality must be kept in the realm of pretense. And so it is, exemplarily so, in father-son relations which assure the genealogy of patriarchal power, its laws, its discourse, its sociality. These relations which are operative everywhere can neither disappear—in the abolition of the family or of monogamic reproduction, for example—nor be displayed openly in their pederastic love, nor be practiced in any other way but in language without provoking a general crisis. A certain symbolic order would come to an end.

"Other"—masculine—homosexual relations would be equally subver-

"Des marchandises entre elles" [When the goods get together] in *Ce sexe qui n'en est pas un* [This sex which is not one] (Minuit, 1977).

sive and thus, forbidden. By interpreting openly the law of social functioning, they risk indeed the displacement of its horizon. Moreover, they
bring into question the nature, the status, the "exogamic" necessity of
proceeds from trade. By short-circuiting the commercial transactions,
would they also expose what is really at stake in such dealings? Masculine homosexual relations devaluate the exalted worth of the standard
of value. When the penis itself becomes simply a means of pleasure, and
indeed a means of pleasure among men, *the phallus loses its power.*
Pleasure, so it is said, should be left to women, those creatures so unfit
for the seriousness of symbolic rules.

Trade relations, always among men, would thus be *both required and
forbidden by the law.* These masculine subjects would be traders only
at the price of renouncing their function as goods.

All economic management would thus be homosexual. The management of desire, even the desire for woman, would also be homosexual.
Woman exists only as the possibility of mediation, transaction, transi-
tion, transference—between man and his fellow-creatures, indeed between man and himself.

If this strange status of the aforementioned heterosexuality has been
able to pass unnoticed and can still do so, *how can one account for the
relations between women in this system of trade?* Except by affirming
that as soon as she desires (herself), as soon as she speaks (herself, to
herself), the woman is a man. Within this system of trade, as soon as
she relates to another woman, she is a *male* homosexual.

That's what Freud demonstrates in his analyses of female homosexuality.[1]

A female homosexual's choice can be determined only by a "virility
complex." Whether it is the "direct prolongation of infantile virility"
or the "regression toward the former virility complex," it is *only as a
man that the female homosexual can desire a woman who reminds her
of a man.* Thus, in their relation one to the other, female homosexuals
"play indiscriminately the role of mother and child, or of husband and
wife."

Mother: phallic power; the child: never anything but a little boy;
husband: man-father. Woman? "Doesn't exist." She borrows the disguise which she is required to assume. She mimes the role imposed upon
her. The only thing really expected of her is that she *maintain, without
fail, the circulation of pretense by enveloping herself in femininity.*
Whence the error, the infraction, the misconduct, the torture which

[1] Cf. "Psychogénèse d'un cas d'homosexualité féminine" [The psychogenesis of a case
of female homosexuality] *Névrose, psychose et perversion,* P. U. F.

female homosexuality entails. How can female homosexuality be diminished? By reducing it to "acting like a man."

Thus the female homosexual, Freud's at any rate, "clearly adopted the masculine pattern of behavior vis-à-vis the object of her love." "Not only had she chosen an object of female sex, but also she had adopted vis-à-vis the object of her love a virile attitude." She became "a man and, putting herself in her father's place, she took her (phallic) mother as the object of love." Her fixation on "the lady" is nevertheless explained by the fact that "the slimness of this lady, her harsh beauty and coarse manners reminded [Freud's patient] of her own brother who was slightly older than she."

How can one account for this "perversion" of the sexual function assigned to a "normal" woman? The psychoanalyst's interpretation is no easy matter. Female homosexuality seems to be a phenomenon so foreign to his "theory," to his (cultural) imaginary, that he can only "disregard the psychoanalytic interpretation."

In order that science not be too shaken up by this embarrassing question, Freud has only to attribute it to an anatomo-physiological cause: "The constitutional factor is, in this case, of undeniably decisive importance." And Freud will be on the watch for anatomical indices which justify the—*masculine*—homosexuality of his "female patient." "The girl's physical characteristics certainly did not deviate from the womanly pattern." She was "beautiful and well proportioned," and "had no menstruation problems either," but "she had, it is true, the tall bearing of her father and pronounced features rather than femininely gracious ones." These features, in addition to her "intellectual qualities which indicate a virile character," "can be considered as indications of somatic virility." In certain cases, however, "the psychoanalyst is in the habit of forbidding himself a thorough physical examination of his patients."

Otherwise, what would Freud have found as anatomical proof of the —*masculine*—homosexuality of his "female patient"? What would his unavowable desire of disguise have made him "see"? In order to cover over his/these fantasies with an objectivity which is always anatomo-physiological in nature, he speaks only of "probable hermaphrodite ovaries." And— he sends the girl away, advising her to "continue the therapeutic endeavor with a female doctor, if she still considered it worthwhile."

Nothing about *feminine* homosexuality has been mentioned. Neither the girl's, nor Freud's. The "patient" even seemed absolutely indifferent to the progression of the cure, although "intellectually she participated a great deal." *Could it be that the only transference concerned is that of Freud himself?* Negative transference, as they say. Or rather, denied transference. How could he possibly identify with a woman who moreover was of "bad sexual reputation," had "loose morals," and "lived quite simply from the traffic of her charms"? How could his "superego" have permitted him to be "quite simply" a woman? That would have been the only way however, not to prohibit his "female patient's" transference.

Thus female homosexuality escaped the psychoanalyst. That does not mean that what Freud writes is simply inaccurate. The dominant sociocultural economy permits "female homosexuals" only the choice between a sort of *animality* that Freud seems to disavow or the mime of *masculine models*. The interplay of desire among women's bodies, sexes, and speech is inconceivable in the dominant socio-cultural economy.

Female homosexuality exists, nevertheless. But it is admitted only in as far as it is prostituted to the fantasies of men. Goods can only enter into relations under the surveillance of their "guardians." It would be out of the question for them to go to the "market" alone, to profit from their own value, to talk to each other, to desire each other, without the control of the selling-buying-consuming subjects. And their relations must be relations of rivalry in the interest of tradesmen.

But what if the "goods" refused to go to market"? What if they maintained among themselves "another" kind of trade?

Exchange without identifiable terms of trade, without accounts, without end— Without one plus one, without series, without number. Without a standard of value. Where *red blood* and *pretense* would no longer be distinguished one from the other by deceptive packaging that masks their respective worth. Where use and exchange would mingle. Where the most valuable would also be the least held in reserve. Where nature would spend itself without exhaustion, trade without labor, give of itself—protected from masculine transactions—for nothing: there would be free enjoyment, well-being without suffering, pleasure without possession. How ironic calculations, savings, more or less ravishing appropriations, and arduous capitalizations would be!

Utopia? Perhaps. Unless this mode of exchange has always undermined the order of trade and simply has not been recognized because the necessity of restricting incest to the realm of pure pretense has forbidden a certain economy of abundance.

Translated by Claudia Reeder

Marguerite Duras

Men are regressing everywhere, in all areas. At present, women possess a much greater aptitude for intelligence. The criterion on which men judge intelligence is still the capacity to theorize and in all the movements that one sees now, in whatever area it may be, cinema, theater, literature, the theoretical sphere is losing influence. It has been under attack for centuries. It ought to be crushed by now, it should lose itself in a reawakening of the senses, blind itself, and be still.

Men must cease to be theoretical imbeciles. The solid stand taken all over the world (and brought about by young people) on the minimal human condition (of which women and workers are prime examples) implies that men must renounce their theoretical rattle and accept the silence which is common to all oppressed people.

Men must learn to be silent. This is probably very painful for them. To quell their theoretical voice, the exercise of theoretical interpretation. They must watch themselves carefully. One has scarcely the time to experience an event as important as May '68 before men begin to speak out, to formulate theoretical epilogues, and to break the silence. Yes, these prating men were up to their old tricks during May '68. They are the ones who started to speak, to speak alone and for everyone else, on behalf of everyone else, as they put it. They immediately forced women and extremists to keep silent. They activated the old language, enlisted the aid of the old way of theorizing, in order to relate, to recount, to explain this new situation: May '68.

They acted as theoretical policemen and this widespread, quiet commotion that was rising from the crowd—here silence is precisely the sum

From an interview in *La création étouffée* [Smothered creativity] (Horay, 1973). The first half of this book is an analysis by Suzanne Horer and Jeanne Socquet of practical and cultural obstacles encountered by women creators. The second part is a series of interviews with "creative" women, including anonymous and well-known writers, artists, film makers, composers, chefs, and scientists.

of the voices of everyone, the equivalent of the sum of our collective breathing—they stifled it.

They were afraid, basically; they were disoriented. Suddenly there was no longer any forum for eloquence and they grabbed onto the old discourse; they brought it to their aid. There was no silence after May '68. And this collective silence was necessary because it would have been through this silence that a new mode of being would have been fostered; it would have been from common obscurity that collective actions would have sprung into being and found direction.

No, men had to disrupt everything and stop the flow of silence.

I am profoundly discouraged when I think of this crime. For it was a crime and a masculine one. It is men who made me nauseous at the thought of any activism after 1968. It is not by chance that the women's liberation movement followed immediately.

It is an extraordinary thing, but men still see themselves as supreme authorities on women's liberation. They say: "In my opinion women should do this or that to liberate themselves—" And when people laugh they don't understand why. Then they take up the old refrain—their veneration of women. Whatever form this veneration of women takes, be it religious or surrealist, and even Georges Bataille is guilty of it, it is still racism. But when you point this out to men, they don't understand.

How could they understand that the women they revere are the same ones who appear before them in the society that they oversee, these slaves, these functional objects? Men don't see their idols, so, as a last recourse, they speak about the charm that today's women have lost— as they would evoke the various skies over Verdun—and they are filled with self-pity.

We will have to wait until whole generations have disappeared, whole worlds of men. In this area I think only young people will transgress stereotypes and bring about change. At present, by the time men are thirty they are condemned as far as this is concerned. Not only will they never be able to understand, they will never be able to see, to look around them. They are a lost cause. Men don't know what's what any more. Their most backward attitude is their desire to continue ruling. Men are like old kings who think they are still in power when they have ceased to reign. And I think that the various other aspects of their retrograde behavior stem directly from their most important regressive stance: they still want to rule.

Many men whom I know, even young men, have incredibly antiquated, old-fashioned, grotesque attitudes when it comes to women's liberation. It is as if suddenly their intelligence ceased functioning, as if it were switched off. It's strange. Besides, look at how they have recourse to ridicule: it is their major defense, the defense of the weak of course.

Q: Do you think women will gain power through a revolutionary movement or through day to day struggle, whatever the cost?

It has already begun. It won't stop. It will proceed faster than the revolution. It has begun in all the countries of the world. It's striking. I don't see anything that can stop it, not even the backward attitude of 60 percent of the female population who want to remain functional.

Translated by Virginia Hules

Warnings

This section introduces dissenting voices. They offer various objections to some of the more extreme anti-theoretical, anti-male positions that could lead to new forms of marginality and isolation for women. They question the correlation between sexual and linguistic specificity. They fear a new "feminine" terrorism within the feminist movement.

Antoinette Fouque

In May 1968 I was at the Sorbonne. The revolutionary fête seemed to me to be threatened by "isms," including feminism, that conferred dignity on the ruling ideologies. Three of us, then ten of us, formed a group of women in which top priority was given to making connections between two "discourses": psychoanalytic discourse and historical materialism. . . .

The actions proposed by the feminist groups are spectacular, provoking. But provocation only brings to light a certain number of social contradictions. It does not reveal radical contradictions within society. The feminists claim that they do not seek equality with men, but their practice proves the contrary to be true. Feminists are a bourgeois avant-garde that maintains, in an inverted form, the dominant values. Inversion does not facilitate the passage to another kind of structure. Reformism suits everyone! Bourgeois order, capitalism, phallocentrism are ready to integrate as many feminists as will be necessary. Since these women are becoming men, in the end it will only mean a few more men. The difference between the sexes is not whether one does or doesn't have a penis, it is whether or not one is an integral part of a phallic masculine economy. . . .

Women cannot allow themselves to deal with political problems while at the same time blotting out the unconscious. If they do, they become, at best, feminists capable of attacking patriarchy on an ideological level but not on a symbolic level. An example? *The Last Tango in Paris*. A liberated young woman kills a man in order to escape from being raped. She kills a poor psychotic with her father's revolver. That's the typical feminist! Bourgeoise, in revolt, wearing boots. She commits a heinous crime in the name of the father and with absolute impunity.

Quoted in Nicole Muchnik's "Le MLF c'est toi, c'est moi" [The MLF is you, is me] in *Le nouvel observateur*, September 1973.

If capitalism is based on the sexual division of work, the women's struggle is based on sexual difference. The only discourse on sexuality that exists is the psychoanalytic discourse. Therefore the women's struggle must of necessity deal with the dialectical relationship between historical materialism and psychoanalysis. . . .

Woman's primary, fundamental homosexuality should only be a passage toward a rediscovered and truly free heterosexuality.

Translated by Elaine Marks

Denise Le Dantec

I fear that women's speech and women's writing are being rapidly institutionalized, and it's a shame. It invades almost everything. You have to become a "terrorist" again in order to be heard and what you have to do to yourself to become a terrorist is by nature hateful and I don't like it a bit: I don't like women warriors even if at one time they were necessary and it is thanks to them that we can write at all.

"They" are publishing us all over the place: yes there is a modishness that I can't stand and that makes me suffer. Because we are losing our song, that quality of "effusion" (though that is not the word I would use)— In any case, people are buying us (at a bad price like all writers in France) and selling us (rather well, even if it is bad). We risk falling into the trap and, once again, questions such as "Who and how are we?" are asked. Power fascinates us as much as it fascinates men, except that we don't have any. But so much the better. Because by repeatedly saying "it's their fault, the fault of the men" we may finally realize our own responsibility in the story, and in History with a capital "H." We may have to accept the fact that accepting the role of slave is exactly the same as accepting the role of master.... We must leave behind that particular dialectic for a momentary pessimism that is both critical and necessary. I realize that I am very harsh, but it is because all of that is difficult for me.

Translated by Marilyn R. Schuster

From an unpublished interview by Elaine Marks, Summer 1976.

Maria-Antonietta Macciocchi

The development of the feminist movement (this movement is perhaps the most solid bastion that has resisted fascism in Europe since 1968) allows us at last to ask the question: if we do not analyze the kind of "consent" or of relationship that there was (or that there is?) between women and fascist ideology—in other words if we do not analyze how and why fascism mystified women—feminism itself (as well as avant-garde politics) will be cut off from its historical hinterland, suspended like a balloon atemporal, immemorial, and therefore deprived of the essential dialectic necessary to an understanding of today's risks and the direction of the main thrust of the feminine and revolutionary struggle.

Translated by Elaine Marks

From "Sexualité féminine dans l'idéologie fasciste" [Feminine sexuality in fascist ideology] in *Tel quel*, Summer 1976. This is an extract from a speech delivered at the International Conference on Sexuality and Politics held in Milan, November 28, 1975.

Arlette Laguiller

Aubenas:[1] During your electoral campaign you concentrated both on the class struggle and on women's liberation.

Laguiller: Yes. As long as there is a class struggle, there will be women's oppression but also, and independently from this class oppression, there is women's oppression. In my campaign I addressed myself to women in general. Marxists think that there is contempt for and oppression of women at every level of society. It's not by accident that bourgeois women become the first feminists: they are slaves in gilded cages. As for the workers, they suffer more from their boss than from their husband, from not having enough money to support their family more than from washing the dishes alone. The struggle for their liberation as women, however, is also easier for women who work: when you begin to struggle against the boss, this automatically becomes the road that brings you to struggle for sexual equality. You gain confidence; like a man you are able to defend your comrades at work. In the militant consciousness it is by struggling on the level of class that you rid yourself of a whole lot of prejudices.

As long as we are not in a socialist society, the problem of women will subsist. In the USSR the great momentum of the October Revolution was brought to a standstill by economic difficulties and since they couldn't give women the means to liberate themselves from familial and domestic tasks they once again started to glorify the family and the eternal feminine. They justified it from a theoretical point of view but they should have said that it was a step backwards for the revolution

---

From an interview by Jacqueline Aubenas in *Les Cahiers du GRIF*, March 1975. *Les Cahiers du GRIF* is a Belgian feminist review. Each issue contains articles and a bibliography organized around a specific topic. There are also book reviews and summaries of important feminist events.
[1] Jacqueline Aubenas, co-editor of the review with Françoise Colin, is writing a book in collaboration with M.-A. Macciocchi entitled *Lutte des femmes* [Women's struggle].—Ed.

because they lacked the material means. The liberation of women from domestic chores is very important but the solution is not to say that it is up to the men to assume these. You have to get rid of those chores, to live differently. I lead an easier life than women who have children. I prefer to eat in a restaurant rather than do the shopping and the cooking— It's a question of one's possibilities. When you can live differently, you do so. In order for this to be true for all women, for all couples, there has to be the wherewithal. Consciousness must change too, but you'll only get there by changing the system. The ideas about women are relative to the economic and political problems: we're entering a period of unemployment and it's going to be women who will pay the price. They're going to be told that ideologically their liberation consists in cooking cheaper cuts of meat and that this is more economical than if they work and grill a steak in five minutes.

Aubenas: The MLF is also struggling for women's liberation.

Laguiller: I agree with the MLF on a certain number of points: equality of the sexes, women being maids or whores, day-care centers, women's strikes. Where I disagree is on the subject of an organization consisting only of women. I think it is a political problem: if a strong revolutionary movement existed we could afford the luxury of such an organization. But we constitute very small groups, terribly weak ones, and our attempt to penetrate the working class is essential. We'll change nothing without it. First of all, the most important thing for us is to build an organization of revolutionary men and women. Secondly there's one thing that bothers me: it's a certain way of not fighting. Women must fight within the existing political organizations. They seek refuge in the policy of segregation in order to be sure of working alone, on their own, etc. Women in the feminist movements are not politicized: for them there are women's problems and then there are the larger problems of humanity which are to be settled by men. I disagree. In the revolutionary organizations it isn't in our interest to talk uniquely about women's problems just because we are women: we want to work on all of the big problems.

Women's problems can definitely be coopted by the bourgeoisie. Not right now because we are entering a difficult period: an economic crisis, unemployment. In a period of full employment, the feminist theses can be coopted by the bourgeoisie. I am not saying that within the revolutionary organizations there are no problems, including some vis-à-vis the women; but to be a feminist means to fight within your own party, your own organization. Women will not be acknowledged if they hide behind women's problems. I belong to an organization where I have no such problems and if I belong to it, it's for this reason. We're revolutionary, our comrades are revolutionary; I'm not saying that in terms of individual behavior there's nothing to discuss because we are conditioned by society and have our prejudices (women too), but it is the role of the revolutionary political organization to change these militants. We militate for a society in which men and women will be equal and we are trying to concretize this right now within our personal relationships. My group picked me in order to stir up prejudices. If the political parties pick so few women as their candidates, it's because they take the prejudices of their constituencies seriously. (Marchais explains it in *L'humanité*:[2] a woman representative for lots of people, is unimaginable, therefore it only leads to the loss of electoral seats.) As far as we were concerned, we knew that in the working classes there are very powerful anti-feminist prejudices; so it was a matter of provoking these and in addition to this it also corresponded to our internal structure: there are women at the head of "Lutte ouvrière" ("Workers' Struggle"). It wasn't just a gimmick, for us it was real.

Sexism is like racism. The further down you go into the poor segments of society, the deeper are those secular prejudices. The more a person is exploited the more a person needs to exploit someone else— It can be said that many bourgeois are not racists whereas it is really they who are the carriers of racism. As far as behavior is concerned, workers are more racist but it is the bourgeoisie who is responsible for this ideology. When you're oppressed you're anesthetized by a lot of things.

Aubenas: But what about feminism?

Laguiller: Feminism, except on very limited issues (abortion) cannot bring together all women in a common struggle. Class oppression is stronger. Men are as hassled as women within the couple and in their militant action. I belong to you, you belong to me. There are guys who don't go out at night in order to avoid problems with their wives. Their situation gives men more privileges but they would also have a lot to gain from a change in the relationship between men and women.

In my milieu—which is a workers' milieu—I have never known women who had emancipated themselves on the woman question before they had emancipated themselves on the political question. When a woman reaches political consciousness and becomes aware of trade unionism, it is infinitely easier to get her to fight in the area of her personal life than the other way around. That's normal. It's the class oppression that is the stronger one. This is less true in the other, upper segments of society. The first oppression women feel there is much more that of sexism than of social oppression since they have no problem in that area. There are two ways of approaching the problem of women

---

[2] French Communist newspaper, the official organ of the party. Georges Marchais is one of the party's leaders.—Tr.

according to social class, and feminists will always run into this obstacle. Personally I am not a feminist but I would not have militated in an organization that did not fight on that issue.

Aubenas: What do you think of the creation of a Secretary of State for the Status of Women? [3]

Laguiller: The Secretary of State for the Status of Women is a kind of G-string which the government gave itself. It won't solve anything. A woman in a rightist regime can't do much for the workers, and the problem of women concerns female workers in particular. Day-care centers—nothing will be done, no credits will be allotted for day care. Françoise Giroud is a kind of weathervane.... What she's obtaining, flexible working hours and all that, already existed and these things will be enforced only if they're convenient for the bosses. There are several little things. But even her line about no longer being able to refuse employment to a pregnant woman is a joke. If it looks obvious they'll find another reason not to hire her, otherwise they'll find a reason later on. All bosses have ways to turn the law around. The law that concerns equal salaries is also a joke in its application. In order to apply it you'd have to drag the bosses into court, something that is unthinkable in the system as it is.

In my own campaign I denounced the absence of women in social and political life, I denounced the inequality of salaries, I spoke at the time about abortion. But I insisted on the global aspects of changing society more than on making a list of women's demands. For me the most important thing is to bring women to the political battleground. You have to change everything from top to bottom: education, etc. You have to have a society which has the means to raise its children— I don't have any ready-made plans. I think that all women are hassled in today's society and at that level I don't mind being called a feminist but that is not my priority in terms of struggle, it is only a parallel struggle for me.

Aubenas: What can be done now?

Laguiller: The fact that there are no women within the political structure is only the normal reflection of their position of inferiority. But if there were more of them this would not necessarily change things. Women heads of government do not automatically make society better; it's a question of political regime. Political power cannot exist without the daily control of the workers. I don't believe in a feminist victory within a capitalist society. We will lick that problem in another kind of society.

Translated by Isabelle de Courtivron

[3] This position, held by Françoise Giroud between 1974 and 1976, no longer exists. In 1978 a new Ministry for the Status of Women was created with Madeleine Pelletier as Minister.

Madeleine Vincent

... But only the revolutionary movement, as it becomes stronger, will provide the real solutions. That is why the feminism of today, especially when it is called the new feminism, has an obsolete, out-of-date sound to it, which takes us back a century, and cannot give a true orientation to women's struggle.

Where, in fact, are we? Today, the objective conditions have changed as much on the national level as on the international level. In France there is the possibility of a new democratic government that might be followed by socialism. There is an influential Communist party which for a long time has considered the problem of women's situation as an important national question that must be dealt with, and it acts accordingly. Unions, especially the [Communist] C.G.T. (Confédération Générale du Travail), also consider that the defense of women's interests is indispensable to the success and unity of the working class. And women play a particularly important role in these organizations. The workers' movement supports women's interests. Is there need for another stimulus? Where could a better one be found than in the workers' movement itself? We must remember that 30 percent of the Communist party, for example, is made up of women. How could we possibly not listen to women when we have such antennae? We've come a long way since the nineteenth century!

The proposals of the French Communist party answer the essential aspirations of women. Millions of women no longer look for the causes of the inequalities that have made them victims. How could one substitute for that, or even try to establish a parallel opposition between men and women which would evade the social question? But since so many wrong reasons and remedies are given for inequality, why is it astonishing that the first violent reaction of women with problems is to blame men, even those who are scarcely better off than the women?

From "Une grande donnée de notre temps" [A basic fact of our time] in *Femmes: quelle libération?* [Women: what liberation?] (Editions Sociales, 1976).

Isn't it the same phenomenon as when the taxpayer blames the tax collector and a failing student's parents, the teacher? But in these cases, the ones who are really responsible get off easily! The immense force that women represent would be lost if the real causes and the real solutions were obscured.

How have ideas progressed?

The influx of women into the work force in this century has given rise to many interpretations. While using women workers for its profit, the bourgeoisie has at the same time maintained in its men workers the negative notion of a rivalry between men and women. It has also developed the idea that work for women is a last resort and also the idea that the man should be the only one to work and to provide for the material needs of the family. At each step a long struggle against all these erroneous ideas has been necessary.

Have reactionary ideas given way? Certainly. They have retreated, thanks to the struggle of the workers' movement, thanks especially to the struggles of the French Communist party. They have retreated with the massive entrance of women into heavy industrial production, and through all sorts of work for women's rights. For a large number of women it is becoming clearer that their fate is linked to that of workers as a whole. And it has become clear to many male workers that the discriminations suffered by women prejudice their own condition.

Individual consciousnesses have without doubt evolved along with these struggles (which themselves could only be victorious by defeating reactionary theories and ideas). That's evident. But obviously, these backward ideas regularly resurface, according to the interest of the moment. Is it necessary to point out the violence of the campaigns criticizing working women in terms of their relation to their children, and those who stay at home in relation to other women? The reader will also remember that a campaign against day care began a few years ago in order to mask the negligence of the government in this area.

Who, if not the bourgeoisie, refused for so long to grant suffrage to women? Bear in mind that this refusal was still effective scarcely thirty years ago. Those who govern us prove their hypocrisy when they attribute to the democratic movement the cause of the delay of women's participation in the elected bodies.

For example, in electing women to municipal councils when they were still ineligible to participate in them, who better than the Communist party could contribute to the retreat of reactionary perspectives on the right to vote? In contrast, who, if not the *grande bourgeoisie*, has multiplied the images of woman as an object submissive to man? Who propagates them today by means of the important audio-visual media, women's magazines, and film?

It is necessary therefore to call on men and women, together and at the same time, to reject out-of-date ideas and false solutions. Opposing women to men without analyzing the social structures and social givens, refusing to see the fundamental reasons for inequalities, does not contribute to the improvement of women's condition. On the contrary, it only prolongs the inequality from which women suffer. It retards any possible progress.

But the struggle against the inferiority of women's status, by showing the profound reasons for it, and by proposing concrete solutions to remedy the situation now, raises consciousnesses. This is the kind of efficacious action that will rid our ideology of all its old prejudices.

Reconciling the classes?

The followers of the "new feminism" have also stated that they want to "reconcile the classes." But can one reconcile the exploiter and the exploited? Isn't it better, to arrive at a real emancipation of women, to unite all men and women who suffer from the same political situation, a situation managed for the exclusive profit of the rich and the powerful? Actually, the slogans of the "reconciliation of the classes" have always served to prolong the worst of exploitations.

But let it be understood: we are not looking for a useless argument over words. We know that certain women consider themselves feminists because like us they passionately desire a real advancement of women in society.

We are happy to find them taking part in numerous collective actions. We are determined to make use of their real effectiveness in the steps taken by women to "live differently," to "affirm their personality," to "participate wholeheartedly in the affairs of society." And that is why we are fighting against anything that might slow down women's participation in the democratic movement.

Of course, we don't think that all women will come to this action in the same way, no more than men have. The people of our country differ greatly. Different social categories have different needs. And sometimes the same aspiration is expressed in different ways. Marx has shown, and experience proves, that "modes of existence, social practice determine consciousness through a complex network of mediations." This very diversity justifies the necessity of the largest possible alliance, and we are working toward it passionately. We feel very excited when any social category expresses in its own way a demand of similar consequence. We see in this manifestation the expression of a supplementary richness.

However, we are resolutely opposed to anything that ignores the real emancipation of women by depriving the democratic combat of part of its forces.

Not mistaking the target

For example, the "new feminism" is currently developing the thesis that no society, socialist or capitalist, is capable of favorably responding to the aspirations of women. Neither a socialist society nor a capitalist society could really end inequalities, because they are both made, thought, and organized "by men" and "for men."

The danger of this position is better grasped when we understand how the aspiration toward a better life is always linked with the idea of socialism. Of course, the amalgam between socialist and capitalist societies (this theme of convergence) is not a specifically feminist theme.

However, it is used to obscure the true conditions of the liberation of women. Equality in work, equality in the family, equality in society, equality in terms of social and political responsibilities, there are really no issues that are more relevant to our struggle for a fairer, more humane, more beautiful society.

And what means are suggested to us? Women's revolt? Revolt in the home? Revolt against love? Must we be content to shout "We want equality"? Is this sufficient to attain equality? Is this sufficient to transform the backward mentalities who on every level are opposed to real and rapid progress?

The struggle against these mentalities, the struggle for immediate improvement and for profound changes constitute one and the same action, against the same causes and the same persons who are responsible. The Communists are today still carrying forward this struggle against reactionary, backward, regressive viewpoints. Whom do they want to win over to their progressive ideas? The great majority of our nation, the working class first and foremost, and in this majority, women. It is therefore for workers and for women that they develop their argumentation. The Communists do not live in a vacuum. Every day more men and women with promising qualities but also often with erroneous ideas are becoming Communists. Clarification of thought is therefore necessary; it is the most effective way to avoid misunderstanding our goal.

If we direct against men the action necessary for women's progress, we condemn the great hopes of women to a dead end.

At the same time, if we consider that the two struggles (one against exploitation of the classes, the other against men) are to be led inde-

pendent of each other, we deprive the democratic fight of forces necessary to its victory. And we resolve none of the problems of women.

To put an end to all kinds of oppression, those born before the
division of society into classes, and those maintained and used to reinforce exploitation in general, we must attack exploitation itself.

For obvious reasons, those in power have every interest in hiding the
real causes of inequalities, and the nature of the obstacles in the way of
the advancement of women.

If the millions of women who today are closely examining the reality
of their situation, aspiring toward equality and wanting to live in a
different way, were to become conscious of the responsibility of capitalist
society for their present state, it would be an important step toward
necessary change.

What it is all about then is a decisive battle that is taking place on
the level of ideas, a battle whose objective is precisely the question of
real change. . . .

Translated by Susan O'Leary

Catherine Clément

Taking a stand as a woman. Every woman, in due course, arrives at that particular consciousness—sooner or later according to the complexities of her own biography. Every woman intellectual working more or less within language is currently solicited, stimulated, awakened at every turn; exasperated or exhilarated, she must finally, come what may, begin to think. Everything that had been, to a greater or lesser degree, suppressed by defense mechanisms is now submitted to an unceasing pressure that explodes the walls around us, or, in a more menacing way, expresses itself at times like a summons: "If you're a woman, show it." To refuse to take a stand, individually or collectively, is tantamount to a "collaboration" with oppression: a betrayal of something like a class or a people. It is, however, impossible to take a stand, and for a good reason: how can one detach a part of a mechanism that is constructed precisely so that one need not account for that part? It is logical then to assert: "If for us the void, which culture abhors, is irresistible, we will jump without a moment's hesitation or resistance, at the most arming our pleasure with some kind of braking parachute that will allow us to keep it in reserve. We would rather learn to land than to give up soaring— We will not allow ourselves to be surrounded or subjected, *we are elsewhere*" (des femmes, *Le quotidien des femmes*, no. 2).[1]

Assuming the *real* subjective position that corresponds to this discourse is another matter. One would have to cut through all the heavy

---

"Enclave Esclave" [Enslaved enclave] in *L'arc*, no. 61 (1975). The occasion that prompted the text was the third evening of the Week of Marxist Thought, which was devoted to Woman and Sexuality. The meeting was held in the large hall of the Mutualité. The speakers were Gisèle Moreau, Catherine Clément, Luce Irigaray, Annette Langevin, and Bernard Muldworf. During the discussion that followed the individual speeches, certain women's liberation groups reacted violently to the theoretical positions of Catherine Clément who, in the Marxist tradition, had insisted that class struggle is more fundamental than the struggle between the sexes.
[1] A newspaper published by the éditions des femmes.—Tr.

layers of ideology that have borne down since the beginnings of the family and private property: that can be done only in the imagination. And that is precisely what feminist action is all about: to change the imaginary in order then to be able to act on the real, to change the very forms of language which by its structure and history has been subject to a law that is patrilinear, therefore masculine. Reflection on feminist action, therefore, calls into question and into play the transformational powers of language, its capacity to motivate change in both ideology and economy. Beyond that, cultural revolution and its place in socialism is seen sometimes as necessary, sometimes as useless: a needlessly long itinerary, an action trap. I see cultural revolution as not only necessary, but dependent on a political, economic, and social revolution. But it is true that such a revolution places such high stakes on the very function of intellectuals, men and women, that the *anticipation* of it requires militant action. No doubt the way in which women are presented is elliptical in relation to a future form; what is manifest in the coming to consciousness of each of us can only be a deformation of an ultimate figure, which will emerge after and through a difficult progression from work to body and from body to language. To represent that future figure today as if it were there, immediately and realizable, free and unshackled, we must resort to a crude sketch; when so many working women are still denied equal pay, to prefigure is to disfigure, like a squiggle drawn by a child, which obscures and spoils the figures that surround it. But a squiggle already shows something; and a sketch can be fleshed out, and anticipation can become reality in the end. So there is no question of *not* anticipating the figure of liberated women; no question of *not* taking into account innovation of the imaginary, the work of language. "Intellectual activity interprets and sometimes anticipates in a specific way, according to its own rhythm and its own methods and laws, both productive activity and social and political battles." [2] The basic problem is therefore to join together the rhythm of intellectual activity—a specificity that it is impossible to enslave—with the rhythm of political struggles and mass movements: if we do not "disenclave" the work of language by mass, political work, it remains an enclave, therefore enslaved.

I was able to measure this problem fully on an evening of crisis; an evening during the Week of Marxist Thought when we were debating "sexuality" in the enormous hall at "la Mutualité": enormous for a theoretical debate, often too small for a public meeting. That evening the hall was packed, animated, and I was on the podium, facing along

[2] Roland Leroy, *Pour la culture avec les intellectuels* [For a culture with intellectuals], p. 28.

with a few others, the public foreclosure of the violences that feminisms stir up, facing their meaning and their range. It is a story I want to transcribe, implicating myself alone in the difficult task; it is moreover a *text in difficulty* that I want to write, in order to keep myself as much as possible in a true position.

Passion, reason. The sound of voices: cries, invectives, not just any invectives, their content is not indifferent. It begins with cries bursting forth, connecting to the speeches being delivered at the podium; thus, after spoken language that produces meaning and seeks to transmit a content of ideas. The interruptions seek to turn the sense around, steal it away, force it to leave the room. For example, someone at the podium says that there should be discussion without passion: what echoes forth from the audience is that it is exactly passion that is needed. The negative sense of passion is thus removed—passion that nullifies wise, discursive reason—and the positive sense of revolutionary passion is put in its place; the ghosts of Pasionaria[3] loom. But that makes discursive speech impossible, argument, persuasion; it nullifies all democratic notion of debate. On the one hand, the conviction that ideas can and should be transmitted through reasoning and reflection and on the other, the practice of speech that proves itself and its strength by imposition. Passion interrupts, punctuates. A long time is needed before its sense can reach the podium: without a speaker it circulates anonymously from woman to woman. At the podium, one is necessarily in a contrary position: nonymous, called to the podium because of one's name, the speaker and designated listener.

Foreseen, unforeseen spectacle. The setting up of a debate at the podium constructs, on the fringe of this particular spectacle, a counterspectacle, from which certain characters begin to emerge. A hall where public meetings are usually held, a hall peopled with political echoes, the ghosts of banners, leaves little room for an exchange of theoretical discourses. It is an untenable structure, a performance straining the limits of the possible: a theoretical debate presented and set forth among intellectuals and for intellectuals on the sexuality of women. Between the audience and the stage, Italian footlights made of lights and wood: the too numerous audience, by convention, cannot intervene. It is on this point that the other spectacle will emerge: implicated yet meant to be mute, "the audience," essential character, will nevertheless intervene. It will speak and cause things to happen: with its own bodies and voices, by moving, shouting, upsetting the order of the other spectacle. It will cause and speak disorder in relation to the order of the debate: but as

---

[3] Dolores Ibarruri, Spanish Republican militant during the Civil War 1936–1939. —Tr.

a character it plays its role in the complex ensemble formed by the podium and its listeners; and that ensemble is no longer a spectacle for anyone. And then the audience splits apart: anything but unanimous, divided, multiple.

Spectacle, women, passions: crisis of hysteria. Hysteria circulated constantly that evening, like an offensive weapon—unremittingly present, tossed about rightly and wrongly, assumed, rejected, badly understood. In order to show how imprisoned feminine sexuality finds escape hatches in crises, I had chosen an example found among contemporary peasant women in Apulia in southern Italy. There, women who are frequently illiterate and always poor, are afflicted with strange problems: they are bitten by tarantula spiders, and then afflicted with languor so that treatment according to an archaic rite is required. In front of an attentive, praying crowd, on a white sheet, they dance for twelve hours, mimicking the spider, crawling on the ground in convulsive gestures, accompanied by a small orchestra. Tarantulas do not exist in that region; and no insect bite produces these precise symptoms: thus we are dealing with imaginary insects which are coddled, named, and described in great psychological detail: Rosina, Peppina, spiders are "lustful," or "sad," or "sleepers." The hysterical peasants dance until they are touched by the grace of Saint Paul; then they are cured for a year, but they must put themselves in a crisis state regularly, for life. When one examines the lives of these women, it becomes obvious that they are bitten when they are in an affective or economic situation that is so conflict ridden that the crisis is the only way out. Salutary, challenging, the spectacular crisis is at once a prison and a liberation: a prison because it reproduces the articulations of a culture in which women are in a miserable position, and a liberation in that it constitutes the only sign that women can articulate even if it is shackled, corporal. There, in a setting analogous to the great crises Charcot[4] unleashed to the delight of the doctors watching around him (and Freud among them), femininity in revolt is played out along with the historical fetters that enclose it on all sides. Sartre, in reference to Flaubert and the crises that were crushing him, speaks of "hysterical commitment" and of *crisis as a positive strategy.*[5] Crisis, therefore, is always twofold: the only possible contestation in a particular social upbringing, in the context of the village community, it is also the lock and key of that society, its safety valve. This language which has not yet reached verbal expression, but is held within the confines of the body, which signifies the body on all sides but does not transmit it in the form

---

[4] French neurologist under whom Freud studied in Paris.—Tr.

[5] J.-P. Sartre, *L'idiot de la famille* (Gallimard, 1971), 2: 1923. [Sartre's monumental study of the writer Flaubert.—Tr.]

of a thought-content, remains convulsive. Men watch, but do not understand.

Mirrored, echoed. The "feminist" part of the audience rises up and in its turn assumes a crisis state. Words, then progressively a barrage of shouts. It is hard to listen to this barrage in which the aggressiveness of the shouts goes along with premeditated political action: women's crisis and obstruction. How can one hear correctly? They cry out: "We are all hysterics," just as once before we cried out, "We are all German Jews." [6] Thus, "hysteric" is construed as an insult, a racial slur; it would be true if this psychiatric category designated a reality in itself, an entity. That "hysteria," to which I add quotation marks visible in the written text, to show that it is a relative nosography, should be an integral part in fact, of the history of women, seems to constitute a provocation: when I point out the feminist crisis as if it were taking place in Apulia ("les Pouilles" in French)—is it the signifier "pouilleux" (lice-ridden, poor, miserable) working subconsciously?—the shouts amplify. "We women are all hysterics": if to be a hysteric is, as I think it is, to suffer in one's body from something that does not come from the body but from elsewhere; if to be a hysteric is to suffer in order to understand, then yes, in this society where one must sell one's ability to work in order to live, we are all hysterics. There is nothing in this syndrome that qualifies women particularly, only the history of mentalities, jurisdictions, revolts, witch burnings bears witness to the long association of the female body with what Greek doctors were the first to call "hysteria." That association is coming to an end.

At least. If one would only consider the feminine situation in the context in which it is inscribed, and not by itself, all alone, removed. The same goes for women as for madmen: in a *manifest* position of exclusion, they keep the system together, *latently*, by virtue of their very exclusion. Crisis signifies that as well. "In every society it is inevitable that a percentage . . . of individuals find themselves placed . . . outside of the system or between two or several irreducible systems. The group asks and demands of those people to figure certain forms of unrealizable compromises, on the level of the collectivity, to figure certain imaginary transitions, to embody incompatible syntheses. . . . Their peripheral position in relation to a local system, does not keep them from being by the same token, an integral part of a total system." [7] One can consider women as these abnormal individuals, afflicted with nervous disorders,

[6] Slogan of May 1968 showing solidarity with one of the most radical leaders, Daniel Cohn-Bendit.—Tr.

[7] C. Lévi-Strauss, Introduction to *Sociologie et anthropologie de Marcel Mauss* (Presses Universitaires de France, 1950) p. xx.

"bitten": compromises that are impossible to live, syntheses that are unrealizable, they are "women" in past societies, from which we are beginning to emerge, only because of the imaginary glue that keeps social figures in their respective roles: there, the man, the master; here, the woman, the hysteric, one comforting the other, the other demanding the one. But even if crisis resolves, it is only momentarily; if it liberates, it is only "for laughs." To be in crisis is to play the game of the one who demands the crisis: that one is always the same, the public.

"*Bravo, sir.*" A woman, among the others, sends forth this salutation from the balcony. It tumbles, falls. To speak, then, and still worse, to put oneself in a public position of theoretical premeditation, is to assume the position of "the man." That explains the shouts, mimicking, gestures, and, soon, the piercing cries of "Hey, hey"; though theory and articulated speech are inadmissible, shouted speech is allowed. In other words, more seriously and irremediably: that would mean that dialectics, for example—but there is nothing else—would be inaccessible to women, and it then becomes impossible to understand all contradiction and hence, all struggle. That would mean that by their nature—innate or acquired in oppression—women could not use thought to help free themselves; that the only scansion of violence permitted them is obtuse, unthinking in its expression. That would mean that language is always masculine, that it is determined according to sex, and that discursiveness is not an integral part of feminine discourse. Even if somewhere it is true that rhetoric and vocabulary are formed by centuries of male cultural domination, to renounce the exercise of thought, to give it to them, is *to perpetuate,* as always when it is a matter of "not being part of the system." "Be a feminist and shout"; an unchanged variant of "Be beautiful and keep your tongue."

To transmit. Knowledge, thought, dialectic, is to make things happen, to upset, change even a little, the conditions of consciousness in relation to the dominant ideology. Intellectual action is that in part; but if it is true that alone this action repeats unknowingly the inner workings of the ideology, even if at the outset it escapes it, then the real problem is political; in feminist struggles, the problem must pass through an alliance between intellectuals and the working class. Lack of harmony is inevitable; distortions, momentary misunderstandings, bits of discourse that, exchanged, are not received when they are sent out. But knowledge of the real relationship between intellectual activity and the overall totality of forces that seek to change society is the condition of all intellectual action. Feminine crisis does not truly signify, it does not produce any change: it signals and repeats. Enclosed as an enclave by all of the group and individual constraints, feminine crisis remains enslaved. That women's language must first be a stuttering, when it's about real suffering, is true in fact; can we make a weapon of this shackle? A means must be elaborated to unhinge entire panels of ideology; a rigorous activity is needed which for the sake of rigor must think out and measure its relation to social activities as a whole.

Translated by Marilyn R. Schuster

Julia Kristeva

psych & po: A different[1] relationship to the text becomes manifest in our practice,[2] and it is one in which you participate. Could you be more specific with regard to how your work is the "work of a woman," or rather, how does being a woman have a bearing upon this type of endeavor? How does the women's struggle, an activity in which you seem to want to involve yourself more and more, transform something in your relationship to writing, to the text, to theoretical and textual production?

Kristeva: The belief that "one is a woman" is almost as absurd and obscurantist as the belief that "one is a man." I say "almost" because there are still many goals which women can achieve: freedom of abortion and contraception, day-care centers for children, equality on the job, etc. Therefore, we must use "we are women" as an advertisement or slogan for our demands. On a deeper level, however, a woman cannot "be"; it is something which does not even belong in the order of *being*. It follows that a feminist practice can only be negative, at odds with what already exists so that we may say "that's not it" and "that's still not it." In "woman" I see something that cannot be represented, something that is not said, something above and beyond nomenclatures and ideologies.

From "La femme, ce n'est jamais ça" [Woman can never be defined], an interview by "psychoanalysis and politics" in *Tel quel*, Autumn 1974. This interview was to appear in the radical feminist journal *Le torchon brûle*. Like many of the feminist journals, *Le torchon brûle* had a relatively short existence, 1971–1973. The interview was published for the first time in the avant-garde journal, *Tel quel*, and later in a collection of Kristeva's writings entitled *Polylogue*. The title, "La femme, ce n'est jamais ça," stresses the conviction of Kristeva and other feminist thinkers that women cannot be defined, indeed should not be defined, since the term is a social and not a natural construct.

1 "Different" refers back to Julia Kristeva's opening statement in which she describes the theoretical discourse developed in her book *La révolution du langage poétique* (Editions du Seuil, 1974).—Tr.
2 In French *pratique* suggests a relationship between theory and practice, the process of moving from one to the other.—Tr.

There are certain "men" who are familiar with this phenomenon; it is what some modern texts never stop signifying: testing the limits of language and sociality—the law and its transgression, mastery and (sexual) pleasure—without reserving one for males and the other for females, on the condition that it is never mentioned. From this point of view, it seems that certain feminist demands revive a kind of naive romanticism, a belief in identity (the reverse of phallocratism), if we compare them to the experience of both poles of sexual difference as is found in the economy of Joycian or Artaudian prose or in modern music—Cage, Stockhausen.[3] I pay close attention to the particular aspect of the work of the avant-garde which dissolves identity, even sexual identities; and in my theoretical formulations I try to go against metaphysical theories that censure what I just labeled "a woman"—this is what, I think, makes my research that of a woman. Perhaps I should add something here, and it's not contradictory to what I just said. Because of the decisive role that women play in the reproduction of the species, and because of the privileged relationship between father and daughter, a woman takes social constraints even more seriously, has fewer tendencies toward anarchism, and is more mindful of ethics. This may explain why our negativity is not Nietzschean anger. If my work aims at broadcasting to the public precisely what this society censures in the avant-garde practice, then, I think, my work obeys ethical exigencies of this type. The whole problem is to know whether this ethical penchant in the woman's struggle will remain separated from negativity; in which case the ethical penchant will degenerate into conformity, and negativity will degenerate into esoteric perversion. The problem is on the agenda of the women's movement. But without the movement, no work of any woman would ever really be possible.

psych & po: You have just returned from China. We would like very much to visit China, but it seems to us that our real China is here, where we transform reality. What we want to know is: "Where is *your* China?" The results of the work we do here with women, among women, often overlap with what is being produced, or so we hear, by men and women in China; among other things, an upheaval, perhaps the disappearance, or the lack of phallic dominance in both struggle and celebration. During your trip, what did you experience with regard to this "difference"?

Kristeva: I have returned from China after a three-week trip to Peking, Shanghai, Luoyang, Xian, and back to Peking where I met many men and women: workers, peasants, schoolchildren, teachers, artists— But with all this, and regardless of my own studies in Chinese, there is

---

[3] James Joyce, Antonin Artaud, John Cage, Karlheinz Stockhausen: writers and musicians included in the avant-garde canon.—Tr.

nothing less certain than having been in China, in its space and time. Traveling to China is tantamount to examining what is new and novel on this planet, phenomena that are both sexual and political upheavals. In the eyes of a Westerner, China joins the two: the struggle for the emancipation of women, the trend toward abolishing social inequalities, together with the emergence of an immense repressed culture into the worldwide political arena. But all of this interests me, especially with regard to this impossible phenomenon that is attempting to assert itself in our society; the avant-garde, the women's struggle and the battle for socialism, are merely symptomatic of the "impossible," on different levels. How will the West greet the awakening of the "third world" as the Chinese call it? Can we participate, actively and lucidly, in this awakening when the center of the planet is in the process of moving toward the East?

If you don't care about women, if you don't like women, you needn't bother going to China; you won't hear anything, you'll be bored, and you'll even run the risk of getting sick, either with understanding nothing, or understanding everything. First of all, ancient China was, if not a matriarchal society as modern Chinese historians follow Engels in asserting, then at least the best known and most highly developed matrilinear society. Later, even during the period of Confucius when women were considered "slaves" or "little men," wives played an essential role in family life and even in the sacred representation of reproductive relations. But most important is the fact that today an immense effort is being made to give women an active role not only in the home, but on all levels of political and social activity: this is one of the main stakes in the present critical campaign waged against Lin Piao and Confucius. Freedom of abortion and contraception, equal pay for equal work, encouragement in aesthetic, political, and scientific endeavors, educational opportunities, adequate health care for mothers and young children, safe nurseries and play areas—these are just a few of the things that I could see in each production unit that we visited in China. Furthermore, in all the performances that we saw (films, plays, operas), not one of them had a man as its main character: there was always a heroine. It's very difficult to describe briefly the relationship between the trend toward emancipation and the "phallic" principle, or let's say its relationship to "power." I shall discuss this very issue in greater detail in my forthcoming book on Chinese women to be published by the éditions des femmes.[4] What is clear is that the problems that face Chinese women who are emerging from a feudal Confucian society have nothing to do with the problems of Western women who are trying to get out from under the

---

[4] The book was published in France in 1974. See the Selected Bibliography.—Tr.

thumbs of capitalism and monotheism. Therefore, it is absurd to question their lack of "sexual liberation," just as it is absurd to project the realization of a so-called universal revolutionary ideal upon their style of life and struggle.

Here are a few empirical observations. In spite of the value assigned to women in today's campaign, in spite of man's dominance in the Confucian patriarchal family, I did not get the impression that reproductive and symbolic representations were determined by what we, in the West, call the "phallic principle." First, the differences between the sexes is not as huge as you might imagine; men and women are not two races at war with one another: "man" is in "woman," and "woman" is in "man." The so-called sexual relations do not seem to be centered around transgression: the quest for partial objects, perversion, etc. Genitality, in other words, the passage through the Oedipal stage (if I may use certain psychoanalytic concepts, but oh so very carefully), seems to underlie this scene and creates a relaxed, calm, "maternal" atmosphere in public, on the job, even during holidays such as May 1; it is an ambiance without the allure of romance; there is firmness or strength without the threat of violence. Chinese writing is what corresponds best to this rhythm.

In any case, it is impossible to talk about Chinese socialism unless we take into account the fact that it is structured around a different distribution of sexual difference and hence, the roles women will occupy within this structure. Of course, nothing has been accomplished, and nothing guarantees that the present efforts will not be engulfed by the ever-present revisionist tide or by a return to the bourgeois system. On this level, just as in economics and politics, "the struggle between the two defense lines" is not a slogan, but an everyday truth.

psych & po: Just as feminine is the reverse of masculine, feminism can be seen as the reverse of humanism. We struggle against this ideology that produces only inversion; without, however, forgetting what each one of us must recognize as our own minimum feminism, our own temporary arena. In this regard, it seems to us that the women's struggle cannot be divorced from revolutionary struggle, class struggle, or anti-imperialism. The issues that are crucial in our practice involve the notion of the subject, its fragmentation, the inscription of heterogeneity, difference— These are issues that feminism skirts, by postulating that women are "separate complete individuals" with their "own identity," or by demanding such things as "names for women," etc. How can we conceive of a revolutionary struggle that does not involve a revolution in discourse (not an upheaval in language as such, but rather a theory of this very upheaval)? We run the risk of creating within feminism an enclosed ideology parallel to the ideology of the dominant class. And what of the impasses these "demands" will meet if they remain on the "social level"?

Kristeva: Feminism can be but one of capitalism's more advanced needs to rationalize: Giscard d'Estaing, wishing to liquidate certain gaullist archaisms, invented the Secretary for the Status of Women. It's better than nothing, but it's not exactly right either. In the twentieth century, after suffering through fascism and revisionism, we should have learned that there can be no socio-political transformation without a transformation of subjects: in other words, in our relationship to social constraints, to pleasure, and more deeply, to language. What is politically "new" today can be seen and felt in modern music, cartoons, communes of young people provided they do not isolate themselves on the fringes of society but participate in the contradiction inherent in political classes. The women's movement, if it has a raison d'être, seems to be part of this trend; it is, perhaps, one of its most radical components. In every political apparatus, whether on the Right, or the Left, the movement, by its negativity, indicates what is otherwise repressed: that "class consciousness" for example, is not unrelated to the unconscious of the sexed speaker. The trap that is set for this demystifying force, a force that the women's movement can be, is that we will identify with the power principle that we think we are fighting: the hysterical saint plays her pleasure against social order, but in the name of God. The question is: "Who plays God in present-day feminism?" Man? Or Woman—his substitute? As long as any libertarian movement, feminism included, does not analyze its own relationship to power and does not renounce belief in its own identity, it remains capable of being coopted both by power and an overtly religious or lay spiritualism. Besides, it is spiritualism's last great hope. The solution is infinite, since what is at stake is to move from a patriarchal society, of class and of religion, in other words from pre-history, toward— Who knows? In any event, this process involves going through what is repressed in discourse, in reproductive and productive relationships. Call it "woman" or "the oppressed social class": it's the same struggle, and you never have one without the other. It seems to me that the movement's most urgent task is to make the ideological and political machines understand this complicity. But this implies that we change our style, that we get out a bit from "among women," from among ourselves, that each one of us in our respective fields fights against social and cultural archaisms.

Translated by Marilyn A. August

Simone de Beauvoir

Schwarzer:[1] When you wrote *The Second Sex* in 1949 you believed that socialism was the only true remedy for the inequality of the sexes. Then, last November, 22 years later, you became actively involved in the feminist movement by taking part in the international woman's march in Paris. Why?

Beauvoir: Because I realized that in the past 20 years, the position of women in France had not really changed and that socialism, as it has evolved—for example, in Russia—hasn't changed women's position, either. Frenchwomen had won a few minor legal victories in terms of marriage and divorce; contraceptive devices had been distributed, but very inadequately, since only 7 percent of Frenchwomen use the Pill. There may be a few more women working than before, but not many, and they are secretaries rather than heads of businesses, and nurses more often than doctors. They are almost completely barred from the most interesting careers, and their advancement is blocked even in those professions they can enter. All these factors made me reconsider. Also, before the Women's Liberation Movement formed in 1970, the women's groups in France were reformist and legalistic. I had no desire to join them. The new feminism, however, is radical. It reiterates the 1968 slogan—change life today; don't gamble on the future; act now.

When the women of the MLF got in touch with me, they asked me to help formulate an abortion manifesto, making public the fact that I and others had had abortions. I thought that this was a valid way of drawing attention to the problem. So it was quite natural that I should decide to march with the militants of the MLF last November, and to support their slogans: free abortion on demand, free contraception, voluntary motherhood.

From an interview by Alice Schwarzer in *Ms*, July 1972.

[1] Alice Schwarzer, German feminist, author of *A Small Difference A Great Consequence*, editor of the radical feminist monthly, *Emma.*—Ed.

Schwarzer: You spoke of the situation in Russia. What are women's lives like there?

Beauvoir: Almost all Soviet women work, and those who don't—the wives of a few highly placed functionaries and other important men— are looked down upon by the rest. Soviet women are very proud of working. They have quite extensive social and political responsibilities and a sense of these responsibilities. However, the number of women with any real power in the Central Committee or in the Assemblies is very small in relation to the number of men. For the most part, women practice the least agreeable and least respected professions. In Russia, almost all the doctors are women. This is because the medical profession is extremely hard, tiring, and poorly remunerated by the state. Women are herded into medicine or teaching—more important careers, like the sciences, engineering, etc., are much less accessible to them. On one hand, women are not professionally equal to men. On the other, responsibility for housework and care of children fall entirely upon them, exactly as in other countries. Perhaps even more so than in France, where a woman in a comparable position would have a housekeeper. One must conclude that even in the Soviet Union there is no real equality between men and women.

Schwarzer: Why is that so?

Beauvoir: Well, first of all, the socialist countries are not really socialistic. The socialism Marx dreamed of, that would truly change mankind, has not been realized anywhere. The means of production have changed hands, but as time goes on we see that this is not really enough to change society, change humanity. So in spite of a different economic system, the traditional roles of man and woman remain the same. This relates to the fact that men have deeply internalized the idea of their own superiority. They are not ready to give up what I call their superiority complex. To validate themselves, they need to see woman as inferior. And she is so used to thinking of herself as inferior that only a few women dare to fight for equality.

Schwarzer: There are many misunderstandings about the concept of feminism. What is your definition?

Beauvoir: At the end of *The Second Sex,* I said I wasn't a feminist because I thought that the solution to women's problems must depend on the socialist evolution of society. By feminist, I meant fighting for specifically feminine demands independent of the class struggle. Today my definition is the same, but I have come to realize that we must fight for an improvement in woman's actual situation before achieving the socialism we hope for. Besides this, I realized that even in the socialist countries, women's equality has not been won. So it is necessary for women to fight for their rights. That is why I have now joined the MLF.

Another reason is that even in the French leftist movements, there is serious inequality between men and women. Women always do the humblest, most boring, and least visible jobs. The men speak, write articles, do the most interesting things, and have the greatest responsibilities. In the bosom of these movements, in principle formed to liberate everybody—including youth and women—women remain inferior.

It goes even further. Many male leftists are aggressively hostile to women's liberation. They despise us and let us know it. The first time a feminist meeting was held in Vincennes, a number of male leftists broke into the hall shouting, "Power to the phallus!" I think they are beginning to revise that position, just because women are demonstrating that they can conduct a militant action independent of men.

Schwarzer: What are your reactions to the new feminists, the young radical women in the movement?

Beauvoir: In America, where the movement is most advanced, there is a whole range of tendencies—from Betty Friedan, who is fairly conservative, to what is called s.c.u.m. (Society for Cutting Up Men), a movement to emasculate men. In France, too, at the heart of the movement there are a number of different tendencies. My own is to want to link women's liberation with the class struggle. I feel that women's struggle, while it is unique, is connected to the wider one in which they must join with men. As a result, I reject any wholesale repudiation of men.

Schwarzer: What do you think of the principle of women-only in meetings? Most parts of the Women's Movement have adopted it for the time being.

Beauvoir: I think that, for the moment, it's a good thing for several reasons. First, if men were admitted to these groups, they wouldn't be able to restrain their masculine compulsion to dominate, to impose. At the same time, many women, consciously or unconsciously, still have certain feelings of inferiority, a certain timidity; many women would not dare to express themselves freely in front of men. Specifically, it is vital that they should not feel judged by the individual men who share their individual lives, because they also need to liberate themselves from them. For the moment, neither men's nor women's mentalities permit really honest discussion in mixed groups.

Schwarzer: But isn't the temporary exclusion of men also a political question? Since they represent the system—and since it is also the individual man who oppresses a woman—don't the feminists consider them "the first enemy" in this primary stage?

Beauvoir: Yes, but it's very complicated, because, as Marx said of capitalists, they are victims, too. But it is too abstract to say, as I've thought sometimes, that only the system is to blame. Men are to blame, too. The man of today did not establish this patriarchal regime, but he profits by it, even when he criticizes it. And he has made it very much a part of his own thinking.

One must blame the system, but at the same time be wary of men, and not let them take over our activities, our potentialities. The system and men both must be attacked. Even when a man is a feminist, one must keep one's distance and watch out for paternalism. Women don't want to be *granted* equality, they want to *win* it. Which is not the same thing at all.

Schwarzer: In your life, do you have this hatred and mistrust for men?

Beauvoir: No. I have always gotten along very well with the men in my life. Many of the women I know in the MLF have no hatred for men either, just an attitude of caution, a determination not to allow themselves to be devoured.

Schwarzer: Do you think it's a good thing, politically, that some women go farther?

Beauvoir: Actually, it isn't a bad thing at all that there are women who repudiate men. They will influence those who are inclined to compromise.

Schwarzer: What do you think about the argument that sexual relations with men are oppressive?

Beauvoir: Is it really true that all sexual relationships between men and women are oppressive? Instead of refusing all such relations, couldn't one work toward having a kind which would not be oppressive? I find it absurd to assume that all coitus is rape. By saying that, one agrees to the masculine myth that a man's sex is a sword, a weapon. The real problem is to find new sexual relationships which will not be oppressive.

Schwarzer: You said in a commentary on *The Second Sex* that the problem of femininity had not touched you personally, and that you felt you were in a "highly impartial position." Did you mean that a woman can, as an individual, escape her feminine condition? On the professional level and in her relations with others?

Beauvoir: Escape her condition as a woman? No! But actually I've been very lucky. I've escaped most of woman's bondages: maternity, the life of a housewife. Also, in my day there were fewer women who pursued advanced studies. To have a postgraduate degree in philosophy was to be in a privileged position as a woman. I received immediate recognition from men—they were ready to accept friendship with a woman who had succeeded on their own level, because it was so exceptional. Now that many women are advanced students, men are afraid of losing their own status. More generally, if you admit, as I do, that a woman is not obliged to be a wife and mother to have a complete and happy life, there are a certain number of women who can achieve full lives without submitting to women's limitations.

Schwarzer: You once said, "The greatest success of my life is Sartre." Yet you express a great need for independence and a fear of being dominated. Although egalitarian relations between men and women are so difficult to establish, do you think that you personally achieved them?

Beauvoir: Yes. Or rather, the problem never came up, because Sartre is in no way an oppressor. If I had loved someone other than Sartre, I still would not have allowed myself to be oppressed. Some women escape masculine domination by means of their professional autonomy. Some arrive at a balanced relation with one man. Others have meaningless affairs.

Schwarzer: You have spoken of women being an inferior class—

Beauvoir: Not a class. In *The Second Sex*, I said that women are an inferior *caste*. In principle, one can leave one class to move into another, but caste is the group into which one is born and which one cannot leave. If you are a woman, you can never become a man. And the way in which women are treated on the economic, social, and political levels makes an inferior caste of them.

Schwarzer: What do you think of the political analyses that equate patriarchal oppression of women as unpaid domestic labor with the capitalist use of workers?

Beauvoir: I don't think those analyses are accurate. Housework produces no profit—it's a different situation from that of the worker who is robbed of the profit from his work. I would like to know exactly what relationship exists between the two. Women's entire future strategy will depend on it.

This particular point has not been examined thoroughly enough in any of the books I've read; only Shulamith Firestone, who is less well known than Millett or Greer, has suggested something new. In her book *The Dialectic of Sex*, she associates Women's Liberation with children's liberation. This is right because women will not be liberated until they are liberated from children, and children are at the same time to some degree liberated from adults.

Schwarzer: How do you see the relationship between the class war and the war between the sexes?

Beauvoir: Abolishing capitalism will not mean abolishing the patriarchal tradition as long as the family is preserved. I believe that not only must we change the ownership of the means of production, but that we must also change the family structure. And even in China this has not been done. It is true that they got rid of the feudal family, which made great changes in woman's condition. But to the extent that they still accept the conjugal family, which is basically a legacy of the patriarchal family, I don't believe that Chinese women have been liberated at all. I am in complete agreement with the attempts that have been made by women and some men to replace the family by either communes or whatever forms remain to be invented.

Schwarzer: Would you say that, while the class struggle doesn't necessarily change woman's condition, radical feminism and the reexamination of the social structure would resolve the class struggle?

Beauvoir: No, not necessarily. If one begins by abolishing family structures, it is very probable that capitalism would be deeply shaken. But that will not be enough to reorganize the means of production, the conditions of work, and the relationships of human beings to each other. There has not yet been enough analysis of this point because the women who were active in feminism were middle-class women who weren't thinking in economic terms. In economics, on the other hand, we've been too content with Marxist formulas to ask the important question. When socialism is achieved, will there then be equality between men and women?

When *The Second Sex* was published, I was very much surprised to find it badly received by the Left. I remember an objection from the Trotskyites. They said that the problem of woman is not a true problem. There is no point in raising it. When the revolution comes, women will find their place quite naturally.

Also the Communists, with whom I was in very bad political repute at that time, ridiculed me harshly. They wrote articles about how the workingwomen of Billancourt had no time for or interest in the woman problem. After the revolution, women would be the equals of men. But what was to happen to women in the meantime didn't interest them.

Schwarzer: In concrete terms, what possibilities for liberation do you see for the individual woman?

Beauvoir: The first thing is work. Then refuse marriage if possible. After all, I could have married Sartre. But I believe that we were wise not to have done so. When you are married, people see you as married, and you begin to see yourselves as married. This is quite different from the relationship you have with society when you are not married. Marriage is dangerous for a woman. Having said this, I acknowledge that a woman may have reasons for marrying—if she wants to have children, for example. It's still very difficult to bring children into the world when the parents aren't married; they encounter all kinds of hardships.

To be really independent, what counts is to have a profession, to work. It means that when you are married, if you wish to divorce, you can leave; you can support your children; you can make a life for yourself. But work is not the solution for everything. It has both liberating and dehumanizing aspects. As a result, women often have to choose between two forms of dehumanization: being a housewife or working in a factory. Work is not a general panacea; nevertheless, it is the first condition for independence. When women strike in factories, as they did in Troyes and Nantes, they become conscious of their power, their autonomy, and as a result they are less submissive at home. It's all connected.

Schwarzer: Can women limit liberation to the individual level?

Beauvoir: Individual emancipation is not enough. Women must go on to collective action. I have not done so myself until now because there had been no organized movement in which I could believe. But writing *The Second Sex*, after all, was an act beyond my own personal liberation. I wrote that book out of concern for the whole feminine condition, not just to understand what the situation of women was, but also as an act, to help other women understand themselves. During the past 20 years, I have answered a great number of letters from women who told me that my book helped them very much to understand their situation, to resist, to make decisions for themselves.

In France and elsewhere, most women are very conservative. They want to be "feminine." However, new conditions in housework are liberating women a little and leaving them time to think: they must be led further, into revolt. In a capitalist country, women will never get jobs while there is unemployment among men. That is why I think that women's equality cannot be won unless there is a total overthrow of the system.

I think the Women's Movement, like the student movement, which was limited at first but later ignited strikes all over the country, could cause an explosion. If women manage to get a foothold in the world of work, they will really shake up the system. For the moment, the weakness of the French and the American movement, too, is that they include very few working-class women.

Schwarzer: Are you in favor of violence in women's struggle?

Beauvoir: In the present situation, yes, up to a point, because men use violence toward women, both in language and in action. They attack women, they rape them, they insult them. Women should defend themselves with violence. Some are learning karate and other ways of fighting. I am in favor of that. They will feel much more at ease in their own skins and in the world when they don't feel helpless in the face of aggression.

Schwarzer: You often speak of American women. Have you had much contact with them?

Beauvoir: Yes. First of all through their books. We have to admit that the American movement is more advanced. I've received many letters from Americans, and invitations to go to America. But my reply to them today is: I am working with Frenchwomen. I must first work at home.

Schwarzer: Now that you consider yourself a militant feminist, what immediate action do you plan?

Beauvoir: First, we are holding special meetings to expose the crimes committed against woman. The first two sessions were held on the 13th and 14th of May. They dealt with problems of maternity, contraception, and abortion. A committee of inquiry interrogated witnesses—biologists, sociologists, psychiatrists, doctors, midwives—and, most important, women who had suffered directly from the conditions that this society has imposed on womankind.

We hope to convince the public that women must be assured the right to procreate freely, that is, the public must help provide the expenses of maternity—child-care centers, especially—and the right to refuse undesired pregnancies through contraceptive devices and abortion. We demand that these be free, and that only the individual woman decide whether or not to make use of them. But contraception and abortion are only a point of departure for women's larger liberation.

Later on we will be organizing meetings at which we will expose the exploitation of female labor: the housewife's, the white-collar worker's, and the women of the working class.

Schwarzer: In *The Second Sex* you quoted Rimbaud's vision of a future world in which woman would be liberated. What do you think that new world will be like?

Beauvoir: Women's Liberation will surely bring about new kinds of relationships between human beings, and men as well as women will be changed. Women, and men, too, must become human beings first and foremost. The differences which exist between them are no more important than the differences which exist between individual women, or individual men.

I don't believe that when women have won equality they will develop specifically feminine values. The fact is that culture, civilization, and universal values have been made by men because they were the ones who represented universality. When the proletariat rejected the bourgeoisie as a dominant class, they did not reject the entire bourgeois heritage, and in the same way, women, when they have won equality with men, will have to make use of some of the tools created by men. It is true that in creating universal values—I would call mathematical science a universal value, for example—men have very often given them a specifically masculine, male, virile character and have confused the two in a very subtle, sly way. It becomes a matter of separating the two, of getting rid of the contamination.

Schwarzer: After the publication of *The Second Sex*, you were often reproached for not having developed any battle plan for women, for having gone no farther than analysis.

Beauvoir: That is true. I recognize this as a shortcoming in the book.

I stopped on a note of vague confidence in the future, in the revolution, and in socialism.

Schwarzer: And today?

Beauvoir: Today I've changed my mind. I have become truly a feminist.

Translated by Helen Eustis

Simone de Beauvoir

Schwarzer: Five years have passed since you came out publicly as a feminist. You, Simone, the writer who most strongly inspired the new femininism, you were anti-feminist until the birth of the women's liberation movement. You were opposed to any autonomous movement. You thought that the socialist revolution would be the automatic solution to woman's oppression.

Much has happened since then. In 1971 you were one of the women who admitted, in public, to having had an abortion. You participated in a certain number of feminist actions and demonstrations. What is your relationship to the young feminists today?

Beauvoir: They are personal relations with women, not with groups or tendencies. I work with them on precise subjects. For example, on the editorial staff of the *Temps modernes* we regularly write a page on "everyday sexism."

I also chair the "Ligue du droit des femmes" [League for women's rights], and I help with efforts to create shelters for women who have been beaten. I am therefore not a militant in the strict meaning of the word—I'm not thirty, I'm sixty-seven, and I am an intellectual whose weapons are words—but I do follow the activities of the MLF and I am at their service.

I find this project for battered women particularly important because, like abortion, the problem of violence concerns almost all women—independently of their social class. It goes beyond the frontiers of class. Women are beaten by husbands who are judges or magistrates as well as workers. So we created an "SOS Battered Women" and we try to organize centers that would give shelter at least temporarily—for a night or a few weeks—to a woman and her children if she can't go home because she might be beaten by her husband, sometimes beaten to death. . . .

From an interview by Alice Schwarzer in *Marie-Claire*, October 1976.

Schwarzer: In your opinion, what role does sexuality, as it is conceived of today, play in the oppression of women?

Beauvoir: I think that sexuality can be a dreadful trap. There are women who become frigid—but that's not the worst thing that can happen to them. The worst thing is for women to find so much happiness in sexuality that they become more or less slaves of men and that strengthens the chain that binds them to their oppressor.

Schwarzer: If I understand you, frigidity seems to you, in the present state of discomfort created by the power play between men and women, a more prudent and reasonable reaction because it reflects this discomfort and therefore makes women less dependent on men.

Beauvoir: Exactly.

Schwarzer: There are women in the MLF who, in this world dominated by men, refuse to continue to share their private lives with men, to have sexual and emotional relationships with them. These women make of homosexuality a political strategy. What is your opinion?

Beauvoir: I understand fully the political refusal to compromise. Exactly for the reason I gave. Love can be a trap that makes women accept many things.

But this is only true in the present circumstances. In itself, homosexuality is as limiting as heterosexuality. The ideal should be the capacity to love a woman as well as a man, one or the other, a human being, without feeling fear or constraint or obligation.

Schwarzer: Your most famous sentence is: "One is not born, but rather becomes a woman." Today we can prove scientifically this "fabrication of the sexes" whose result is that men and women are very different: they think differently, they have different emotions, they walk differently. They are not born this way, they become this way. It is the result of their education and their daily life.

Almost everyone is in agreement about acknowledging this difference. But it is not only a difference: it implies at the same time an inferiority. So it is all the more astonishing that with the new revolt of women there should appear a rebirth of the eternal feminine, in short a mystification of the feminine.

That's what Jean Ferrat sings about in his latest hit: "Woman is the future of man." And even in the women's movement, some groups are brandishing these slogans.

Beauvoir: I think that today certain masculine shortcomings are absent in women. For example, a masculine manner of being grotesque, of taking oneself seriously, of thinking oneself important. Note that women who have a masculine career can also adopt these shortcomings. But all the same, women always retain a little nook of humor, a little distance between themselves and the hierarchy.

And that way of squelching competitors: in general, women do not act that way. And patience which is, up to a certain point, a quality (later it becomes a shortcoming), is also a characteristic of women. And irony, a sense of the concrete, because women are more strongly rooted in every day life.

These "feminine" qualities have their origin in our oppression, but they should be preserved after our liberation. And men, too, should acquire them. But we must not exaggerate in the other direction. To say that woman has special ties to the earth, the rhythm of the moon, the tides, etc., that she has more soul, that she is less destructive by nature, etc. No, if there is something true in all that, it is not in terms of our nature, but of the conditions of our life.

"Feminine" little girls are also made and not born that way. Numerous studies prove this. A priori, a woman has no special value because she is a woman. That would be the most retrograde "biologism," in total contradiction with everything I think.

Schwarzer: Then what does this rebirth of the "eternal feminine" mean?

Beauvoir: When men say to us: "Just keep being good little women. Leave all the tedious things to us: power, honors, careers— Be happy to be there, bound to the earth, busy with human tasks—" That's very dangerous! On one hand it's a good thing that a woman is no longer ashamed of her body, of her pregnancy, of her menstruation. I think it is excellent that she should get to know her own body.

But it would be an error to make of it a value and to think that the feminine body gives you a new vision of the world. It would be ridiculous and absurd, it would be like constructing a counter-penis. The women who share this belief fall again into the irrational, into mysticism, into a sense of the cosmic. They play into the hands of men who will be better able to oppress them, to remove them from knowledge and power.

The eternal feminine is a lie, because nature plays an infinitesimal role in the development of a human being. We are social beings. Because I do not think that woman is naturally inferior to man, I do not think either that she is naturally superior to him.

Translated by Elaine Marks

Evelyne Sullerot

*"Destiny is written at the same time as
it is fulfilled, not before."*
Jacques Monod, *Chance and Necessity*

For a long time, women appeared to be more dominated by nature than
men, if only because of their function as mothers. It seemed that nature
both created and justified women's place in society in the realm of tasks,
roles, status, power. References to female physiology were so extensive and such credence was given to the way myths and ideologies
represented women, that we lost track of all the other economic and
socio-cultural facts and of their control mechanisms.

Even though it may seem paradoxical, natural sciences such as physiology, biology, and, later, genetics (without even intending to do so)
were to undo the prevailing explanatory system and ask different basic
questions about women in relation to men. Finally, because these sciences provided women with efficient tools, they allowed women to start
their gradual liberation from nature.

The discovery of the ovum in female mammals at the end of the
seventeenth century allowed natural scientists of that period to establish
a complementary relation between male testes and female ovaries. This
led to the radical reevaluation of the woman's role in conception and
later to the recognition that both parents contribute equally to the
hereditary constitution of their progeny. The woman was no longer
exclusively considered a passive receptacle destined to receive the sperm
—the only seed of life—as the Greeks and Romans believed and many
generations after them, including socialists like Proudhon at the end
of the nineteenth century. It was acknowledged instead that the woman

---

"Préface au fait féminin" [Preface to the Feminine (matter of) Fact] in *Le fait
féminin* (Fayard, 1978). *Le fait féminin* is the account of a colloquium organized
by Jacques Monod and Evelyne Sullerot and held at the Royaumont Center for the
Human Sciences. The colloquium, whose goal was to study the question "What is a
woman?" was closed to the public. Participants included European and North
American psychologists, anthropologists, historians, sociologists, gynecologists, and
pediatricians, among them Philippe Ariès, Leon Eisenberg, André Lwoff, Eleanor
Maccoby.

actively participates in the formation of the original configuration of the embryo. A whole naturalist school even went overboard and claimed that women, and women only, were equipped with "little foetus machines" whereas "male liquor" was a mere starter in the embryo's growth process.[1] At the beginning of the twentieth century, progress in genetics gave this question its definitive answer. Moreover, the discovery of sex chromosomes and of their role in determining the child's sex saved women from being held totally "responsible" for their children's sex: from then on no society could allow a man to repudiate his wife because she was producing daughters only, and to do so today would seem strictly speaking "unnatural." After that, the discovery of the fertility cycle in women led to the recognition that nature had programmed female sexual pleasure independently from the needs of reproduction. Between World War I and World War II, the discovery of the sex hormones that regulate this cycle fostered the development of oral contraceptives—the Pill—which gave women the power to make decisions on whether they wanted to conceive or not. At the same time, knowledge acquired in the physiology of reproduction gave women other reliable methods of contraception such as the IUD. Last and not least, enormous progress in hygiene and medicine cut down the number of women dying in childbirth or from puerperal fever, thereby substantially lengthening women's life expectancy. At the same time, the proportion of a woman's life devoted to procreation because of infant mortality was considerably reduced: for thousands of years, the average woman had to give birth to four or five children in order that two of them might reach adulthood, but today two pregnancies are usually enough for the same result. The development of formulas and adequate baby foods freed women from obligatory breastfeeding and men are now able to participate in the baby's "breeding" from birth, which means new possibilities in role sharing.

These discoveries, and many others, resulted in the separation of domains hitherto linked together: sexuality, procreation, motherhood, child rearing. To separate domains and to act on each of them individually gives multiple choices and creates freedom. But as women, thanks to natural sciences, are liberated from their bondage to nature and given freedom, they are at the same time given responsibility and anxiety. They are in a position more similar to that of men than in the past, when the only specific leeway that philosophy would grant women was acceptance, whether it be through resignation or revolt. All these discoveries made clearer the cultural aspects—theologies and overt or covert ideologies—or the socio-economic aspects—power structure, economic

[1] Cf. F. Jacob, *La logique du vivant*, p. 78. [Gallimard, 1970.]

benefits, or sex-role divisions—which underlay women's position and which up to now had been concealed by an obsessive adherence to "natural determinism."

Consequently, sociological studies of women and feminist thought were characterized by a deliberate break with the past and in particular a deliberate refusal to refer to "natural determinism" or to nature itself because such terms had been previously so universally, so profusely, and so abusively used to produce systems of representation, values, and education which buttressed male domination. At the same time, sociology was also focussing on the study of domination and exploitation as systems: colonial, class, ethnic systems. Sociology was also strongly influenced by research on the structure of power strategies (the main focus of research for the sociology of politics and labor) as well as by research on the mechanisms of social conditioning (the major thrust of sociological research on education, communication, mass media, culture, etc.).

As a consequence, feminist thought and research in the sociology of women have been strongly ideological and rather unscientific because they constantly tried:

—in as much as possible, to get rid of references to nature and to their by-products ("feminine nature," "feminine temperament") because such references seemed to draw attention to differences in order to mask the socio-economic and socio-cultural mechanisms of domination which prevent equality between the sexes.

—to distance themselves from descriptions, explanations, and theories of women elaborated by men (many of them MDs) and to create a women's thought based on the reality of women's experience.

These two approaches can strengthen each other and at the same time be contradictory. The first approach insists on equality between the sexes and purports to isolate all obstacles to this equality in order to pull apart their mechanisms. This approach therefore avoids any reference to "natural differences" between man and woman. The other approach insists on specificity—feminine specificity—which is still poorly defined and poorly experienced in our societies. Such an approach purports to give women the full right "to be different" and to pursue their "difference."

Such contradictions do not necessarily have a sterilizing effect and they can be overcome because it is possible to study the causes of social inequities and to oppose them by encouraging the development of feminine specificities. But to do so requires great clarity in research and in the interpretation of facts before attempting—and it is still premature to do so—any global theory. Debates and publications that want to prove these contradictory hypotheses (not to mention their popularized versions) have greatly suffered from confused reliance on some facts and great mistrust of other facts which were consequently ignored or even deliberately not mentioned. Because of their lack of scientific rigor, the analyses so far offered are often powerful and relevant but they remain fragile and the important opinion trends that they created are likely to be of short duration.

Having lived through this period as a woman, as a practicing activist, and as an analyst of social realities, I gradually became more conscious of the dangers caused by this lack of rigor. The refusal to integrate into the study of women all the biological facts that are linked with differences might lead us to dead ends, with a proliferation of cliques each building to its own interpretive system without taking into account observations based on reality. I realized that thought and theory were no longer possible without a thorough dialogue with specialists in various biological sciences.

On the one hand, several of the observations I made about women—in the sociology of labor for instance—raised questions that studies limited to the mechanisms of socio-cultural conditioning and to economic factors could not fully answer. If, as a social activist, I wanted to act on these facts and change the lives of women, I had to be thoroughly familiar with all possible biological causes in order not to waste my efforts in applying my knowledge to poorly chosen areas.

On the other hand, biology and medicine keep discovering and offering ways of changing and manipulating female physiology. Some, for instance, suggest the permanent elimination of menopause through constant hormone intake, so that a woman will keep menstruating until she dies. Others suggest the elimination of menstruation and of the inconvenience of the menstrual cycle. There are those who show that the left and right cerebral hemispheres have different functions in men and women and that cognitive mechanisms therefore operate differently in both sexes. Is it not necessary to study the implications of these discoveries and to survey all the possible scientific interventions in the life of women?

In short, in order to assess the past and the future development of women, we had reached a point where it became imperative—despite the unfavorable ideological climate—for the human sciences to ask the biological sciences to face the social implications of their research and discoveries. . . .

I, who have been studying the social aspects of women's problems for the past twenty years, was deeply "shaken up" by my work on the Royaumont Colloquium. Although I desperately needed to know more on the "biological nature of women," I dreaded this approach. I saw the dangers of anything that might cause the issue of female destiny to be inexorably and permanently settled. I kept on thinking secretly that hope for change would be found in social facts only. But in the course of this long debate on nature vs. culture, I discovered that, given the present state of science and civilization, *it seems to be much easier to change natural than cultural facts.* It was much easier to relieve women from obligatory breastfeeding than to make fathers give babies their bottles. It is much easier to develop contraceptives that eliminate the menstrual cycle than to change women's attitude toward menstruation. It is inertia built into cultural phenomena that seems to slow down our control over natural phenomena. Simone de Beauvoir said in a now famous statement: "One is not born a woman, one becomes a woman." After reading this book, every reader will understand that this statement can be reversed: one is indeed born a woman, with a physical destiny programmed differently from that of a man and with all the psychological and social consequences linked to this difference. But one can change this destiny and become what one wants to be, one can comply with this destiny or deliberately move away from it.

What do we want? To be more like men? To live better and to express our specificity? I would like to make a closing statement: all through this book differences between girls and boys or women and men are frequently mentioned. But since they are natural differences—genetic, embryological, physiological—any advantage appears to be paired with a drawback. These differences never indicate the undeniable and global superiority of one sex over the other, because superiority and inferiority are fragmentary evaluations linked with subjective judgments in a given domain. Each of us will draw his or her own conclusions from these discussions since the human species, which is cultural by its very nature, is the only living species to be capable of conceiving of itself as a species, to conceptualize sexes, and to search for its own reasons to exist.

Translated by Yvonne Rochette-Ozzello

Creations

These selections point to the importance, in the French feminist investigation, of the attempt to connect the exploration of woman's unconscious and woman's language with the specificity of woman's body.

Xavière Gauthier

In French the word "writer" does not have a feminine form. For "poet," there is "poetess," a ridiculous word, it is synonymous with foolish innocence, nature (a prototype is Minou Drouet[1] in the woman-child myth), or old-lady respectability.

There are, however, women who write. Is their writing different from men's? *In what ways does their writing call attention to the fact that they are women?*

There are two popular positions on this subject. Both are extreme and hence they clash. On the one hand, we could conceive of feminine literature in the traditional sense of the word, that is—flowers, sweetness, children, tenderness, submission, and acceptance, etc. "With Mallarmé, I change worlds. With Louise or Marceline,[2] I learn to love the firm solid world in which I live. Feminine poetry brings with it a sublime acceptance of the human condition," writes Alain Bosquet in his preface to *Hanches* [Haunches] by Claude de Burine. "I have often found comfort and freshness in the texts of women," writes Jean Breton in his introduction to *Poésie féminine d'aujourd'hui* [Feminine poetry today]. On the other hand, denying the difference between the sexes, we could say that there exists only one type of literature—it is neuter, and therefore it is the one in which women participate at the same rate at which they "progress" both socially and economically. "When women finally celebrate Mass, when they are equal in number to men in the

---

"Existe-t-il une écriture de femme?" [Is there such a thing as women's writing?] in *Tel quel*, Summer 1974. This selection and the one that follows were originally intended to be part of a double page spread on women's writing in *Le monde des livres*. The editor, Jacqueline Piatier, refused to publish the texts on the grounds that they were "completely incomprehensible, absurd, meaningless. . . ." They were published instead by the journal *Tel quel*.

[1] A child poet whose work created considerable attention in the 1950s.—Tr.

[2] Louise Labé (1524?–1566) and Marceline Desbordes-Valmore (1785–1859), France's best-known women poets.—Tr.

fields of journalism and medicine, in law courts, the Cabinet, and other governmental offices, when they are taxi drivers, office managers, then they will be architects, novelists, musicians, and poets as well. When their physical inferiority no longer blemishes their status as people, when their condition is comparable to man's, then I believe that, just like men, they will create. Women leave their children, their knitting, their procrastination, their gossip and suddenly begin to sing! Like us!" (Jean Fanan, avant-propos to *Poésie féminine d'aujourd'hui*.)

Regardless of their apparent differences, these two points of view are perfectly symmetrical; they are alike and should be condemned as the flip sides of the same prejudiced coin dependent on the same humanist ideology. In the first case, certain qualities are attributed to women, and are seen as particularly "feminine" (intuition, sensitivity, etc.); but it is men who render these judgments. Therefore the writing of "woman" will respond to their expectations and will reassure them. This is a masculine point of view. In the second case, the woman (though slightly retarded) is considered to be "like" a man or is in-the-process of becoming a man. This point of view is equally masculine and reassuring—it is one that can emanate only from a phallic system—and many women give in without any problem at all. Some women writers when asked the questions we are raising now, namely, "What about the specificity of women's writing?" confess to having never wondered about it.

But perhaps if we had left these pages blank, we would have had a better understanding of what feminine writing is all about. In fact, what surprises us is the fact that men and women seem to speak approximately the same language; in other words, women find "their" place within the linear, grammatical, linguistic system that orders the symbolic, the superego, the law. It is a system based entirely upon one fundamental signifier: the phallus. And we can marvel (like Thérèse Plantier in *C'est moi Diego* [I am Diego]) at the fact that women are alienated enough to be able to speak "the language of Man." "*If there is a madman, then it's definitely the Woman.* Believing themselves to be emancipated, women had access to universities where they were fed by force a language in which everything, verbs and subjects, was masculine. And so, having lost their minds, women believed they could be men, equal their masters in adopting their grammar syntax. Completely divorced from themselves without knowing it, women were transformed into this Crazy Sex which was named the 'Second Sex.' "

Women are, in fact, caught in a very real contradiction. Throughout the course of history, they have been mute, and it is doubtless by virtue of this mutism that men have been able to speak and write. As long as women remain silent, they will be outside the historical process. But, if they begin to speak and write *as men do*, they will enter history subdued and alienated; it is a history that, logically speaking, their speech should disrupt.

If, however, "replete" words (*mots pleins*) belong to men, how can women speak "otherwise," unless, perhaps, we can *make audible* that which agitates within us, suffers silently in the *holes of discourse*, in the unsaid, or in the non-sense. "The women say, the language you speak poisons your glottis tongue palate lips. They say, the language you speak is made up of words that are killing you. They say, the language you speak is made up of signs that rightly speaking designate what men have appropriated. Whatever they have not laid hands on, whatever they have not pounced on like many-eyed birds of prey, does not appear in the language you speak. This is apparent precisely in the *intervals* that your masters have not been able to *fill* with their words of proprietors and possessors, this can be found in the *gaps*,[3] in all that which is not a continuation of their discourse, in the zero, the o, the perfect circle that you invent to imprison them and to overthrow them" (Monique Wittig, *Les guérillères*).

One might think that Nathalie Sarraute's work is moving in this direction since her texts tend to manifest "tropisms," formless, trembling, imperceptible, moving, which literary language tries to crush and bring back into the fold, and restore to order. "Upon these numerous movements, both subtle and complex, conventional language poses immediately the cement slab of its definitions" ("Ce que je cherche à faire" in *Nouveau roman: hier, aujourd'hui* ["What I am trying to do" in *The New Novel: Yesterday, Today*]).

Since the "Name of the Father" (the no of the father)[4] is what psychoanalysis designates as that which determines submission to the law and to any "conventional language," we conceive of the problems that women writers frequently encounter—women who escape from the reproductive scheme in order to risk themselves in a productive endeavor —with "their" name, in other words, their father's or their husband's name. Marguerite Duras, in order to write, had to choose her own name (what we call a pseudonym). When I asked her if a woman could write if she kept her father's name, she told me: "That's something which never seemed possible, not for one second. Like many women I find this name so horrible that I barely manage to say it." Women, in fact, and even less so than men, do not have a proper name: "That which identi-

---

[3] Xavière Gauthier's italics.—Tr.

[4] In French *nom* (name) and *non* (no) are homophonic words. Lacanian psychoanalysis has used this resemblance to underline the role of the father in the child's coming to language and the child's separation from the desired mother. In the Lacanian paradigm, this coming to language marks the passage into the symbolic world governed by the laws of language.

fies them like the eye of the cyclops, their single forename" (Monique Wittig). Knowing, more or less consciously, that in order to make a name for themselves in literature, women have to be men, they often used masculine pseudonyms, George Sand for example and Daniel Stern (Marie d'Agoult). But it is not only women of the past who disguised themselves in this way. Dominique Desanti for one, admits to having done exactly "as the nineteenth-century ladies. Early in my career as a journalist, I took advantage of the fact that I had a first name ambiguous enough to use masculine adjectives and pretend that I was a man. Otherwise, I feared *that I would not be taken seriously*, since I was interested in international politics—"

Editors are familiar with this phenomenon, as they often require their female journalists to use only the first initial of the first name when they are dealing with a so-called masculine topic. (See the case of Agnès Van Parys for a book on deserters.)

The choice of women authors questioned here had nothing to do with any similarities among them. We can only say that all of them—each in her own way and to varying degrees, implicitly or explicitly—allude to Freudianism and Marxism which are the only possible bases for a materialist analysis of libidinal and political economies.

And then, blank pages, gaps, borders, spaces and silence, holes in discourse: these women emphasize the aspect of feminine writing which is the most difficult to verbalize because it becomes compromised, rationalized, masculinized as it explains itself. . . . If the reader feels a bit disoriented in this new space, one which is obscure and silent, it proves perhaps, that it is women's space.

Translated by Marilyn A. August

Julia Kristeva

X.G.: Before asking ourselves if there is a feminine writing, what is a subject who writes, a writing subject?

J.K.: For at least a century, the literary avant-garde (from Mallarmé and Lautréamont to Joyce and Artaud) has been introducing ruptures, blank spaces, and holes into language. It is what Mallarmé called "the music in letters": Maldoror's explosive *Chants* or the multiplied condensation of myths, philosophy, history, and verbal experience in *Finnegans Wake*. All of these modifications in the linguistic fabric are the sign of a force that has not been grasped by the linguistic or ideological system. This signification renewed, "infinitized" by the rhythm in a text, this precisely is (sexual) pleasure (*la jouissance*).

However, in a culture where the speaking subjects are conceived of as masters of their speech, they have what is called a "phallic" position. The fragmentation of language in a text calls into question the very posture of this mastery. The writing that we have been discussing confronts this phallic position either to traverse it or to deny it. The word "traverse" implies that the subject experiences sexual difference, not as a fixed opposition ("man"/"woman"), but as a process of differentiation. The word "deny" means that the subject constitutes a fetishistic shelter in order to avoid castration. Only the truly great "literary" achievements bear witness to a traversal, and therefore, to sexual differentiation. In this way, the subject of the writing speaks a *truth* proper to any speaking subject, a truth that the needs of production and reproduction censure. All speaking subjects have within themselves a certain bisexuality which is precisely the possibility to explore all the sources of signification, that which posits a meaning as well as that which multiplies, pulverizes, and finally revives it.

In Western societies, (sexual) pleasure (the advent of non-sense

From "Oscillation du 'pouvoir' au 'refus'" [Oscillation between power and denial], an interview by Xavière Gauthier in *Tel quel*, Summer 1974.

which multiplies sense) is granted to women provided it isn't discussed. In the same way, writer and literature in general are considered feminine.

Women who write are brought, at their own pace and in their own way, to see sexual differentiation as interior to the praxis of every subject. There are two extremes in their writing experiences: the first tends to valorize phallic dominance, associated with the privileged father-daughter relationship, which gives rise to the tendency toward mastery, science, philosophy, professorships, etc. This virilization of woman makes of her, ideally, a typical militant who can, in fact, become a veritable striking force in the social revolution (just as it was in the USSR, and just as it is today in China); this doesn't at all justify any dogmatic interpretations that call for "happy sexuality" because it's taken over by society— On the other hand, we flee everything considered "phallic" to find refuge in the valorization of a silent underwater body, thus abdicating any entry into history.

If women have a role to play in this on-going process, it is only in assuming a *negative* function: reject everything finite, definite, structured, loaded with meaning, in the existing state of society. Such an attitude places women on the side of the explosion of social codes: with revolutionary moments. But women tend to move immediately to the other side—the side of symbolic power. Women can become the most solid guarantee of sociality because they can make decisions concerning procreation (in the "developed" countries and as the final arbiters), and because they tend to identify with power after having rejected it.

X.G.: Can the writing of women be an answer to this oscillation between "power" and "denial"?

J.K.: Women generally write in order to tell their own family story (father, mother and/or their substitutes). When a woman novelist does not reproduce a real *family* of her own, she creates an imaginary story through which she constitutes an identity: narcissism is safe, the ego becomes eclipsed after freeing itself, purging itself of reminiscences. Freud's statement "the hysteric suffers from reminiscence" sums up the large majority of novels produced by women.

In women's writing, language seems to be seen from a foreign land; is it seen from the point of view of an asymbolic, spastic body? Virginia Woolf describes suspended states, subtle sensations and, above all, colors —green, blue—, but she does not dissect language as Joyce does. Estranged from language, women are visionaries, dancers who suffer as they speak.

However, this estrangement has recently begun to dissipate. One symptom: *Le pays où tout est permis* [The country where everything is permitted] by Sophie Podolski. Here is a twenty-year-old woman who today produces an incredible innovation. In Podolski I read not only what is traditionally considered feminine (sensations, colors, etc.) but a certain sensitivity to language, to its phonetic texture, its logical articulation, and throughout this entire written and sketched universe, the ideological, theoretical, political conflicts of our time. The avant-garde has always had ties to the underground. Only today, it is a woman who makes this connection. This is important. Because in social, sexual, and symbolic experiences, being a woman has always provided a means to another end, to becoming something else: a subject-in-the-making, a subject on trial.

If we call the moment of rupture and negativity which conditions and underlies the novelty of any praxis "feminine," we understand that this moment is also present in the elaboration of theorems, theories, and science. No "I" is there to assume this "femininity," but it is no less operative, rejecting all that is finite and assuring in (*sexual*) *pleasure* the life of the concept. "I," subject of a conceptual quest, is also a subject of differentiation—of sexual contradictions.

Translated by Marilyn A. August

Claudine Herrmann

*You ask what is supreme happiness here
on earth?
The sound of a little girl's song as she
walks away, having asked you for her
way.*
Li-Tai-Po

The term "space" refers to very different concepts: there is a physical space and a mental space for everyone. These two categories have in common the capacity to be invaded: one by violence, the other by indiscretion.

In our world, physical space is linked to different functions: one is domination and bondage (one "occupies" a region, a country is "occupied," one rules, one is ruled), another function is hierarchy: one is seated at a greater or lesser distance from a sovereign or from the master of the house, a professor is enthroned behind his desk and his students are seated on benches, a lawyer in chambers is assigned to a place that distinguishes him from his client.

Moreover, a court of law is a good example of the hierarchical function of space: at one level, the judge and the bench (in French *le Parquet*, where the prosecutor sits, originally meant a "little park," a reserved space) at another level, the court recorder, in the front the brothers at the bar, further off, their assistants.

In other words, this conception of space reflects systems and hierarchies perfectly: some spread out, others crowded in together, some higher, others lower. In length, width, and height, order is established by division, the disposition of space for man is above all an image of power, the maximum power being attained when one can dispose of the space of others, as is well illustrated by this excerpt from Victor Segalen's *Bricks and Tiles*:

> Here is the heart of the city, the vagabond Center of the Mongolian, Chinese, and Manchurian City. Princes created it at will, or tore it down in anger. They played with it, moving it five li[1] to

---

From "Les coordonnées féminines: espace et temps" [Women in space and time] in *Les voleuses de langue* [The tongue snatchers] (des femmes, 1976).
[1] A "li" is a Chinese measure equal to approximately one third of a mile.—Tr.

the North or the South as we would move around a heavy piece of furniture. Too big? One cut the cities back. They surrounded these immense cities with walls, changing them as you would alter a wooden cabin; and when the Master wanted another one, he designed it as you would lay out the walkways of a little garden planted according to your whims.[2]

The functioning of mental space is not as far from this as one might think: "to put people in their place," means assigning them to a well-defined position in relation to oneself, with attendant rights to think and feel and the possibility of speaking according to such a language. Some ideas or words are "out of place" when certain people—because of their social position, age, or sex—say them, and these differences, in a variety of forms, subsist everywhere today.

The space of the mind is divided according to rules that are just as strict as the rules governing physical space: everyone must conform or risk a social sanction ranging from silent scorn to exclusion from the group, pure and simple.

As soon as everyone takes his assigned position, it is easy for someone from the outside to theorize about such and such a group which behaves in one way or another, which expresses itself in this way or that (when it has no other choice) and to insert the group in a nice literary or scientific system; then he will reap the glory of determining the rules that govern it.

Physical or mental, man's space is a space of domination, hierarchy and conquest, a sprawling, showy space, a *full* space.

Woman, on the other hand, has long since learned to respect not only the physical and mental space of others, but space for its own sake, *empty* space. It is because she needs to maintain a protective distance between herself and the men she has not chosen. As for those she may have chosen, there too, in order to avoid total annihilation, to escape man's habitual urge to colonize, she must conserve some space for herself, a sort of *no man's land*, which constitutes precisely what men fail to understand of her and often attribute to stupidity because she cannot express its substances in her inevitably alienated language.

The *void* is for her, then, a respectable value. Therefore it is hardly surprising that it was a woman—Simone Weil—who wrote the following passage in a chapter of *Waiting for God* entitled, significantly: "Accepting the Void": "Loving truth means tolerating the void ..." and later: "Not exerting all the power at one's disposal, is to tolerate the void. It is contrary to all the laws of nature: only grace can achieve it."

It is interesting that Simone Weil, totally alienated by her upbringing

2 Victor Segalen, *Briques et tuiles* (Editions Fata Morgana, 1975), p. 30.

in masculine culture, should confuse what is masculine with what is natural (as opposed to what is supernatural).

And from that point on, what is feminine (and repressed for her since she was not even a feminist, according to her biographer Simone Pétrement)[3] becomes "supernatural." "Tolerating the void" is not in fact "supernatural," it is simply feminine.

These observations are not meant in any way to reduce Simone Weil's work to meanings imposed by her condition. They do not exclude other interpretations. Works are like dreams: they can have several meanings. We would take great pains not to reduce any work to one meaning.

However, the notion of the *void* as a positive value merits attention and signals Simone Weil as a precursor of modern thought (was it not Claude Lévi-Strauss who wrote that if nature abhors a vacuum, culture abhors fullness?)....

The human mind seems to establish a revealing link between absence of space/time and absence of grammar.... And, in fact, women who for centuries have been *cut off* from space, subjected to time without any means of recuperating it through action, have written poetry, uniquely, much longer than men.

There is one vision of spatial ensembles which is linked to geography and the articulation of elements among each other, and there is another vision which is just as interesting, which focusses on each one of the elements and not on the relationship between them. Jan Morris who after having been a man, became a woman, expressed it this way in *Conundrum*:

> I don't believe men feel this instant contact with the world around them; for me it is one of the constant fascinations and stimulants of my new condition.
>
> What do I notice, on my way down the hill to the shops? Perhaps not quite so dreamily as I once did the perspectives of square and crescent; instead, the interiors of houses, glimpsed through the curtains, the polished knockers, the detail of architrave or name-plate. I look at the place more intimately, perhaps because I feel myself integral to the city's life at last. I am no longer the utterly detached, the almost alienated observer of the scene; I am one with it, linked by an eager empathy with the homelier things about it.... [4]

[3] Simone Pétrement, *La Vie de Simone Weil* (Editions Fayard, 1973), p. 118. In English: *Simone Weil: A Life*, trans. Raymond Rosenthal (Pantheon Books, 1976).
[4] Jan Morris, *Conundrum* (Harcourt Brace Jovanovich, Inc., 1974), pp. 157–58. In French: *L'énigme* (Gallimard), p. 194.

This opinion seems to be in full agreement with Virginia Woolf in *Orlando* where she imagines precisely the same situation that Jan Morris found her/himself in, that is, the transformation of Orlando into a woman: "She was unversed in geography, found mathematics intolerable, and held some caprices which are more common among women than men, as for instance, that to travel south is to travel down hill." [5]

However, as soon as woman conceives space as a function of rapprochement rather than in terms of its separating function, she becomes at once an intrepid traveler and, if need be, a topographer like Alexandra David Neel, able to get around without a map in the Himalayas as she tells it in *Travels of a Parisian to Lhassa*: "I tried to remember exactly all that I knew about the topography of the place. One road went from Dayul to Dowa, it didn't interest me. The main trail to Tsawa Tinto where I wanted to go, went along the left bank of the Nou Tchou. Other paths led to the same village along the right bank. I could, then, as I saw fit, cross the river or not—all the peasants had told me—I wanted to stay on the path along the left bank in order to avoid the monastery, therefore I had taken the wrong route." [6]

Women today have displayed a remarkable appetite for travel. Usually they are not motivated by a taste for conquest—even scientific conquest—but rather by the desire to know other human beings, other customs and climates—and although they do not admit it, they want to fight against time, to multiply perspectives and comparisons and to draw into life itself, into their most intimate self, that composition and architecture of the world that men generally pass on to their works rather than to themselves.

It is because time is harder on women than men. Aging, separated from her children, strength no longer consoles her. More than anyone, from childhood to old age, she lives the negative aspect of time: only her childhood is truly free. She stands out without trying to in youth, then she finds herself little by little ignored as her beauty disappears. Her talents do not matter much. Man's love is for her body.

Her most mortal enemy then is time—time our torture, as Simone Weil said, and rather than constantly measure up to the ever triumphant monster, she prefers to deny it (like Simone Weil who tried to short-circuit it by "giving in" to it) or to peel away the scales, passing moments, like Virginia Woolf, or to protect herself by forgetting—even pathologically—like some of Marguerite Duras's heroines.

---

[5] Virginia Woolf, *Orlando* (Harcourt Brace Jovanovich, A Harvest Book, 1928), p. 190.—Tr.
[6] Alexandra David Neel, *Voyage d'une Parisienne à Lhassa* (Gonthier, 1964).

If man lives in an organized temporal perspective, delineated by the realization of goals he sets for himself, woman, like the natives of impoverished countries, prefers to consume immediately, without keeping anything in reserve and prefers one happy moment to a momentary deprivation that would assure future advantages.

Because for her, affective values are still the most important, and they are exactly the ones that one cannot keep in reserve.

It is not only because woman produces and raises children that she is associated with them, it is because often, like them, she lives in the present, and does not project herself into the future.

Men's time is, in effect, just another system, but the most frightening of all, the one that deprives you of the present in the name of the future and puts off the present moment indefinitely by crushing it under the past and the future.

As soon as a woman speaks up, it is usually to reclaim the right to the present moment, to affirm the refusal of a life alienated in social time which is so hostile to interior time.

Also, women seldom treat time as a positive element in their works, a dimension that enriches vision by adding another complexity and a factor of truth. . . .

Time and space respond to the mind's rhythm, which is at one with the biological rhythm of pulsation such as the circulation of the blood or nervous response. Time and space no longer participate in the artificial continuity imposed by social life, but in a reality that is simply that of intimate life.

The continuity becomes evident in light of a primarily social preoccupation. Masculine system has until now required women to assume material continuity—of daily life and of the species—while men assume the function of discontinuity, discovery, change in all its forms, in essence, the superior, differentiating function.

It follows that in order to recuperate the indispensable and complementary lost function, woman must provide another division of time and space, refusing their continuity, fragmenting them into moments and places that are not linked together, in such a way that each is a sort of innovation in reference to its temporal or geographical context.

Her life—and her work, in the case of Virginia Woolf—often resembles an archipelago, a series of little islands that point toward an uncharted sea and that the waves conceal and reveal at whim.

This vision preserves the freshness of life by refusing to consider it as a landscape that goes by while one thinks about something else: "Your days and hours go by like the tree branches and forest moss landscapes for the hunting dog running along a trail. . . ."

On one side, then, there are men who see in the present moment a means for arriving at their goal, and on the other, there are women who sink into it, stretch and prolong it because for them it is an end in itself. These visions are frequently contradictory whereas they should be complementary, as they are for artists; instead they lead to quarrels: women "waste their time" and men "don't know how to live."

These different observations help us understand why Professor Anastasi of Fordham University was able to conclude his experiments in differential psychology with this remark: "On the whole, girls are better than boys in subjects that rely primarily on verbal activity, memory, and perceptual speed. Boys are better in subjects involving numerical reasoning, spatial aptitudes, and in certain informational subjects like history, geography, or the sciences in general."

It remains to be seen whether women, once conscious of their identity and without trying to imitate what has been done until now, could inaugurate a new culture. Our knowledge has been following a path that is not necessarily the only one possible. In the last few years there has been a renewal in the principal disciplines that has led to the following consideration: not only have the discourses of knowledge been arbitrarily chosen, but their object as well.

Set theory in mathematics does not constitute progress so much as a change in point of view: the passage from monovalence to polyvalence. And just as in art, the Impressionists' concern with the relative character of colors in relation to each other is not necessarily preferable to such and such a school of thought that went before it, but is simply concern with something else, in the same way, relativistic physics does not weaken the physics of our fathers: it stands to one side and looks elsewhere.

What remains to be discovered is always so great that everyone can adjust his or her lens at will without necessarily imposing a limit on others.

However, when one considers the bitterness of our most distinguished intellectuals when old age catches up with them, one cannot help but think that a knowledge that would also help one know how to live and die, in other words, perhaps, wisdom, would be highly desirable, just as it would be preferable, as we have seen in recent years, to establish a science based on harmony rather than domination.

Translated by Marilyn R. Schuster

Marguerite Duras

I think "feminine literature" is an organic, translated writing ... translated from blackness, from darkness. Women have been in darkness for centuries. They don't know themselves. Or only poorly. And when women write, they translate this darkness. ... Men don't translate. They begin from a theoretical platform that is already in place, already elaborated. The writing of women is really translated from the unknown, like a new way of communicating rather than an already formed language. But to achieve that, we have to turn away from plagiarism. There are many women who write as they think they should write—to imitate men and make a place for themselves in literature. Colette wrote like a little girl, a turbulent and terrible and delightful little girl. So she wrote "feminine literature" as men wanted it. That's not feminine literature in reality. It's feminine literature seen by men and recognized as such. It's the men who enjoy themselves when they read it. I think feminine literature is a violent, direct literature and that, to judge it, we must not—and this is the main point I want to make—start all over again, take off from a theoretical platform. The other day you were telling me, "Yes, but women can also be ideologues, philosophers, poets, etc., etc." Of course. Of course. But why go over that? That should go without saying. We should be saying the opposite: can *men* forget everything and join women? ....

You know, in his *Discourse on Politics*, Aimé Césaire, the black poet, says that when someone is brown, people always wonder if he or she has black blood, but never do they wonder if he or she has white blood. And when we have a male in front of us, we could ask: does he have some female in him? And that could be the main point. That's it: reverse everything, including analysis and criticism. ... Reverse everything. Make women the point of departure in judging, make darkness the point of

From an interview by Susan Husserl-Kapit in *Signs*, Winter 1975.

departure in judging what men call light, make obscurity the point of departure in judging what men call clarity. . . .

I know that when I write there is something inside me that stops functioning, something that becomes silent. I let something take over inside me that probably flows from femininity. But everything shuts off—the analytic way of thinking, thinking inculcated by college, studies, reading, experience. I'm absolutely sure of what I'm telling you now. It's as if I were returning to a wild country. Nothing is concerted. Perhaps, before everything else, before being Duras, I am—simply—a woman. . . .

Just as when you are grown up you forget the child you once were. You no longer know anything about that. Men have gotten lost in the same way, whereas women have never known what they were. So they aren't lost. Behind them, there is darkness. Behind men, there is distortion of reality, there are lies. . . .

The silence in women is such that anything that falls into it has an enormous reverberation. Whereas in men, this silence no longer exists. . . .

Because men have established the principle of virile force. And everything that emerged from this virile force—including words, unilateral words—reinforced the silence of women. In my opinion, women have never expressed themselves. It is as if you asked me: "Why aren't there writers in the proletariat? Why aren't there musicians among the workers?" That's exactly the same thing. There are no musicians among the workers just as there are no musicians among women. And vice versa. To be a composer, you must have total possession of your liberty. Music is an activity of excess, it is madness, a freely consented madness. . . .

Do you know the thesis by Michelet about witches? [1] It's admirable. (By the way, I think, and many people think, on the basis of letters and journals, that Michelet did not have a normal sex life—which is certainly in his favor.) He says that in the Middle Ages, when the lords went off to war or on the Crusades, when the women stayed alone for months at a time on the farms, in the middle of the fields, hungry and lonely, then they simply started talking. To whatever was around them: trees, animals, forests, rivers. . . . Perhaps to break the boredom, to forget the hunger and the loneliness. The men burned them. That's how witches came into being. Men said, "They're in collusion with nature," and they burned them. That's how the reign of witches began. I add, personally, that what they did, in effect, was punish those women because they turned a little away from them and became less available to them. The women who began to come into contact with nature, as if by osmosis,

---

[1] Jules Michelet, *La sorcière* [The sorceress], 1862, a text that has been assimilated by many new French feminist writers, particularly Cixous, Clément, and Gauthier. It is a part of their canon.—Ed.

took part of themselves away from men. So men killed them to punish them. And that madness—talking to animals, trees, that part of themselves which suffocates and explodes, that transference—you find it in all women, including women of the middle class. It's what I call their neurosis. Neurosis in women is so ancient, thousands of years old—all women are neurotic in my opinion—that people are used to their behavior. And much female behavior that one finds normal would be considered neurotic if exhibited by males. Of course women express this neurosis differently in our day. They no longer talk to animals or trees, because, apparently, they aren't alone. In fact, however, they are completely alone in their millions, in their poverty, in their comfort, and in their slums, in all their completely functional marriages—whether rich or poor. They are as alone as before. And everywhere. Madness has found other expressions, but it is still there. It is still the same madness.

Translated by Susan Husserl-Kapit

Chantal Chawaf

Isn't the final goal of writing to articulate the body? For me the sensual juxtaposition of words has one function: to liberate a living paste, to liberate matter. Language through writing has moved away from its original sources: the body and the earth. Too often GOD was written instead of LIFE. Classicism and rationalism have mutilated the verbal paganism of the Middle Ages and the Renaissance. Linguistic flesh has been puritanically repressed. Abstraction has starved language, but words must die. They have a sensorial quality. Their role is to develop consciousness and knowledge by liberating our unconscious as well as to bring back hope.

Words have the power to deny destruction and our writing must prove this. We need languages that regenerate us, warm us, give birth to us, that lead us to act and not to flee. And the imaginary must be a form of contact. The novel and its traditional narrative style summarizes, it is a yardstick for measuring distance. But when I write, on the contrary, I move in close and what I see is enormous. I magnify the word with a close-up lens. I examine it at close range: it has its own way of being granulated, ruffled, wrinkled, gnarled, iridescent, sticky. I try to respect its variations in elevation, its sheen, its seeds, and like an artisan I offer them so that they may be touched and eaten. The word must comfort the body. I cannot hurry. I will not rush the word. I want to lose no part of it. The word has its own organic life and to conserve that life is of the utmost importance. In order to reconnect the book with the body and with pleasure, we must disintellectualize writing. The corporality of language stirs up our sensuality, wakes it up, pulls it away from indifferent inertia. Theories deprive us of whirlpools sparkling and free which should carry us naturally toward our full blossoming, our rebirth. For me the most important thing is to work on orality. For women, the old material language corresponds to our historical place which is actually

---

"La chair linguistique" [Linguistic flesh] in *Nouvelles littéraires*, May 26, 1976.

birth. And this language, as it develops, will not degenerate and dry up, will not go back to the fleshless academicism, the stereotypical and senile discourses that we reject. If a music of femininity is arising out of its own oppression, it materializes through the rediscovered body.

I feel that feminine writing is social, vital. I feel the political fecundity of mucus, milk, sperm, secretions which gush out to liberate energies and give them back to the world. Feminine language must, by its very nature, work on life passionately, scientifically, poetically, politically in order to make it invulnerable.

Translated by Yvonne Rochette-Ozzello

Madeleine Gagnon

Taking over this language which, although it is mine, is foreign to me.
Arranging it in my fashion and I don't translate. This meant, at first,
learning on the writing slate in order not to squander. Writing meant
learning not to spend; it meant erasing as I went along all that had been
inscribed on the slate; a sharpened memory would compensate for the
loss of the signs. My body, at the time, was losing nothing yet, my periods
would come much later, yet everything was preparing me for it. Learning to exchange blood, milk, tears in the loss of the body, learning to
flow, and remembering the traces on the day when they had been erased.
For me words have always flowed as freely as the signs on the writing
slate. I did not learn about the powers or the rights associated with them.
Copyrights, rights of survival or immortality, the power of what is written down and remains, the obsessions with translations or with death, I,
a woman, don't understand much about all this. I have learned to efface[1]
myself a thousand times and each time I return triumphant with pleasure. For me death is daily and monthly, it comes and goes. It doesn't
mean ONE unique death to be feared; ever since I started to exist I have
been dissolving into all that disappears and comes to life again. "To
invent a language that is not oppressive, a language that does not leave
speechless but that loosens the tongue" (*Parole de femme*),[2] this is
where we stand, that is we men and women who are still struggling
against all of the varied forms of exploitation, against all the forms of
domination, for we have lived these for thousands of years within the core
of our bodies; regardless of their origins, be they of sex or class, we have
experienced them in our sexes. That's why we can only speak in a

---

From "Corps I" [Body I] in *La venue à l'écriture* [Coming to writing] (Union Générale d'Editions, 10/18, 1977).
[1] In French *effacer* means "to erase" and *s'effacer*, "to self-efface."—Tr.
[2] Madeleine Gagnon is quoting Annie Leclerc in *Parole de femme*. See the Bio/
Bibliography at the end of this book.—Tr.

loosened tongue, why we are unable to utter anything besides what flows out, and is dissolved, and knows that what obliterates it from all power at the same time conserves it in men's memories.

We have never been the masters of others or of ourselves. We don't have to confront ourselves in order to free ourselves. We don't have to keep watch on ourselves, or to set up some other erected self in order to understand ourselves. All we have to do is let the body flow, from the inside; all we have to do is erase, as we did on the slate, whatever may hinder or harm the new forms of writing; we retain whatever fits, whatever suits us. Whereas man confronts himself constantly. He pits himself against and stumbles over his erected self. For him, crossing out a word is a drama, erasing one is death. It is the tragedy of his power, of his force, of his sex. He is constantly double, he and his phallus. He has established, from the farthest of ages and without giving birth, the binary relation. He has set up the mirror, projected the fantasm. He has become his own representative, his own reference point. He has to become master of himself since it is in himself he finds his second, his diminished other, his slave. Then he can become Master of others.

The phallus, for me at this time, represents repressive capitalist ownership, the exploiting bourgeois, the higher knowledge that must be gotten over; it represents an erected France that watches, analyzes, sanctions. The phallus means everything that sets itself up as a mirror. Everything that erects itself as perfection. Everything that wants regimentation and representation. That which does not erase/efface but covets. That which lines things up in history museums. That which constantly pits itself against the power of immortality. Yet I snatch this language that is foreign to me and turn it about in my fashion. I thread together truths that will be reproduced. But on the slate I wrote with a sovereign chalk. It told which part of me was to prevail. I am a foreigner to myself in my own language and I translate myself by quoting all the others.

Translated by Isabelle de Courtivron

Viviane Forrester

We don't know what women's vision is. What do women's eyes see? How do they carve, invent, decipher the world? I don't know. I know my own vision, the vision of one woman, but the world seen through the eyes of others? I only know what men's eyes see.

So what do men's eyes see? A crippled world, mutilated, deprived of women's vision. In fact men share our malaise, suffer from the same tragedy: the absence of women particularly in the field of cinema.

If we were responsible for this absence, couldn't they complain about it? "After all," they would say, "we have communicated our images, our vision to you; you are withholding yours. That is why we present a castrated universe, a life whose essential answers are unknown to us. We make films, we attempt to say, to translate, to destroy, to know, to invent, and you condemn us to a monologue that confines us to stale repetition, an isolation such that we are becoming petrified in endless narcissism. We have only fathers. We see only through our own fantasms, our malaise, the tricks we play on you, our renunciations (this network of conventions which replaces you and propagates itself dangerously at every level of our work) and the vacuum created by your absence and the dolls who fill it and whom we have fabricated. And we do not know how you see us. You do not look at us, etc."

We don't hear such complaints and for obvious reasons. Because this blindness to women's vision, which in fact prohibits any global vision of the world, any vision of the human species, has been fashioned by men for our mutual impoverishment.

How can male directors today not beg women to pick up the camera, to open up unknown areas to them, to liberate them from their redun-

---

"Le regard des femmes" [What women's eyes see] in *Paroles ... elles tournent* [Speak up ... women are shooting films] (des femmes, 1976). This book is a collection of essays written by feminist film makers and actresses who belonged to the group "Musidora."

dant vision which is deeply deformed by this lack? Women's vision is what is lacking and this lack not only creates a vacuum but it perverts, alters, annuls every statement. Women's vision is what you don't see; it is withdrawn, concealed. The images, the pictures, the frames, the movements, the rhythms, the abrupt new shots of which we have been deprived, these are the prisoners of women's vision, of a confined vision.

The quality of this vision is not the point—in the hierarchical sense—it is not better (how absurd to speak of a "better" vision), it is not more efficient, more immediate (certain women will assert that it is, but that's *not* the point); but it is lacking. And this deficiency is suicidal.

Women are going to seize (they are beginning to do so) what they should have acquired naturally at the same time as men did, what men after this bad start should have eventually begged women to undertake: the practice of film making. Women will have to defend themselves against an accumulation of clichés, of sacred routines which men delight in or reject and which will frequently trap women as well. They will need a great deal of concentration and above all of precision. They will have to see, to look, to look at themselves unaffectedly, with a natural gaze that is so difficult to maintain; they will have to dare to see not only their own fantasms, but also, instead of an old catalogue, fresh, new images of a weary world. Why will they be more apt to rid themselves of whatever obstructs men's vision? Because women are the secret to be discovered, they are the fissures. They are the source where no one has been.

Translated by Isabelle de Courtivron

Christiane Rochefort

A man's book is a book. A woman's book is a woman's book. A crowd of fathers-husbands-big brothers-lovers are watching, not our capacities as writers, but our behavior. We are allowed to write, OK. But not anything. "I like your books very much, but why do you insist on using crude words?" "That's the way the character talks you know," I would say, "and besides it's the way you talk, yourself." "Yes, maybe, but is it necessary that you write it?" We have to be decent. Exceptions are tolerated if they are without ambiguity, part of the right erotic game. We have a body: university degrees don't obliterate the fact. When Kristeva got a prize not long ago, a critic wrote in a so-called liberal newspaper: "She has beautiful legs."

We have a physiology: after Beauvoir's novel *La femme rompue* [The woman destroyed], the critic of *Le monde*[1] said, "She's an old woman." He himself was about to die, but he was a man and consequently had no age. The quantity of whisky that Françoise Sagan absorbed was carefully measured. And I saw with my own eyes, almost with tears, Marguerite Duras, just coming out of a clinic after a breakdown, questioned, I mean tortured, by a TV reporter, about how she feels now and if she is inspired as before and if she is not frightened by the blank page. Indiscretion with women is regular.

We have a psychology: I got some free analysis after my first book was published. One journalist wrote that I probably was ugly and frustrated— till, meeting him at a cocktail party, I patted him on the shoulder saying: "Ho, sir, I'm the ugly, frustrated one." He ran away while the others laughed. He himself was a piece of fat.

From Are Women Writers Still Monsters?—a speech given at the University of Wisconsin—Madison, February 1975.
[1] The most highly regarded French newspaper because of its extensive reporting and the thoroughness of its articles.—Ed.

We have a private life: dozens of times I was asked if I really went to bed with my hero. I didn't notice that such questions were asked of a normal writer (a man).

I'm perfectly sure that if my first book[2] were written by a man, it would not have been a scandal, and, consequently, not a bestseller. There are sometimes good sides to oppression. But it took time for me to recover, and come up with the correct analysis: I was a woman, so emphasis was put on the smallest sexual issues appearing in my writings. If *they* see anything, this is all that they see.... In brief, we are read below the belt—men are at the glorious level of brain.

In spite of everything, I think creativity is a natural activity of human-kind. All babies are born with a fantastic potential. But our present-day society doesn't need all that. It needs sheep, for production and consumption. In terms of potential, what is not necessary is not awakened, or it is stifled, or it is cut off: this is the enormous business of children's oppression. Of *all* children's oppression. This mutilating surgery which affects every child goes further for the poor, for the oppressed races, and for females....

I know with certainty that my salvation as a creator (I mean as a person) is due to the fact that I was dumb enough, blind and deaf enough, not to understand that I was a female. Although it was obvious, and I received all the necessary information about it (don't do this, don't say that, don't, don't, a little girl does not), I remained deaf, blind, and reluctant: not *me*, not for me. "Me" was something else. Somewhere else. Since reality was a lie, I had a reality of my own: a secret life in dreams. There, a double of mine with no defined sex (I didn't know that I meant: with no defined role) would do such great things as riding horses, sailing boats, rescuing animals from hunters and people from fire, plague, Indians from white people, inventing stories, drawing, dancing, making music, sculpting stones (I sculpted so many stones in dreams that the first time I had a chisel in hand I knew exactly how to use it). In the world of appearances, I didn't feel real. Schizophrenia? I was lucky that my parents were not in a position to take me to a therapist: he would have discovered my trick, brought me back to "reality" and it would have been the end of me. This brave secret of mine rescued me: *it* has kept alive my creative possibilities.

I learned later on, in consciousness-raising groups, that it is a pretty common experience—female children are driven mad, schizophrenic—because there is a total antagonism between what they are and what

[2] *Le repos du guerrier* (Grasset, 1958). In English: *The Warrior's Rest*, trans. Lowell Bair (David McKay Co., 1959).—Ed.

society wants them to be. Among them, a remarkable proportion is defeated in this combat. I almost was, between twelve and twenty: then I was rescued by a small light of political consciousness: I learned that I was an oppressed person. . . .

The husband of a friend of mine once read what his wife did write (when the housework was over). He said: "You know, you are so much better in helping me?" She stopped writing on the spot. Now she is pretty desperate, for she wants to work again but dares not. So I told her my own story: When I finished my first book—it was a novel of course, it is easier for a woman to begin with a novel, for this is what they are supposed to do more or less and this is another story, the influence of discrimination on choices—when I finished my novel, my first movement was to show it to the man I lived with at the moment. He said: "My poor girl, you better darn stockings." I stopped writing on the spot for three years—till I parted from my husband, swearing that never again in my life was I going to show anything to a man who *loves* me. Recently, I found this forgotten manuscript, which in my memory was the pretty bad work of a beginner; not only did it have some qualities—but it was feminist: I even had forgotten this remarkable point, congratulations. I had a good moment laughing at me, at us, at History . . . I gave the book a title: "You better darn stockings." And I put it back in its tomb. . . .

Well. So, here you are now, sitting at your writing table, alone, not allowing anybody anymore to interfere. Are you free?

First, after this long quest, you are swimming in a terrible soup of values—for, to be safe, you had to refuse the so-called female values, which are not female but a social scheme, and to identify with male values, which are not male but an appropriation by men—or an attribution to men—of all human values, mixed up with the anti-values of domination-violence-oppression and the like. In this mixture, where is your real identity?

Second, you are supposed to write in certain forms, preferably: I mean you feel that in certain forms you are not too much seen as a usurper. Novels. Minor poetry, in which case you will be stigmatized in French by the name of "poetesse": not everybody can afford it. I must confess that, although I write poems, I couldn't afford showing them, except to close friends. They are in a drawer.

You are supposed, too, to write *about* certain things: house, children, love. Until recently there was in France a so-called *littérature féminine*.[3]

---

[3] A traditional category in French literary history since the end of the nineteenth century.—Ed.

Maybe you don't want to write *about*, but to write, period. And, of course, you don't want to obey this social order. So, you tend to react against it. It is not easy to be genuine. . . .

Has literature a sex? With dignity, I, and most of my sisters, we would answer: No.

But. But. But, do we have the same experience? Do we have the same mental structures? The same obsessions? Death, for instance, is a specifically male obsession. As well as essential solitude.

After all, we don't belong to the same civilization.

Written directly into English by Christiane Rochefort

Manifestoes–Actions

*"Manifestoes–Actions" translates
the presence of feminism in France,
acknowledges the actions of groups
involved in concrete issues such
as contraception, abortion reform,
and prostitution, and accompanies
the launching of significant feminist journals or special issues.*

Women Arise!

Debout les femmes!

We who are without a past
Without history, outcast
Women lost in the dark of time
Women whose continent is night.
  Together slaves arise
  To break our chains asunder
  Arise!

Subjugated, humiliated
Women bought and sold and raped
Shut away within the walls
Women banished out of sight.
  Together slaves arise. . . .

Women cut off from each other
Each alone to bear her fate
From our sisters separated
Women we have been betrayed.
  Together slaves arise. . . .

Women we must greet each other
See and speak to one another
Women all enslaved together
All together will arise.
  Together slaves arise. . . .

The days of wrath for us have come
By the thousands we are here
Women we shall know our power
Women this must be the hour.
  Together slaves arise
  To break our chains asunder
  Arise! Arise!

Nous qui sommes sans passé les femmes
Nous qui n'avons pas d'histoire
Depuis la nuit des temps, les femmes
Nous sommes le continent noir.
  Levons-nous femmes esclaves
  Et brisons nos entraves
  Debout!

Asservies, humiliées, les femmes
Achetées, vendues, violées
Dans toutes les maisons, les femmes
Hors du monde reléguées.
  Levons-nous. . . .

Seules dans notre malheur, les femmes
L'une de l'autre ignorée
Il nous ont divisées les femmes
Et de nos soeurs séparées.
  Levons-nous. . . .

Reconnaissons-nous, les femmes
Parlons-nous, regardons-nous
Ensemble, on nous opprime, les femmes
Ensemble, révoltons-nous.
  Levons-nous. . . .

Le temps de la colère, les femmes
Notre temps est arrivé
Connaissons notre force, les femmes
Découvrons-nous par milliers.
  Levons-nous femmes esclaves
  Et brisons nos entraves
  Debout! Debout!

Translated by Germaine Brée

MLF Song. To the tune of "The Peat Bog Soldiers."

Manifesto of the 343

A million women have abortions in France each year. Because they are condemned to secrecy, they are aborted under dangerous conditions. If done under medical control, this operation is one of the simplest. These millions of women have been passed over in silence. I declare that I am one of them, I have had an abortion. Just as we demand free access to birth-control methods, we demand freedom to have abortions.

> Signed:
> Simone de Beauvoir,
> Christiane Rochefort,
> Françoise Sagan,
> Colette Audry,
> Violette Leduc,
> Gisèle Halimi,
> Romy Schneider,
> Delphine Seyrig,
> Jeanne Moreau,
> Catherine Deneuve,
> Micheline Presle,
> among others.[1]

"Un appel de 343 femmes" in *Le nouvel observateur*, April 5, 1971.
[1] Many of these names appeared on other manifestoes in the early 1970s.—Ed.

Simone de Beauvoir

"Perturbation, ma soeur...."[1] This issue comes to you under the sign of perturbation. The reader who expects to find a methodical and complete exposé of woman's condition will be disappointed. It is not our intention to denounce all the injustices suffered by women, or to draw up a list of their demands, even less to propose revolutionary tactics: our only desire is to disturb. We were guided in the choice of texts by the principle of freedom. We did not establish any preconceived plan. Women—some of whom have remained anonymous even to us—spontaneously chose to speak about topics that were closest to their hearts and we welcomed their writing. There was one thing they had in common: a radical refusal of woman's oppression. Consequently there were certain resemblances which allowed us to group under a few headings the articles that we received. There exist, nonetheless, among these articles serious differences and even occasionally contradictions. Feminist thought is not monolithic; every woman who struggles has her own reasons, her own perspective, her particular experience, and she offers them to us in her own way.

It is possible that some readers will be upset by some of the texts. Among the women who choose to express themselves, some think that the language and the logic currently used in our world are universally valid instruments even though they have been fashioned by men: the problem is to steal the tool. Others, on the contrary, think that culture itself is one of the forms of their oppression. Because of this oppression, because of the way they reacted to it, women have created a cultural universe different from that of men. They want to refer to their own

Introduction to "Les femmes s'entêtent" in *Les temps modernes*, April–May 1974.
[1] These words are from a book of collages by Max Ernst whose title is *La femme 100 têtes* (The Woman with 100 heads). For a discussion of the title "Les femmes s'entêtent" see the introductory essay, "Contexts of the New French Feminisms," n. 4.—Ed.

values by inventing a form of speech that reflects their specificity. A difficult, often uncertain, invention, but when this effort succeeds it enriches us with a truly new contribution.

In both cases the voices you are about to hear want above all to *disturb* you. The oppression of women is a fact to which society has grown so accustomed that even those among us who condemn it on the whole, in the name of abstract democratic principles, consider that many aspects have been improved. Because I more or less played the role of token woman, it seemed to me for a long time that certain inconveniencies inherent in the "feminine" condition should be either left alone or passed over and that there was no need to attack them. What made me understand the new generation of women in revolt is that my off-handedness involved complicity. In fact, if one accepts the slightest inequality between the two sexes one accepts Inequality. Some people think it childish, petty, that feminists attack vocabulary and grammar: for example, the fact that in French for three feminine nouns and one masculine noun the adjective is masculine. This is certainly not the terrain on which to begin the battle. But to overlook this means to run the risk of not seeing many things. Vigilance must be one of our passwords. And, in fact, the new feminists look at the world with the same ingenuous, demanding look of a child. The child is weak, we listen and smile. Women are strong and want to be stronger: they are troubling and that is why there is an attempt to discredit their vision of things, to make them seem ridiculous, to call them viragos.

The readers—women or men—who come to these texts in good faith run the risk, when they have finished reading, of feeling that they have been challenged. The anti-sexist struggle is not only directed, as the anti-capitalist struggle is, against the structures of society as a whole: the anti-sexist struggle attacks in each one of us what is most intimate and what seemed the most secure. It challenges our desires, the very forms of our pleasure. Let us not retreat in front of this challenge; beyond the suffering that it may provoke in us, it will destroy some of our shackles, it will open us up to new truths.

Translated by Elaine Marks

Editions des femmes

The women's liberation movement is a historical, international reality which, from now on, can be neither subjugated nor censored.

Since May 1968 women have been struggling with great intensity to form a revolutionary force.

Along this same route, and in order to extricate ourselves from the dead ends of feminism, the group "politics and psychoanalysis" which initiated the publishing house éditions des femmes also initiated, six years ago, the specific inscription of this struggle on the double front—practice and theory—of the unconscious and of history.

Translated by Elaine Marks

Notice on the back cover of Julia Kristeva's *Des chinoises* [About Chinese Women] (des femmes, 1974).

Rape Is an Abuse of Power

—Men rape because they own (have) the law.
—They rape because they are the law.
—They rape because they make the law.
—They rape because they are the guardians of the peace, of law and order.
—They rape because they have the power, the language, the money, the knowledge, the strength, a penis, a phallus.

Men say that:
—in any case we're asking for it,
—that we are not careful enough,
—that we shouldn't follow strangers,
—but that you can't say no to your father,
—that we provoke it,
—that we are accomplices,
—that we should learn a good lesson from it,
—that we shouldn't go out without a protector,
—etc.

We say to ourselves:
—what is it that dies in a woman when she has been raped?
—rape leaves you helpless, voiceless, paralyzed, frigid, traumatized,
—what woman does not live in fear of being raped?
—how many little girls are "raped" just by seeing men expose themselves in public gardens?
—why is it that rape is never punished?
—why is rape impossible to prove?
—why do they always refer a raped woman to a law that favors rapists?
—why is a woman not a "real woman" until she has been raped?

"Le viol est un abus de pouvoir" in *Le quotidien des femmes*, May 3, 1975.

Bodily rape is merely the acting out of a daily ideological reality.
Rape is an initiation
   they say that we are becoming women,
   we say that we are being forced to enter the legal system.
Rape does not exist
   they say it's natural,
   we say: it's the law.
Rape exists; it's a reality. The raping of silent little girls by fathers, by
brothers; the raping of isolated women by men.
   in any case it exists in women's minds as fear, as anguish.
   it exists in men's minds as a right.

                              Translated by Isabelle de Courtivron

The Women Prostitutes of Lyon Speak to the People

We asked the State to listen to us as women.

Poniatowski[1] answers us with billy clubs, takes our money, puts us in prison, insults us, hits us, ejects us forcibly from churches in order to put us in brothels, and takes away our children.

He refuses to see us as women.

He only accepts us as sex factories.

He speaks about procuring, but he takes our money and goes free!

So we say:

NO TO PROCURING,

NO TO BROTHELS,

NO TO POLICE REPRESSION,

NO TO PRISON SENTENCES.

YES TO JUSTICE

YES TO ALL THE ADVANTAGES AND RIGHTS OF BEING WOMEN!

More united than ever, in dignity, for the creation of an Estates General of women prostitutes, we come together again in the struggle.

Action Committee of Women Prostitutes

Translated by Elaine Marks

"Les prostituées de Lyon parlent à la population" in *Le quotidien des femmes*, June 1975.
[1] Michael Poniatowski: Minister of the Department of the Interior (1974–1977) in Giscard d'Estaing's government.—Tr.

C.D.

Feminism is first of all a *social* movement. Like any movement of revolt, its very existence poses—explicitly or implicitly—two fundamental postulates.

The situation of women is a cause for revolt. That's a platitude, but a platitude that involves a much less accepted corollary. One does not revolt against what is natural, therefore inevitable, or inevitable, therefore natural. As soon as there is revolt there is concurrently and inevitably the notion of a process that can be *resisted*. That which can be resisted is not inevitable; that which is not inevitable could be otherwise; it is arbitrary therefore social. The logical and necessary implication of women's revolt, as of any revolt, is that the situation can be changed: if not, why revolt? The belief in the possibility of change implies belief in the social origin of the situation.

The rebirth of feminism coincided with the use of the term "oppression." The ruling ideology, i.e., common sense, daily speech, does not speak about oppression but about a "feminine condition." It refers back to a naturalistic explanation: to a constraint of nature, exterior reality out of reach and not modifiable by human action. The term "oppression," on the contrary, refers back to a choice, an explanation, a situation that is *political*. "Oppression" and "social oppression" are therefore synonyms or rather social oppression is a redundancy: the notion of a political origin, i.e., social, is an integral part of the concept of oppression.

This term is thus the basis, the point of departure for any feminist study or strategy. Its use radically modifies the foundations not only of sociology but of all the social sciences. . . .

A feminist- or proletarian-science must succeed in explaining op-

From "Pour un matérialisme féministe" [For a materialist feminism] in *L'arc*, no. 61 (1975). The author of this article, C.D., is Christine Delphy. She signs some of her articles with her complete name.

pression; in order to do so, oppression has to be the starting point. If this science is coherent it will inevitably lead to a theory of history written and described in terms of the domination of social groups over each other. This science cannot consider a priori any domain of reality or of knowledge as exterior to this fundamental dynamic. . . .

Materialist feminism is therefore an intellectual procedure whose advent is crucial for social movements and the feminist *struggle, and* for knowledge. For the former it corresponds to the passage from utopian socialism to scientific socialism and it will have the same implications for the development of the feminist struggle. That procedure would not —could not even if it wanted to—limit itself to women, to women's oppression. It will not leave untouched any part of reality, any domain of knowledge, any aspect of the world. In the same way that feminism-as-a-movement aims at the revolution of social reality, so feminism-as-a-theory (and each is indispensable to the other) must aim at the revolution of knowledge.

Translated by Elaine Marks

Xavière Gauthier

Why witches? *Because witches dance.* They dance in the moonlight. Lunar, lunatic women, stricken, they say, with periodic madness. Swollen with lightninglike revolt, bursting with anger, with desire, they dance wild dances on the wild moors. Wildwomen, uncivilized, as the white man says of other races; wildcats, as the government and the unions say of some strikes; as they say of some of our schemes. The witches dance, wild and unjustifiable, like desire.

They tried to make us believe that women were impotent, immobile, paralyzed. That is because they tried to make women walk a straight line, in lock step, in goose step. In reality, they dance, they creep, they fly, they swim in every sea. They coil themselves up, they twist, they jump, they crouch, they leap.

Witches can fly for they are light; they submit to no law least of all that of gravity. A broom? They fly very well all by themselves. Their mount is but a slight modification of the housewife's tool....

Why witches? *Because witches sing.* Can I hear this singing? It is the sound of another voice. They tried to make us believe that women did not know how to speak or write; that they were stutterers or mutes. That is because they tried to make women speak straightforwardly, logically, geometrically, in strict conformity. In reality, they croon lullabies, they howl, they gasp, they babble, they shout, they sigh. They are silent and even their silence can be heard.

"Pourquoi Sorcières?" [Why witches?] in *Sorcières*, no. 1 (1976). *Sorcières* is a literary review edited by Xavière Gauthier that is dedicated to exploring women's creativity, women's language. Each issue is organized around a theme ("Food," "Voice," "Smells," "Prisoners," etc.) and includes a variety of poetic and narrative pieces as well as book and film reviews and announcements concerning activities of the MLF. The contributors may be well-known writers as well as younger women who sign their first names. "Why Witches?" is the opening statement of the first issue.

The frightful masculine fashion of speaking always surprises me. Speaking in order to be right—how ridiculous! In fact, to put someone else in the wrong. Speaking to nail the listener's trap shut. Speaking to put her in her place: man's language, man's rod. Meaning something. Speaking as if speech were not vocal, as if it did not resonate with a million modulations, as if it did not blend with the listener. Speaking as if speech were not spoken, independent of the mutilation of meaning. It seems completely absurd to me that women have considered borrowing and imitating this machine-gun language, and hoped to use this war machine to say something different. While a new voice is beginning to be heard on behalf of the gaps in the socio-symbolic order, on behalf of the unsaid, the unmeaningful, the repressed holes in masculine discourse.

How imposing the phallocratic system must be for women to have doubted themselves to the point of asking for equality (?!) with men! How great our alienation must have been to let us think for one instant that we should be like men, to let us be tempted for one instant to take our (?) place inside that hierarchical jungle where, as an Argentine proverb has it, the one who sits on the upper rung in the chicken coop shits on the one who sits on the lower. Let's leave the practice of everyone-out-of-my-way-or-else to the football players. Now that women are coming into history as women, it would be heart-rending if they were in a hurry to become men. All the more so since women are in the midst of literally blowing the system to bits, undermining it, sapping it, during a fearful witches' sabbath. A new history is beginning.

Why witches? *Because witches are alive.* Because they are in direct contact with the life of their own bodies and bodies of others, with the life force itself.

Now not only do we live apart from our garments and finery, but apart from our bodies. Completely apart. We know nothing about our bodies; there are specialists for this. And when our bodies do speak to us through sickness, we feel surprised, attacked as if by something outside ourselves. We do not feel, we do not control, we do not seek our own health. Our bodies do not belong to us. We live with them, but without them, in spite of them, against them.

Witches did not work miracles. They knew their bodies; they were not cut off from their bodies by nature or by others. They let the information that our bodies, that nature, that others constantly send us get through; they let the messages flow. That is how they were able to cure. Or to poison. There was nothing supernatural about it. In real, direct contact with nature, they breathed, touched, learned each flower, each plant, each herb. To the sick they gave Soianines, plants called

Consolers, which calmed their pains; they gave Belladonna as an anti-
dote for serious illnesses. Plants which were also poisons. Witches knew
the therapeutic dose. They were the caretakers, the healers of the people. They were midwives helping women to give birth, to give life. They
were also able to liberate women from unwanted pregnancies by abortion
and contraception.

All this was a bit too much! For the authorities who were exclusively
religious, it left women too much room for happiness, for freedom, for
power over their own bodies. "The Church declared in the fourteenth
century that if a woman dares to heal without having studied she is a
witch and must die" (Michelet). It is on the deaths of millions of women
that medical science was erected. Medical science, that masculine system where a small number of specialists who studied in medical schools
has the power to restrain and repress the bodies of everyone else.
   What still remains after this gigantic manoeuvre which expelled us
from our bodies? A few remedies called—with justifiable scorn—"old
wives' cures"— But most of all an immense movement that is beginning
to blossom, from every corner but particularly from women, to shake
off this bodily oppression. It is no accident that the struggle for the right
to abortion is one of the first great women's battles right now. *Like
witches burned by the Church for the benefit of medical science, millions of women have been killed in our time by the repressive machinery
of the Church and the medical profession.* Like witches, these women
die amidst general disapproval, martyred by society. And why? Because
they dared to live their bodies, to live their sexuality, to explore their
sensuality freely, because they dared to go into rapture.

Why witches? *Because witches are rapturous.* They tried to make us
believe that women were frigid, chaste, prudes. That is because they
tried to force us to have proper sex, according to a masculine model, with
masculine limits, in terms of conquest, of possession. In reality, witches
are bursting; their entire bodies are desire; their gestures are caresses;
their smell, taste, hearing are all sensual. Their pleasure is so violent, so
transgressive, so open, so fatal, that men have not yet recovered. Such
a great number of women were burned—some say eight million in two
centuries—out of fear, that one is forced to conclude that they tried to
have the female sex disappear from the earth. (Sometimes men who had
the misfortune to let the feminine in them be expressed were also sent
to the stake.)
   The *Malleus maleficarum,*[1] the indictment against witchcraft, said:

[1] *The Hammer of Witchcraft.* See Introduction II: Histories of France and of Feminisms in France, p. 12.

"All witchcraft comes from the carnal desire which is insatiable in women." And even Freud-the-Father had the intelligence to recognize that a girl's sensuality is otherwise greater than a boy's since her upbringing is devoted to repressing it with such vigor. Repressing her sensuality and therefore her sexual curiosity, and her desire to know, to think.

Female eroticism is terrifying; it is an earthquake, a volcanic eruption, a tidal wave. It is disquieting and so is mystified. It is made a mystery. It has been said that witches possessed a magic power. In fact, this was sexual. It was not a power, but powers, even forces. Forces that pass through a woman, that flow through her and that do not come from any Devil (= God) but from the unconscious, from the body. *The Force of the body.*

It has been said that witches cast spells, curses, that they performed magic rites. And doubtless anyone who surrendered to their desire was lost. Lost for a certain type of social productivity or conformity. But what is more vital than this extreme surrender to desire?

In traditional pictures the witch is not only disturbing, but old, ugly and wicked.[2] Which summons up the opposite image in fairy tales: the good fairy, young and beautiful. The good fairy has magnificent blonde curly hair, and the witch has a horrible straight black mop— If the standard image of female beauty today is that of the fashion model, good (dumbly smiling), young (eternal freshness, naïveté, stupidity), and beautiful (obligatory conformity to a certain stereotype of "beauty"), I understand the temptation to prefer to identify with the wicked witch. But that is a trap. Why must we choose between these two extremes that are mutually dependent? Why let ourselves be locked into a choice of opposites that are two sides of the same coin, which is the exclusion of women: idealized/scorned, sanctified/satanized, worshipped/martyred, burdened with every virtue/with every vice? Why do we have to be relegated to Heaven or Hell? Some words chanted by a group of women in the street come back to me: "We are not beautiful; we are not ugly; we are angry." Yes, and we are inflamed with desire, with struggle, with work, with life.

We know—women have always known—that men are paper tigers. That does not exempt us from a long and difficult struggle against the masculine system, against phallocratism. The Vietnamese knew that their enemies were paper tigers. But it took all those years of revolutionary struggle—of real, popular, collective force—to get rid of American imperialism, a false force of supertechnological warfare. Our woman's struggle is not easy; it is irreversible, indomitable.

[2] Even if historically this was not the case: "Many perished precisely because they were young and beautiful" (Michelet).

If the figure of the witch appears wicked, it is because she poses a real danger to phallocratic society. We do constitute a danger for this society which is built on the exclusion—worse, on the repression—of female strength. If women were not dangerous for this society they would not have been gagged, imprisoned, repressed for centuries. And the repression has been immense, enormous, in proportion to the strength. And the liberation that is coming is in proportion to the long repression of the strength that "justifies" it: this liberation is going to overturn *everything*; it is irrepressible, inexpiable. Nothing can stop it now. From the moment that women recognized one another, touched, clasped, loved one another, their force is quietly invincible.

This is, of course, *one* way, my way, of seeing witches. Taking off from particular details of history and legend, taking off from the word itself: "witches," I drift, I dream, I rave, I lust. If I propose *Witches* as the title of a journal, it is because I think that this word also resonates strongly in other women. But resonates differently for each one. I propose here *Witches* as a historical anchor, an immense political revolt from the past, probably, but also and especially turned toward the future. Other women will write differently here, as they speak, feel, think about witches, or even as they reject them.

I would like *Witches* to be an open place for all women who are struggling as women, who are seeking and speaking (writing, singing, filming, painting, dancing, drawing, sculpting, playing, working) their specificity and their strength as women. I would like *Witches* to be alive and mobile. As such I did not want to create a permanent, definitive, restrictive, and rigid editorial board, but an editorial board that could be new, different for each issue. It seems to me very artificial, very formal to gather together women who would agree on everything forever. On the contrary, for a particular issue, on a chosen theme, a real work group could be created where each woman could really discuss, suggest, invest something of herself, engage her joys, her questions, her powers, her desires.

Translated by Erica M. Eisinger

Nathalie Roncier
Claudie Landy

It is not our intention (for we "organizers") to draw up a list of accomplishments, any more than it is to put together a "common program" for the women of La Rochelle, but rather to talk about those two days, about ourselves during those two days, so that we may move on, if we so desire, to something else.

Yes, we went through hell, facing the judgment of the guys, of the women. It was a zoo, the weekend's freak show; feminists were there, the guys licked their chops.

Women came.

The women, daughters, mothers, militants, wifies, girlfriends, the isolated, the aggressive, the homosexuals, the cinemaphiles, the married, the not-married, the confused, the defensive, the feminists, the concerned, the not-feminists, the not-concerned, the wives with their guys, without their guys.

Women saw themselves. Women saw.

Themselves, the others, the films made by women, for women, pretext-films, they saw themselves, they were frightened, they liked, they didn't like, one of them even said "Funny how you can recognize yourself in all that."

They distrusted, they rejected, appreciated, rejected, grumbled, exploded.

Women wanted:

—to discuss films, themselves, other matters, to look, to say nothing (and that's not surprising), to stay together. It was enough to say: "How about going up to the lounge" for them to go up, to try and speak, to speak of themselves, to explain themselves without being judged, without being a target, without being a prey.

"Apres 48 heures du cinéma des femmes à La Rochelle" [After 48 hours of women's films in La Rochelle] in *Paroles . . . elles tournent* [Speak up . . . women are shooting films] (des femmes, 1976).

—to stop the film (the last one) we had gone beyond cinema (they cried out fascism when they saw the images of the Arab women).

What are women's films:
—pretext-films?
—slice-of-life films
—feminist films
—films in women's language
—films of revolt
—films that say
—films that cry out
—films that yell
—films that invent
—films that live
—films that move

Now we have:
everything to say, everything to do, everything to live, everything to invent, everything to film, everything to revolt against, to reject, to build for ourselves, to find for ourselves, to talk about ourselves as subjects.

We in the cinema:
We women spectators.

We went, we saw, we listened to what films had made of us, how they made us talk, come across on the screen, how they accept us, how they sell us, how they rape us, how they reproduce patriarchal society. In these films, we experienced the aggression of the images.

We and the cinema:
Men created the technique for themselves and for us, but by themselves.

They built a man's language for men by using it to service their fantasms.

We wanted our own language, wanted to understand, know, exist, find an identity, our identity as women, to film.

To film. We could have written, painted, spoken. To film because sensitized to the cinema, being part of the Rochelle workshop which set as its goal the diffusion and realization of a different kind of cinema.

Our film.
Whether the cinema calls itself feminist, experimental, or other, it fabricates us, it invents us despite ourselves (the star system, the new wave, or Bergman). We wanted to state this, to film it. "Of the utilization and representation of women in film" will be shown during our cinema festival . . . in La Rochelle.

In relation to the history of film making, our undertaking is original because it is subjective. Our film is also: our women's fantasms, the attempt to write in our own language. We have tried to talk about ourselves during this shooting, about our life, our lived experience.

We lived in the film
for the film
by the film
beyond the film
and we felt like talking about it
living it
starting again
doing something else.

Translated by Isabelle de Courtivron

Defense of Violette C.

Sir: Alerted by a woman journalist of *Hebdo* 76, the ITCAW (International Tribunal on Crimes Against Women) has just been informed about the hunger strike continued for forty-three days by your fifteen-year-old daughter Violette. You opposed her legal emancipation and we understand that she prefers to die rather than remain under your guardianship. We do not think that paternal authority gives you the power of life or death over your children, nor the power you already have taken by allowing the health of Violette to deteriorate in an irreversible way. Whatever your reasons for going so far in affirming your rights, we appeal to your sense of humanity in order to return to your daughter her life and her health. This affair has created a strong emotion among women of all nationalities informed by the Tribunal as we have been. We want to affirm our complete solidarity with Violette. You alone will bear the entire responsibility for what has happened to her and for what will happen. We are counting on you to make an end immediately to this drama by emancipating Violette.

Signed: Simone de Beauvoir, Benoîte Groult, Luce Irigaray, Juliette Gérard, Claude Servan-Schreiber, Delphine Seyrig, Jeanne Moreau, Christiane Rochefort, Emilienne Brunfaut, Maude Frère, Gisèle Halimi.

From *Resolutions from the International Tribunal on Crimes Against Women*. 1976. The International Tribunal on Crimes Against Women was held in Brussels (March 4–8, 1976). Over 2,000 women from forty countries attended. The violent crimes reported on include: slavery, polygamy, clitoridectomy, rape, prostitution, discrimination against lesbians, torture, femicide, violence against women in medicine in general and in gynecology and psychiatry in particular. The proceedings of the Tribunal were published in Diana E. H. Russell and Nicole Van de Ven, eds., *Crimes Against Women* (Les Femmes Publishing, 1976).

Gisèle Halimi

Thus came into being the newborn woman-child of the women that we are and we offer it to all the women of this country. The lack of time and the abundance of material account for some of the limitations of our enterprise. But I believe we will have accomplished the main thing. Without preliminary negotiations, without political training, we have summarized for the time being our principal demands as women, and we have set them down.

And so we will be present at the legislative elections. Not as servant-voters or as token candidates, but as spokeswomen for our Common Program and, if we are elected, as deputies for the "Cause of Women." We know that the parties, and oddly enough those of the Opposition, will sooner or later coopt (such is the accepted term) our ideas. They are old hands at this. I must add that, unlike professional leftists—men or women—we don't feel bitter about this kind of cooptation. On the contrary. Remember the abortion issue, remember the fight against rape. Two feminist struggles par excellence launched, and to this day still led, by the women's movements. The bill proposed by "Choisir" for freedom of abortion was taken over, with a few variants, by the Socialist party in 1973; and its fundamental principles influenced in large part the Simone Veil Law.

Two years ago, we denounced rape as a crime against women and

From the Introduction to *Le programme commun des femmes* [The common program for women] (Grasset, 1978). This book is a collective project drafted by the women of " "Choisir la cause des femmes" [To choose, the cause of women], under the direction of Gisèle Halimi, the group's co-founder. It summarizes the chief needs and demands of French women in legal, medical, political, and educational areas, and offers concrete solutions to each of these. The Common Program was designed to inform women voting in the 1978 legislative elections and to encourage them to support those political parties that endorsed the Program's proposals. Also included in the group's strategy were the candidacies of women representing "Choisir" (including Gisèle Halimi), for the office of *député*.

were met with ribald skepticism by the parties. A leftist party accused us seriously of exploiting a cocktail-party topic. Today, our principal demands[1]—criminal courts for rapists, publicity for these trials, for example—appear in the Communist party's bill "aiming to establish for women: advancement, equality, freedom in work, family, and society";[2] our demands are also included in the work being undertaken by the Women's Caucus of the Socialist party. This proves that the leaders have given their endorsement. It also means that there was, and will continue to be, cooptation in the narrow sense of the word.

Is this regrettable? At the conclusion of a superficial, somewhat childish analysis, maybe so. . . . But this would ignore the profound meaning of "Choisir's" struggle. When the Bobigny trial[3] enters the National Assembly through the front door, when the rape trials of Colmar and Aix-en-Provence[4] trigger such widespread debates throughout the country that it forces the political parties to echo these debates, I say that cooptation, for us, means victory.

We do not constitute a party, nor do we wish to become one. We want to remain a women's movement in movement. We consider ourselves a work group and a pressure group. When our manifestoes, our demonstrations, our trials, our public meetings, our press conferences, our writings bring about a new consciousness that forces change, change in the laws, in the habits, in the political platforms, we are moving forward.

If the parties take up our actions, very well. If not, we will take action.

Such is the nature of our Common Program for Women and of our candidacies. Our electoral campaign will not be "classical." Classicism, when it comes to electoral matters means, first of all, money, the party, being used to political jargon, knowing how to form alliances, in other words how to make compromises. Luckily, we will be different, unorthodox, inventive and, by force of circumstance, new.

This book is, to begin with, a working tool in the positive sense: a program. Urgent and short-term, once again. But it is also a tool of revolt: women voters, armed with these considerations, will be able to challenge candidates and will not be duped when it comes to their own

---

[1] On one hand, that the right to choose to have an abortion can only belong to the woman; on the other hand, that there be no law restricting legal abortions to only certain cases.

[2] Bill proposed to the National Assembly on June 14, 1977.

[3] The Bobigny trial was the landmark event that focused national attention on the abortion issue in 1972.—Tr.

[4] Two of the most publicized rape trials defended by Gisèle Halimi and "Choisir." —Tr.

concerns. Depending on the answers they receive, they will decide and they will vote.

And then what? Once the elections are over, we, "Choisir," will resume our work. For years to come the Common Program for Women will be our working tool and our research material. We will deepen our investigations, we will complete them. The contribution of each woman will be taken into account. The suggestions or experience of each woman will help create a new chapter, unlock a new cell, share a new hope. The conquest of half the sky is not played out in the electoral games.

And what about the parties? My only hope is that their words will be backed by progressive decisions, for their supporters and for all of us. And I bet that's exactly what will happen, no matter how they try to rationalize it.

We will meet them again in 1983. And in 1988. And after that. And at every stage we will make new evaluations.

The future cannot be created without women.

Translated by Isabelle de Courtivron

Research on Women

The women's movement, in its different and sometimes contradictory aspects, has, for the past few years, deeply shaken the social habits and the cultural tradition of the modern world. Propelled by this movement or disturbed by what it has left untouched, research on women has recently begun to appear. It took its first steps modestly, but it has become increasingly daring in the various domains of writing and the social sciences, abandoning the vindictive discourse of a modish and already out-dated feminism in order to attack key areas of ideology or of knowledge and to analyze them from a new vantage point—the point of view of women.

This issue inaugurates the regular publication of research on women in this journal. The reader will find contributions by women, illuminating the representation of or giving the opinion of women on diverse problems that relate to literature, linguistics, psychoanalysis, sociology, history, etc., and to women's questioning of them.

Translated by Elaine Marks

"Recherches féminines" in *Tel quel*, no. 74 (Winter 1977).

Variations on Common Themes

A radical feminist theoretical journal

This project was born from the recognition that feminism does not have its own space for theoretical debate, although it feels the need for this space now more than ever. Feminist publications are practically nonexistent in this country, and not only do we need theoretical journals, but we also need widely published monthlies (like *Sparerib* in England, *Emma* in Germany, *Effe* in Italy). And we need not one but several militant newspapers (as were *Le torchon brûle, Les femmes s'entêtent, Les pétroleuses,* and as *Histoires d'elles* still is). It would also be desirable for purely informative publications (like *L'information des femmes*) to be further developed and multiplied. But if we have chosen to devote our efforts to the launching of a "theoretical" journal, it is because such a publication seems to us to be equally necessary, and not because we consider it as a priority.[1]

What meaning do we give to theoretical?

Women frequently react with mixed feelings to this term. We believe in the necessity of an in-depth analysis of women's oppression, but at the same time "theoretical" too often refers to inaccessible texts that are destined for a privileged social elite. Theoretical is then synonymous

---

["Variations sur des thèmes communs"] in *Questions féministes*, no. 1 (November 1977). This lead article was written by the Editorial Collective. The initials in brackets are those of the individuals responsible for different parts.

[1] Since we wrote this editorial (in June 1977) things have moved in the feminist press. The "widely published monthly" we were calling for was born (*F-Magazine*), though it is not as feminist as we would wish. On the other hand, two new militant monthlies have appeared: *Remue-ménage* and *Le temps des femmes,* and a "journal of feminist politics": *La revue d'en face.* This list is not exhaustive since mimeographed newsletters are not mentioned here.

with hermetic, as if the obscure nature of a text established its "scientific value," its "seriousness." Such an equation must be broken. We want to rehabilitate the true meaning of theory and by so doing make theory everyone's concern, so that each of us can not only use it but also produce it. We consider as theoretical *any discourse, whatever its language may be,* that attempts to *explain the causes and the mechanisms,* the *why* and the *how* of women's oppression in general or of one of its particular aspects. "Theoretical" means any discourse that attempts to draw political conclusions, that offers a strategy or tactics to the feminist movement.

Following this particular political definition of "theoretical," our journal will try to bring together texts of different kinds that formulate theories about women's oppression: a one-page brochure, a literary work, a lampoon, a theoretical article can contribute equally to the elaboration of a feminist science. We know that it is not always possible to write simply: certain concepts do not exist in ordinary language and cannot be translated, and the possibility of their reformulation depends on the level of abstraction and specialization of each discourse.

Theory does not only explain facts, it also describes reality: we will therefore also publish texts that offer information on women's life in France and in other countries, on women's status today and in the past.

This diversity we hope to put into practice will bring to the archives of discourse and history texts that are ordinarily banned, and we will offer for a broader discussion topics that today can only be debated in the isolation of feminist groups.

A "feminist science": how and why?

When one analyzes women's oppression, one necessarily studies their material oppression, which is real, and the ideology that has been internalized by women and whose coercive power allows exploitation to exist. Now, one of the privileged breeding grounds for this ideology—it develops constantly and was not produced once and for all—is still "science," and in particular the so-called sciences of man. A feminist approach necessarily includes a criticism of scientific discourse on women but also of the supposedly "general" discourse: what is indeed more revealing than omissions? General theories of society and of the psyche, when they consider sex categories as being natural without asking questions about their development and their social nature and when they do not take into account women's oppression, thereby condone this oppression, thus remaining at the level of the most reductive sexist ideology. Such theories help perpetuate women's oppression while they build a false theory of the object they purport to study.

We wish that a feminist science could come into being, which would account for hierarchical patriarchal structures (and their impact on individual people) and, by so doing, change the global analysis of society. Our daily lives would benefit from this feminist science: the emergence of subversive feminist discourses has allowed us and still allows us to alter the course of our lives. But we also want to know how a feminist viewpoint can intervene wherever the powers that be, whose direct aim is the reproduction of patriarchal structures, are in action. In certain professional domains (medicine, gynecology, psychology, psychoanalysis, social work) the issue of women's oppression is crucial because the problem of "abnormality" keeps arising and leads to normalizing therapeutic interventions.

Radical feminism

Those are the words by which we identify our political perspective. The notion of radicalism starts from the recognition of (and from a political struggle against) the oppression of women by our patriarchal social system. In order to describe and unmask this oppression, arguments that have recourse to "nature" must be shattered, an undertaking that feminists set in motion several years ago and that should constitute one of our most solid gains. But things do not work that way: naturalist evidence, although it has been unmasked, still prevails, slyly and perniciously, in the very heart of the women's movement (where certain groups, strangely enough, delete the word "liberation" between the words "women" and "movement"). The present trend of "neo-femininity," which attracts many women because it appears to be constructive, can be interpreted as a return to anti-feminist classicism, a fall into one of the traps that patriarchy sets for us. For our oppression is not to be found in the fact that "we are not feminine enough" but on the contrary in the fact that we are *too* feminine. Under the pretext that we are "women," "different," we are prevented from fully leading the life of free and independent individuals. It is the patriarchal system which posits that we are "different" in order to justify and conceal our exploitation. It is the patriarchal system which prescribes the idea of a feminine "nature" and "essence."

Radical feminism takes as its preliminary tenet the necessity to work within the area that the first feminists conquered against naturalist ideology. This requires:

—A deliberate refusal to probe, to elaborate, to project any concept of "woman" that would be unrelated to a social context.

—The corollary to this refusal is our effort to deconstruct the notion of "sex differences" which gives a shape and a base to the concept of "woman" and is an integral part of naturalist ideology. The social mode of being of men and of women is in no way linked with their nature as males and females nor with the shape of their sex organs.

In a nonpatriarchal society, the question of being a man or a woman will not be asked in the terms in which it is asked today. All labor, all tasks will be performed by men and women. On the level of sexual practices, the distinction between homo- and heterosexuality will be meaningless since individuals will meet as singular individuals with their own specific history and not on the basis of their sexual identity.

—To destroy the differences between the sexes is to abolish the hierarchy that today exists between two terms, one of which is defined in relationship to the other and in this process is kept in an inferior position. One cannot claim "the right to be different," for this means in today's context "the right to be oppressed." Our top priority is to claim the right to be autonomous (the right not to be the object of, owned by). Our second priority is each person's right to her or his singularity outside of any reference to sexual identity. This does not mean that "we wish to become men," for at the same time as we destroy the idea of the generic "Woman," we also destroy the idea of "Man."

—The destruction of the idea of "Man": this notion represents another patriarchal trap. Unmasking naturalist ideology has allowed us to demonstrate how science and theories are sexist. The next step was to maintain that thought, language, and discourse are "masculine" and therefore hermetically closed to women. Those of us who took that step have reached a defeatist position which hampers all of us. Hence another vicious circle of oppression that we must explore: on one hand, by drawing attention to the fact that we recognize our oppression, we do not sum up our "being." The social system is contradictory since it allows us, despite its oppressive practices, to be feminists, to decipher its oppressive mechanisms, more particularly, to track down what ideologies claim to be self-evident and to do this through language itself; on the other hand, by asserting that nothing in the social system is "masculine." Certain scientific discourses, certain concepts are truncated and phoney insofar as they are based on power relations, not because they are elaborated by "men." The "principal enemy" is a certain type of hierarchical social relation where men are involved as agents but not as biological beings.

Radical feminism also expresses itself in relation to the revolutionary political groups that today challenge the status quo. It rejects any interference in its affairs from established political groups and maintains that certain notions, certain key expressions are basically false (the idea of "primary struggle" and "secondary struggles"; the terroristic use of capitalism as the unique explanation). Radical feminism sets as its goals the rediscovery of a materialistic approach, by making political use of certain concepts. So that, if the notion of class distinction is correctly, i.e., dialectically posited—that is, based on the reality of oppressive dynamics instead of on a static content analysis—it can be said that women belong to the same social class, the same gender. The insistence that *all women belong to the same social class*—along with the breaking away from naturalist ideology—is the preliminary condition for any feminist struggle: the creation of the French women's liberation movement for instance relied on an adhesion to this concept which diverged from the reigning Marxist orthodoxy.

Today the radical feminist trend based on these subversive probings seems to be smothered both as an agent and as a voice. Newborn, or rather reborn, the new feminism is threatened within itself by a two-pronged reaction: leftist cooptation on one side and cooptation via the ideology of neo-femininity. These two factions that, each in its own more or less disguised way, serve the interests of patriarchy, are the only women's groups to be acknowledged by the media.

However, the radical feminist trend exists: it gave impetus to all the important feminist campaigns and it is the force behind all subversive action against womens' oppression, against hierarchical social organization. Moreover, it is acknowledged as a model by many separate and isolated groups all over France. The time has come for radical feminism to speak up, to have a place for theoretical and political encounters in order to share its experiences and analyses, and so that its achievements may be disseminated and discussed.

This is what we intend to contribute, within the limits of a quarterly. We hope that this undertaking will allow those papers that are sadly confined to desk drawers to come right out, and those papers that have not even been written, because there was no hope of their being published, to be written at last. [C.D. & M.P.]

Since the days when, in the feminist movement, we liked to repeat that the theory of women's oppression "remained to be done," much has been written in France and in other countries that adds to one or several analyses of this oppression and leads to definite tactical stances.

The Marxist stumbling block

Early in the movement, two trends in the analysis of women's oppression emerged, one calling itself "revolutionary feminism" (in the United States "radical feminism") and to which we adhere, the other known as the "class-struggle tendency." The latter has attempted to find a point of articulation between women's struggle and class struggle, within a Marxist theoretical framework, but has not attempted to expose what seems to us to be not only inherent gaps in Marxist theory but also inconsistencies in the way it "situates" the oppression of women. This group's solution consists in *adding* various observations about women without ever questioning the principle of the monopoly of the working class that is supposed to contain in its struggle the *total* subversion of "the" system of oppression—capitalism. To oppose sexist mentality and institutions strictly on ideological grounds, without basing the struggle on a materialistic analysis of the oppression of women, is not enough. One must study the connections between sexist mentality, institutions, laws, and the socio-economic structures that support them. These structures are part of a specific system different from the capitalist system, and we call this system "patriarchy." The basic analysis of patriarchy (as a system of production that includes a special production relation between the sexes) has already been elaborated with the MLF and we wish to help disseminate and deepen it in this journal. Let us briefly present this analysis.

If wage-earning men and part of the women (45 percent of women are wage earners) are subjected to a common economic exploitation within capitalist relations of production, all women (those who work "double shift" and those who stay at home) are subjected to a common economic exploitation to which men are not subjected (on the contrary, they benefit from this) in production relations that are not capitalistic, namely the unpaid production of domestic services. It is precisely because such work is not remunerated that it finds itself outside of the capitalist system, one of whose characteristics is wage earning. Housewives are not paid in relation to the work they perform. They are, through marriage (and in principle, for life), economically dependent on their husbands who derive material and psychological power from this dependence. This institutionalized dependency of women has its effects on their position in paid labor: "supplementary" income, part-time work, higher rate of unemployment among women, and so forth. It all points to economic subordination, compulsory housework, and confinement to the domestic sphere.

This analysis allows us to define men and women as two groups with opposite interests. This opposition of interests is not limited to the family. The economic inferiority of women in the work force, their exclusion from power positions, including politics, and their restricted access to knowledge must be linked with the division of labor between the sexes, which itself is based on the family as an institution. The overall power of men over women, the psychological devaluation of women (beyond their material exploitation), the sexual and physical violence against women, all result from this power and help to reinforce it.

Back to essences

First we protected ourselves from the orthodox Left, which is on our right because it eliminates sex struggle. Now we must defend ourselves against another Right: a new attack with the good old rhetoric on sex differences but this time uttered by women, which eliminates historical and dialectical materialism in order to give voice to the naked truth of women's eternal bodies.

Everything that is expressed in the women's movement is not always theoretical, but this does not mean that underlying theories do not exist behind the words. It is important to bring to light these implicit theories of which people are not necessarily conscious, particularly when they seem to go against an overtly feminist discourse.

Today there is a trend that through the concept of "women's words" focusses on a search for feminine identity. To repeat "we are this and we are that, and above all not like you" would be a way to tell men: shit on you! All right. But does such a discourse express a true refusal, a true contesting of masculine ideology and of the system that produces it?

Otherness and the Identity-Body

Some women declare that "language must be shattered," because language is supposed to be male as it is a conveyor of, among other things, male chauvinism. They claim for themselves "another" language, that, in its new form, would be closer to woman's lived experience, a lived experience in the center of which the Body is frequently placed. Hence the watchwords: "liberate-the-body" and "speak-the-body." It is legitimate to expose the oppression, the mutilation, the "functionalization" and the "objectivation" [2] of the female body, but it is also dangerous to place the body at the center of a search for female identity. Furthermore, the themes of Otherness and of the Body merge together, because the most visible difference between men and women, and the only one that we know for sure to be permanent (barring mutations) is indeed the difference in body. This difference has been used as a pretext to "justify" full power of one sex over the other.

When a group is in power it propagates the reigning ideology, it imposes categories. The group in power, which always needs to justify its domination, condemns those that it oppresses to being different: he or she cannot be treated equally because— Therefore colonized people

[2] The tendency to "nominalize" is characteristic of contemporary theoretical discourse in France and corresponds to the preoccupation with process.—Tr.

were generally "lazy" and "incapable" of producing anything from their land themselves, etc. Such "differences" are not explained by specific historical circumstances because history evolves and can bring about revolutions. For the oppressor, it is safer to speak of natural differences that are invariable by definition. That is the basis of racist and sexist ideologies. And thus a status of inferiority is inextricably bound to a status of difference.

Now, after centuries of men constantly repeating that we were different, here are women screaming, as if they were afraid of not being heard and as if it were an exciting discovery: "We are different!" Are you going fishing? No, I am going fishing.

The very theme of difference, whatever the differences are represented to be, is useful to the oppressing group: as long as such a group holds power, any difference established between itself and other groups validates the only difference of importance, namely, having power while others do not. The fact that blacks have "a sense of rhythm" while whites do not is irrelevant and does not change the balance of power. On the contrary, any allegedly natural feature attributed to an oppressed group is used to imprison this group within the boundaries of a Nature which, since the group is oppressed, ideological confusion labels "nature of oppressed person." In the present context, since oppression is not over, to demand the right to Difference without analyzing its social character is to give back to the enemy an effective weapon.

To advocate a "woman's language" and a means of expression that would be specifically feminine seems to us equally illusory. First, the so-called explored language extolled by some women writers seems to be linked, if not in its content at least by its style, to a trend propagated by literary schools governed by male masters. This language is therefore as academic and as "masculine" as other languages. Secondly, it is at times said that woman's language is closer to the body, to sexual pleasure, to direct sensations, and so on, which means that the body could express itself directly without social meditation and that, moreover, this closeness to the body and to nature would be subversive. In our opinion, there is no such thing as a direct relation to the body. To advocate a direct relation to the body is therefore not subversive because it is equivalent to denying the reality and the strength of social mediations, the very same ones that oppress us in our bodies. At most, one would advocate a different socialization of the body, but without searching for a true and eternal nature, for this search takes us away from the most effective struggle against the socio-historical contexts in which human beings are and will always be trapped. If there is one natural characteristic of human beings, it is that human beings are by nature social beings.

Witch-Woman and Cartesian-Man

One could summarize how some women proceed in their quest for identity through the opposition between Witch-Woman and Cartesian-Man. There are several reasons given for using the witch as a positive image of woman. Among them the subversive activities of witches throughout their history, as well as alleged characteristics of witches that some women see as liberation symbols:

—"direct" contact with nature, with their body and the body of others;

—practices, ideas, and a language that are presented as positive models for a specifically feminine culture, as opposed to an oppressive masculine culture;

—on top of everything, a halo of mystery and secrecy that evokes the notion of a private territory or kingdom where women are queens.

Witches were subversive because of their alliance with the devil, their medical practices, and their sexual activities, imagined or real, especially during the Sabbath "orgies." Alliance with the devil was certainly for women, as for the poor, a form of revenge against the Church, but it was not a means of fighting the Church: to believe in the devil or to pretend to do so is to side with the Church in its God-Devil dogma. And to equate Woman with the Forces of Evil, even in a victorious fashion, is also to give in to church ideology.

Witches as healers, poisoners, aborters, and midwives knew about plants and the body not by osmosis but because they had studied them practically. If witches used plants effectively it is because they classified them and experimented with them, and that is a "scientific" approach. It is not a better practice because one calls it scientific, but it means that witches used their brains in the same way as men, who later monopolized medicine.

Witches did dance in the moors and they hid there too. The wilderness was for the most destitute women the only place of survival that society allowed them. The witch, queen of the forest, is like the domesticated wife who is queen of the home. Queen of one domain because excluded from others. Mystery, night, forest, it all resembles the clandestineness of pariahs and heretics. The underground where one may indeed fight is nonetheless not equivalent to freedom.

And what about the sexuality of witches? Michelet points out one interesting facet of the Sabbath, namely contraception: they said that "women never came back pregnant." It appears that there often were simulations or spectacular representations of sexual acts as well as practices "against nature" (because they did not lead to conception, of course!). We are dealing here with very rationally regulated sexual outlets. Procreation was controlled, but can one speak of sexual liberation for women? Michelet describes women who during the Sabbath "bow down," "offer themselves," "let themselves be devoured by the crowd," and so forth. If witches had certain powers, because of which they were feared and respected in the lower classes, they nonetheless apparently remained sexual objects. To conclude: beware of those Thrones for "Woman" that turn her into an altar ("on her back, a devil was conducting a service").

As for the "other" language of witches advocated by some women—a language of the body, singsong, visceral cries, etc.—(silence even, which supposedly can be heard, what was the point of asking for your turn to speak then?), this language of the body, this cry-language, is that enough to fight oppression? If one should not hesitate to cry out one's guts against the words that leave you out in the cold, there is no good reason to reject as "masculine and oppressive" a certain form of conceptual discourse and thus give men the exclusive control over discourse. Oppression must be named and analyzed (its mechanisms exposed) if we want to fight it. Men give us too willingly the exclusive use of visceral cries and intuition; there again the segregation between masculine and feminine has been effective. We are only playing the oppressor's game if we deprive ourselves of knowledge and conceptual tools because he has used them before us. It would be like, for instance, rejecting work on pretext that it is "alienating," circumscribed within the "competitive male" world, when the exclusion of women from the labor force (that is to say, denying them economic independence) is a much greater "alienation" at the very center of our oppression.

When we claim that we are different, and outsiders in the world of men, we are only parroting them:

Nature-Woman: consecration of Culture-Man.
Devil-Woman: consecration of God-Man.
Mystery-Woman: abyss to be filled by the reigning ideology.
Womb-Woman: self-service for stereotypes.

Sphinx-Woman: smile because you can say nothing. Woman is supposed to possess a huge secret, probably that of our origins, just because gestation occurs in her body: consequently she may remain illiterate, she already knows too much! But she does not know what she knows (do her ovaries know?), it cannot be formulated— She is said to be beyond formulation, knowledge, science: in order to keep her away from these skills.

Pleasure-Woman: avatar of body-woman, sex-woman, greedy sex, frigid sex, anything-you-like sex. The special relation to nature and the particular capacities for sexual pleasure attributed to women remind us of the language used about "Negroes" or even workers (in May 1968 this graffiti: "Workers screw better")—in short, the rhetoric of the prevailing ideology on the oppressed. During one century men confine us to frigidity or "purity" in order to better use our bodies. During the next century we are condemned to "total" pleasure in order to make us believe that in "nature's" ghetto we enjoy a form of liberty denied to those who are supposedly alienated in society but who in fact have means of control over us.

In everything that is supposed to characterize women, oppression is always present. We are willing to sacrifice ourselves? No, we "have been" sacrificed. Maternal instincts? No, but the obligation for women to fulfill a certain role. We are close to nature? No, but we are prohibited from using the tools necessary for social mastery, for the knowledge of our own bodies and for creation. As far as creation is concerned we are left, through an ambiguous play on words, with the "creation" of babies, on condition that it be involuntary, regulated, and "inspired" by other minds than ours.

Sex is not our destiny

We must reclaim for ourselves all human potentials, including those unduly established as masculine, that is to say, those monopolized by men in order to enslave us more thoroughly. For instance rational discourse: it's up to us to change its content. For instance violence: it's up to us to choose its forms and its goals. But violence is necessary against the violence of oppression. We want to be able to choose; we want to move out of the equation women = oppressed.

More than women, we are individuals. Up to now, only the masculine is allowed to be neuter (nonsexual definition) and general. We want access to the neuter, the general. Sex is not our destiny. A man, Sacha Guitry, said: "I would gladly agree that women are superior if it would discourage them from becoming equals." This represents the Doormat-Pedestal tactics, or the tactics of "kicking upstairs" to some honorary position someone who must be gotten rid of. What "they" want is simple: we should not step on their turf, we should help them reach their goals by staying in our place. Equality is a threat to men: the threat that their privileges will disappear.

Women whose deliberate feminist approach is to demand for themselves before anything else (and perhaps exclusively) their Difference, are working against the notion of equality: What? demand equality with the oppressor?

But equality-with-the-oppressor is a contradiction in its own terms. If there is equality between two persons, there is no longer oppressor nor oppressed. In the dictionary, the definition for the word "equal" is: "Having the same quantity, size, nature or value, cf. identical, same, equivalent." We have here two notions, that of resemblance and that of same value. The fact that women want to be considered as having as much value as men cannot be criticized. But must women consequently resemble men? If to be equal to men means by definition that men should stop oppressing us, and if at the same time we demand equality for all human beings, i.e., demand that men cease being oppressors, what difference can we claim for ourselves and according to what criteria? In the struggle for an egalitarian society, the only difference that we acknowledge is that of our political choices. What do we assert when, at a rally, we imitate the shape of a vulva with our hands instead of raising closed fists? The specificity of our *struggle* against a specific oppression. We assert that for us women, the main front is the fight for the destruction of the patriarchal system and of phallocracy. From our position as oppressed persons, we do not demand a "feminine" society but a society where men and women would share the same values, those being necessarily anti-phallocratic and anti-hierarchical.

In our struggle, we demand that our history be acknowledged in History: history of our oppression, history of our revolts, history of our cultural and technical contributions, and so on. But one must not forget that our specific contributions have existed and exist because of a division of labor based on sex and hierarchy. If we invented agriculture, pottery, plant science, tapestry, or the art of quilting, we must have these things recognized as general economic and/or cultural contributions, but we don't have to limit ourselves to them. For what we offer and must bring (both on the territory men have left us, but by subversively forcing them to move into it, and on grounds that we must now conquer for ourselves: for example music, mathematics, architecture, as well as political and economic decision making) is finally a global change in society, the sharing of tasks, equal access to the means of production and to cultural tools.

We acknowledge a biological difference between men and women, but in and of itself this difference does not imply an oppressive relation between the sexes. The battle of the sexes is not biological. We acknowledge a difference between men and women in social *hierarchy*; we acknowledge psychological differences that express both the oppression of one sex by the other and the exclusion of both sexes from the potentials attributed to the other. These are the differences that we want to abolish. [E.L.]

A journal "on" women? No.

The word "woman," I can't and never could bear it. It is with this word that men insulted me. It is a word from their language, a corpse filled with *their* fantasms against us. Us, who? Women of course, and the *word* pops up again. And with it they will have "had" us, as *they say.*

A journal, then, in order to try to understand what happens *behind* their words, the very words that they impose upon us, sometimes even in our revolt. To know that we are not only caught *by* their words ("woman," "love," "responsibility," "honesty," "faithfulness," "motherly love," "feminine specificity," and so on) but that we are had *through their* (very) *material institutions* (serfdom-marriage, underpaid work in comparison to theirs, unpaid surplus—work silence imposed upon us, being exploited, and disposed of for them, laws and violence against us, the world). These are realities, not "words." But they play with words. Should we follow them? Because, watch out, they know what they are doing in point of fact. It is all done by the age of five: they know the mysteries of the language of scorn (at that age they go directly to the basics, later they will learn the [same but] censored language for better oppressive use: the language of "feminine" values, of the specific-woman-being). At five it is all done since they already materially possess their woman: their mother (waiting for their wife).

For us, the days of playing with their words are over, and now comes the period of analysis so that their *words* do not subvert our *struggle:* "*They say* [....] that each word must be passed through a sieve." (M. Wittig, *Les guérillères.*) And this is the sieve of reality, which their words obfuscate.

Thus the word "woman": we don't have the right to use it alone any more, we don't have the right to conceive of it alone. The reality "women" is sociological (political), the product of a relation between two groups, and of an oppressive relation. The *real* group of women is defined by its very position in this relation, just as the group of men is also defined by its position as oppressor. It is not because we are "women" but because we are oppressed in this relation, that we and we alone can pull apart (= analyze and destroy) the mechanisms of oppression. And, like any besieged group, we must among ourselves give priority to the study of the aggressors' tactics: their behavior (their violence, so perfectly calm), their rhetoric (their words, through which they hem us in), the fact that they are starving us, and the fact that they try to destroy our morale. At this point, it is not enough to say that our aggressor refuses to give us the right to life, or that he denies that we exist, and to pretend that, consequently, we are among ourselves going to "recover" our self, our "identity," an "other" identity as a woman, and so on. What besieged community can afford such an attitude if it does not want to commit suicide within its walls?

What it's all about is knowing that our social "identity," our real and concrete definition, is that of *besieged persons,* and primarily that. We must find out how and by what strategy the aggressor denies us property, free disposition of ourselves, free access to our own food. Presently, historically and sociologically he denies that we exist by asserting that we are woman and by forcing us into what he decided the "female" condition to be.

Before coming back to this point, let us take up again the siege metaphor and let us study its "moments"—this term meaning both an historical evolution of the situation and the various stances that, given where we are now, coexist.

Femininity, feminitude, feminism: the three "moments" of the battle

1. *First moment: Femininity. Or: "Everything is fine and dandy during a siege."* The besieger is at the ghetto's gates. Food is outside the women's town and the fields have been taken by the aggressor. It is a quiet siege. He has blocked off all exits except the largest gate, which is decorated with flowers (particularly on Mother's Day) and which is connected to his camp by a lowered drawbridge. As long as women accept to follow this route and go out to beg for food (in exchange for what awful work, by the way!) he will hand them out some crumbs. They are still hungry in their dependent state (material aspect of femininity) but the situation seems tolerable; all the more so since the assailant also "provides" them with an "explanation" (the ideology of femininity): their female constitution (biology) is to *be* hungry, they *are* defective and he can fix them (to prove it: the crumbs). Since the women are weakened by serflike work and malnutrition, they tell themselves that he has got to be right, that "that's the way it is." At most they will send back to their masters the "mean things" that men dump on them: *men are* this, they are that and that too is "the way it is." Some women, however, individually refuse femininity and they become mad or are killed.

2. *Second moment: Feminitude. Or: movement that recognizes women. Or:* "Indeed I have been starved by him (first level of consciousness) but I have *value.*" For instance: "I am light, I can jump and dance. I will fly away, build something, *far* from him. I am heavy with my own body; my body is beautiful. I myself give value to the self that they have devalued." But how, "far from him?" But "I" who? Critical questions. Uncertain answers. This feminitude which resembles negritude, this demanded difference with the added notion of "better," this *cultural feminism*

similar to black *cultural nationalism*, will they enable us to be fed by our hunger? You will say that it is necessary to gain self-confidence. This is true and it requires that we be together among ourselves. But the "self" is emaciated with a bloated belly, it is the product of the dynamics of starving, of the dynamics of besieging. We cannot be satisfied with turning around on ourselves, with dancing alone in a circle, while *they are there* hemming us in, obstructing our paths to freedom. To believe that we can find our food in ourselves is to reason in an essentialist (the idea of an auto-nourishing self) or metaphysical (let us wait until manna falls down from the sky) manner. It means playing the game of the other, dwelling on the tactical stratagem of the enemy (hunger, femininity) without seeing his strategy (siege, hemming in), concentrating on the effect without attacking the cause. It means locking ourselves up within a static argument, and pushing reality into a dead end.

Reality is this: the sidewalks and squares of the women's city have been carefully blacktopped by the aggressor and nothing grows in the ghetto that he does not allow to grow (except a few flowers in the cracks of the walls, which could not replace wheat fields anyhow). Even our "feminine" qualities, like our "defects" are the product of the political relation between men and women, the product of a siege relation. At least, if there is one quality—so obligatorily, so harshly acquired during our slavery! —that we must use, it is in fact courage. Courage to recognize each other and to come together, yes, but *in order to* end the siege by force.

3. *Third moment: Feminism. Or: women's liberation movement. Or: an attack on the social roots of difference.* Or: "I will be neither a woman nor a man in the present historical meaning: I shall be some Person in the body of a woman."

The fact is that food and fields are *outside* the ghetto. If there is an "elsewhere" where we must go and get our food, it lies there, in the space of reconquered fields, beyond the siege relation. And if there is "another way" through which we must acquire our food, it is indeed through fighting on the battlefield. No ring-around-the-rosy on the town's main square, the one with the steps, as if we had the power to lift up the drawbridge, to lock ourselves up by ourselves. Because at the heart of the matter is the fact that the machinery of the drawbridge, the chains that keep it lowered toward the assailant, are not in our hands but in *his hands*. The battlefield is the large open door of Femininity, the lowered drawbridge of oppression, the aggressor's campsite. In order to *cut through* them with force we must gather our forces. Each of us will only be able to be "herself" when all of us will have regained access to the real world. (It is only after this that our *imaginaire* ["imaginary order"] [3] like that of men, will be transformed.) For the time being we need the type of concrete tactical imagination that proceeds from an analysis of facts.

Does this mean that utopia should be rejected? Indeed not. Utopias, like cries, are vital to us: they are our words as oppressed persons, our sociological imagination. But utopia proceeds in fact from an analysis, and there are several kinds of utopias, as there are several kinds of analyses to underlie them. Some take into account (and work against) political reality, i.e., women = *a sociologically defined class within* (outside, through) *a material and historical relation of oppression,* but whose oppression is *itself ideologically attributed* by the ruling group *to an alleged biological determination of the oppressed class,* limited to this class. Others, and sometimes without even being aware of it, condone (and against us) the theory of the oppressor in its ultimate ideology, i.e., women = woman.

Biological, ideological, political—

It seems important to us to succeed now in clarifying the relation between what is political and what is "biological." We can say at the same time that there is no relation between a physical constitution and a social "condition" *and* recognize that for the time being, there is just the same, some relation, thus possibly introducing ambiguity and confusion in our analyses. What we must answer is—not the false problem (very in among "scientists") which consists in measuring the "role" of biological factors and the "role" of social factors in the behavior of sexed individuals—but rather the following questions: (1) In what way is the biological political? In other words, what is the political function of the biological? (2) In what way (and why) do social sex classes correspond to biological sex classes? (3) How does ideology operate materially? We certainly have parts of the answers to these questions, but the analysis must be continued.

A. *The biological as an ideology which rationalizes the political.* We know that the political class of men (defined in the relation of oppression) defines us as a biological class in order to justify by nature its power as oppressor. They use "sex difference," but only in *one direction.* Unlike what their loudspeakers lead us to believe, there are in their heads no real differences between *the sexes:* if this were the case, it would pre-

[3] In Lacanian psychoanalysis, the imaginary order is the order of perception, hallucination and their derivatives as opposed to the symbolic order which is the order of discursive and symbolic action.—Tr.

suppose that they acknowledge the existence of two sexed groups. But they conceive of themselves as purely social, purely general beings, not as a "biological group of men." Group of men, yes. But in their mind they possess a *quality*, but we alone would have a "particular" physical constitution (mostly defined by motherhood). We use the term "masculinity" ourselves in answer to "femininity" in a sociological analysis. But for them "femininity" (a given in the biological mode) is opposed to "virility" (which is an act in the psychological, social, and human modes, as they explain it to themselves [and to us] with such pangs and complacency!). We therefore see a social group which decrees, acts, thinks, and organizes its power on the other social group by defining the other as the only biologically determined group.

B. *Ideology as materially effective in reality.* It is indeed on the basis of our physical appearance that they constantly act out their power. (For example, take a job opening with a certain remuneration calculated without reference to the sex of the person who can perform it, i.e., calculated for a man. The remuneration will drop 30 percent if an obviously female applicant answers the job offer.) To put it briefly, our social class of "women," a product of the political, has indeed the material contours of our biological category because of the effects of ideology—

C. *The logical reversal of the political over the biological.* Starting from our raised consciousness about their politics and from our political analysis (which shows that none of the two sex categories exists and that therefore none can be conceived of outside of its relation to the other) we recognize that, as a consequence of their having chosen the biological to define us politically, their own political class coincides also with their physical contours. Thus, when we physically exclude men from our groups, we express at the same time the fact that we have understood their politics and that we consider males, indeed, as a political group. *We have totally politicized anatomy.* Men had used politically only ours (when they ideologically defined us but not themselves as *the sex*). The fact that they are excluded for "anatomical reasons" is the logical backlash of their politics, where one sees the turning of the political against the ideological.

To end the siege by force or to die

If it is on the basis of our women's anatomies that we have been compelled to come together politically, we also did it in order not to forget that this biological category is political, created by the social relation of oppression and the very ideology of the oppressor. So that we may not forget, so that we may have the courage to recognize that if we join our forces of anatomical women, it is to destroy ourselves as sociological women and at the same time to destroy men as sociological men.

We must abolish sex social classes, and in order to do so we must not let ourselves be haunted by the insidious question of identity, of values "specific" to each sex, not be engulfed in the unique valorization of our sex "culture." We must not forget that "specific" means, primarily, "uniquely pertaining to a species." For us there is only one human species, and that excludes all forms of discrimination, of hierarchy (sex, race, class).

For us, the analysis must first of all be the analysis of the power relation that *transforms* women *into* women. Forms of thinking or of practice which would focus on women *as* women run the risk of unwittingly repeating the terms of the oppressor, of closing our category upon itself. By so doing, we would "drop" all the women who do not have the material chance to act as if the aggressor did not exist—those who don't have the possibility of falling into the woman-as-woman value trap. If we accepted these terms, we would turn against ourselves, against our sex social group, by forging an "identity" that hides material exploitation and oppression, this daily relation that creates our class. Because the most womanly women, those who most fully correspond to the present "identity" of our class, are in fact the women with the lowest salaries and those whose husbands won't let them go on strike, the women without any salary at all, the raped women, the battered women, the women abandoned with small children.

It is not a question of reconquering ourselves, as women, it is a question of conquering our freedom. It's not only our feminitude that we must promote. If we must gain in strength, if we must speak and write, if we must act, it is in order to transform now the social, economic, and political relations that lead to the hierarchical classification into so-called "sex" groups of persons who are identically human, identically socializable— In order to destroy it, we must analyze the system of social sexes. We must end the siege by force— or else slowly continue to die. [N.-C.M.]

A *theoretical journal for feminism? Yes*

We want to forbid a member of the National Assembly from saying that aging women cost too much within the national economy and that for the love of them, the Assembly will vote on a law forcing them to retire at sixty so that their employers be saved the bother of having to get rid of them. We want to understand and to expose the historical and social factors that made it possible for one social group to be treated like cattle and that turned us—one half of humanity—into domesticated beings, raised to reproduce and to preserve our species.

We know the meaning of words and we know that "love, abnegation, devotedness" belong to the faked language of scorn, humiliation and fear in our daily lives. We—living beings—are treated like objects because a society based on violence, exploitation, and oppression assumes that our lot is dispossession (no name, no identity, no rights, no body), rape, terror, and murder. We are, depending on circumstances, objects to be used, battered, exchanged, manipulated, or objects linked with wealth, well-being, prestige, power, and science. We are unique among all other historically dominated social groups, in that we have ignored the *social* character of our condition because we are, as women, bound by individual (marriage) contracts to the patriarchy.

We know the meaning of such words as "eternal feminine," "instinct," and our total confinement within "the nature of things." We know that psychology, categories of knowledge, intellectual disciplines, bourgeois values, and idealism are part of a coded language. There is no essence. There is no woman, no femininity, no eternal feminine. There is a social group burdened with lowly tasks, despised because it must do these tasks, and so little "specialized" that the language which refers to us and gives us a form simultaneously describes us as the sex, but also as the sex which has no sex, as the Mother-Goddess and the whore, as the muse and the bluestocking. We know that "women" illustrate a power relation implying a double work load, professional unfitness, the lowest possible salary, the exclusive social responsibility for the care of the elderly, handicapped, and children. Some say: woman. We say: women.

We are feminists because the commercial manipulation of our bodies, of our lives, gives us no choice; because a society which allows the sexual organs of baby girls to be freely displayed (for example, in Denmark) clearly demonstrates the political character of sex hierarchy and shows that it is not pornography that gives enjoyment, but the enjoyment of power that constitutes pornography.

As feminists we must show the historical, social, and therefore arbitrary and reversible character of this sex hierarchy. We must show that "women" only exist in so far as the oppression and exploitation of one social group is the basis of the other group's power. [c.c.-p.]

Translated by Yvonne Rochette-Ozzello

Utopias

This section communicates the vision of the new worlds to which feminist thought and action are dedicated.

Simone de Beauvoir

The free woman is just being born; when she has won possession of herself perhaps Rimbaud's prophecy will be fulfilled: "There shall be poets! When woman's unmeasured bondage shall be broken, when she shall live for and through herself, man—hitherto detestable—having let her go, she, too, will be poet! Woman will find the unknown! Will her ideational worlds be different from ours? She will come upon strange, unfathomable, repellent, delightful things; we shall take them, we shall comprehend them." [1] It is not sure that her "ideational worlds" will be different from those of men, since it will be through attaining the same situation as theirs that she will find emancipation; to say in what degree she will remain different, in what degree these differences will retain their importance—this would be to hazard bold predictions indeed. What is certain is that hitherto woman's possibilities have been suppressed and lost to humanity, and that it is high time she be permitted to take her chances in her own interest and in the interest of all.

Translated by H. M. Parshley

From "Liberation: The Independent Woman" in *The Second Sex* (Vintage, 1974) [*Le deuxième sexe*]
[1] In a letter to Pierre Demeny, May 15, 1871.

Françoise Parturier

With their heads and their bodies finally liberated, with their eyes wide open, women will no longer be like those blinded horses who turn in circles around the well to which they are attached; they will no longer turn blindly, lovingly around you, Sir. You will no longer be the opaque screen between women and the world. . . . They will no longer bury themselves in you, and the day is coming when you will lament having lost what you claimed you couldn't bear. In return, they will no longer judge you because they, too, will know that pleasure and love are powerful gods who cannot always receive simultaneous honors. They will learn that the death of desire is a law that you cannot avoid; it is not a flaw in your character. They will admit that even for a free body happiness is the exception. And finally, they will renounce, if they have not already done so, the unrealizable temptation of the great love.

Will they be any happier?

It is probable that free from both the anguish of passion and biological anguish—since nature always takes her revenge and compensates for one change by another and since everything in life balances out mysteriously—women will know another form of anguish, the one you feel so strongly, Sir, and which was your exclusive luxury: metaphysical anguish. It is then and only then that genius can flourish. . . .

I have the feeling that soon, in twenty years perhaps, there will be a revolt of feminine minds against a world made by men for men where so much horror, blood, weeping, and torture inflicted on what is alive proclaims that domination is a vice.

One day women will refuse the useless suffering added to the inevitable suffering of our mortal condition and perhaps they will plunge headlong, like you, into the mad venture of wanting to reform the world. The result would be a religious crisis without precedent which would undoubtedly oblige the Catholic Church to return to Galilee. . . .

From *Lettre ouverte aux hommes* [*An open letter to men*] (Albin Michel, 1968).

As is often claimed, the twentieth century is indeed a century of demystification; this doesn't mean it is a demystified century. For example, the myth of feminine inferiority, which has been consolidated by instinct and habit, withstands like a concrete block any proof, any demonstration. It is easier to change laws than hearts. The evidence is everywhere and convinces no one, rockets turn around our gibbering heads and the paradox of our century is that we will have lived through a new era with old thoughts and your reign, Sir, will have ended before your preconceived idea of your own superiority.

Translated by Elaine Marks

Françoise d'Eaubonne

Therefore, with a society at last in the feminine gender meaning non-power (and not power-to-the-women), it would be proved that no other human group could have brought about the ecological revolution; because none other was so directly concerned at all levels. And the two sources of wealth which up until now have benefited only the male would once again become the expression of life and no longer the elaboration of death; and human beings would finally be treated first as persons, and not above all else as male or female.

And the planet in the feminine gender would become green again for all.

Translated by Betty Schmitz

From *Le féminisme ou la mort* [*Feminism or death*] (Horay, 1974).

Annie Leclerc

The frightful prison of love will finally be forced open when all those who know how to talk of love, how to want it and live it, will join together and merge lovingly, bursting with the laughter and the pleasure of being both man and woman, and yet neither; of being both young and old, and yet neither, and yet all else as well. That prison will give way when, branding every place and every text with their subversive love, they cause the downfall, the first death rattle of the haters, the vampires, the zombies, atrocious puppets of our history.

Only then will we know what pleasure, knowledge, activity, language, really *mean*. Are you ready to join us? You, and all the others contained within you, my all-loving ones, I love you.

Translated by Isabelle de Courtivron

From "La lettre d'amour" [The love letter] in *La venue à l'écriture* [Coming to writing] (Union Générale d'Editions, 10/18, 1977).

Marguerite Duras

... I think the future belongs to women. Men have been completely dethroned. Their rhetoric is stale, used up. We must move on to the rhetoric of women, one that is anchored in the organism, in the body.

Translated by Susan Husserl-Kapit

From an interview by Susan Husserl-Kapit in *Signs*, Winter 1975.

Maria-Antonietta Macciocchi

I speak for those women who have killed that feminine anti-feminism, artificially nourished by male power, which makes woman the enemy of woman, of the woman who is too something: too intelligent, too active, too militant, too generous, too courageous, too young, too naïve.

I do not believe that the human species merits Freud's pessimism: I do not believe that femininity is accepted by no one, including women. But I believe, on the contrary, that thanks to the uncertain and timid design of *an other* relationship between men and women, we are in the presence of the opening of a *new continent* in history. If all the feminist movements, if all the revolutionaries understand this, one day there will be no more fascism.

Translated by Elaine Marks

From "Sexualité féminine dans l'idéologie fasciste" [Feminine sexuality in fascist ideology] in *Tel quel*, Summer 1976.

Julia Kristeva

In all the theatrical representations that I saw in China there was not a single hero: it's the heroines who rise up in rebellion but also who give a dramatic turn to events because, if the situation remains in their hands it deteriorates and the party has to intervene to set things straight. Chinese women are rebels, a "half of the sky" but *constantly* moving "against the stream" of the sky. They represent a force—probably an essential force—in the cultural revolution that is now under way.

It is impossible to equate their problems with ours. It is also impossible to expect from them, as they emerge from feudalism and Confucianism, the solution to the difficulties of Occidental women wedged in by monotheism and capitalism. But with Chinese women as a starting point, we can examine the weight of a metaphysical tradition and a mode of production which have functioned in this part of the world because of the complicity of our language or our dead silence. We can give a political dimension to our protest: the importance of women's awakening for the structures of a socialist society, its essentially international role because it eats away at the foundations of Occidentalism. We can try to write, to pursue this inquiry "à la chinoise": against what is and with everything that here, today, is moving "against the stream."

Translated by Elaine Marks

From "Les chinoises à 'contre-courant'" [Chinese women against the tide] in *Tel quel*, Autumn 1974.

Julia Kristeva

Other phenomena lead me to believe that the die is cast in China, for a socialism without God or Man, which will accompany, at a distance, the perilous unprecedented renaissance of a new humanity that is gathering momentum here.

Translated by Anita Barrows

From *About Chinese Women* [*Des chinoises*] (Urizen Books, 1977).

Monique Wittig

Moved by a common impulse, we all stood to seek gropingly the even flow, the exultant unity of the Internationale. An aged, grizzled woman soldier sobbed like a child. Alexandra Ollontaï could hardly restrain her tears. The great song filled the hall, burst through doors and windows and rose to the calm sky. "The war is over, the war is over," said a young working woman next to me. Her face shone. And when it was finished and we remained there in a kind of embarrassed silence, a woman at the end of the hall cried, "Comrades, let us remember the women who died for liberty." And then we intoned the Funeral March, a slow, melancholy and yet triumphant air.

Translated by David LeVay

From *Les guérillères* (Minuit, 1969; Viking, 1971).

Suzanne Horer
Jeanne Socquet

We think that it is a bad mistake for women to pursue deliberately the puppets, tinsel, and formulae already worn out by men. If, in the same context, some women are senators, graduates from prestigious technological institutes, corporation presidents, bankers, and creators, and if they perform their tasks in the same manner as the men do, these women will only be adding to the monuments of incompetence, to the lust for power, to the craving for notoriety, to the lures and to the constraints that already exist. We find such a rat race uninteresting and totally without benefit for women.

We think that women must offer other forms of social systems, other forms of creation, other goals, other directions, and by "other" we mean "better": we mean those that stress the value of human beings as a whole, that truly liberate them; that is to say, those that put them directly in front of themselves, instead of in front of a double, a shadow, an image, a golem.

Why, you will ask, would women succeed where men have failed? Why not? Let us try, it is well worth the effort.

We must not follow in the footsteps men have imprinted on this earth. Why repeat the same errors with the same too obviously catastrophic results? We do not believe in social revolutions that aim at "changing man." Such jolts shift problems without ever solving them in depth. They provide only temporary answers, as religions do.

We believe in conscious evolution, consciously conducted by human beings who want to realize the full range of their possibilities, who want to live at last and not be contented with merely surviving.

We are aware of the degree to which such remarks are utopian, but it is exactly this dose of utopia to which we ordinarily refer when we measure what might be truly revolutionary in an idea. We do not enjoy believing that the moon is made of green cheese and we do not like

From *La création étouffée* [Smothered creativity] (Horay, 1974).

ideological dreamers. We prefer a courageous utopia that has at least the merit of questioning the very foundation upon which humanity, up to this day, has erected its monuments. Since, in our judgment, these monuments are failures, we believe that the foundations must be rebuilt.

We think that women have nothing to lose by wanting for themselves a different way of being human and that they have everything to gain by wanting to labor toward this goal by themselves. The point of view of creative women on this world-in-process will be exciting, provided that these creators do not reflect the past but indeed offer a new conception of creation, a new way of seeing, and a new form of expression.

Translated by Yvonne Rochette-Ozzello

Hélène Cixous

I shall speak about women's writing: about *what it will do*. Woman must write her self: must write about women and bring women to writing, from which they have been driven away as violently as from their bodies—for the same reasons, by the same law, with the same fatal goal. Woman must put herself into the text—as into the world and into history—by her own movement.

The future must no longer be determined by the past. I do not deny that the effects of the past are still with us. But I refuse to strengthen them by repeating them, to confer upon them an irremovability the equivalent of destiny, to confuse the biological and the cultural. Anticipation is imperative.

Since these reflections are taking shape in an area just on the point of being discovered, they necessarily bear the mark of our time—a time during which the new breaks away from the old, and, more precisely, the (feminine) new from the old (*la nouvelle de l'ancien*). Thus, as there are no grounds for establishing a discourse, but rather an arid millennial ground to break, what I say has at least two sides and two aims: to break up, to destroy; and to foresee the unforeseeable, to project.

I write this as a woman, toward women. When I say "woman," I'm speaking of woman in her inevitable struggle against conventional man; and of a universal woman subject who must bring women to their senses and to their meaning in history. But first it must be said that in spite of the enormity of the repression that has kept them in the "dark"—that dark which people have been trying to make them accept as their attribute—there is, at this time, no general woman, no one typical woman. What they have *in common* I will say. But what strikes me is the infi-

---

"The Laugh of the Medusa" in *Signs*, Summer 1976. This is a revised version of "Le rire de la méduse," which appeared in *L'arc* (1975), pp. 39–54.

nite richness of their individual constitutions: you can't talk about *a* female sexuality, uniform, homogeneous, classifiable into codes—any more than you can talk about one unconscious resembling another. Women's imaginary is inexhaustible, like music, painting, writing: their stream of phantasms is incredible.

I have been amazed more than once by a description a woman gave me of a world all her own which she had been secretly haunting since early childhood. A world of searching, the elaboration of a knowledge, on the basis of a systematic experimentation with the bodily functions, a passionate and precise interrogation of her erotogeneity. This practice, extraordinarily rich and inventive, in particular as concerns masturbation, is prolonged or accompanied by a production of forms, a veritable aesthetic activity, each stage of rapture inscribing a resonant vision, a composition, something beautiful. Beauty will no longer be forbidden.

I wished that that woman would write and proclaim this unique empire so that other women, other unacknowledged sovereigns, might exclaim: I, too, overflow; my desires have invented new desires, my body knows unheard-of songs. Time and again I, too, have felt so full of luminous torrents that I could burst—burst with forms much more beautiful than those which are put up in frames and sold for a stinking fortune. And I, too, said nothing, showed nothing; I didn't open my mouth, I didn't repaint my half of the world. I was ashamed. I was afraid, and I swallowed my shame and my fear. I said to myself: You are mad! What's the meaning of these waves, these floods, these outbursts? Where is the ebullient, infinite woman who, immersed as she was in her naiveté, kept in the dark about herself, led into self-disdain by the great arm of parental-conjugal phallocentrism, hasn't been ashamed of her strength? Who, surprised and horrified by the fantastic tumult of her drives (for she was made to believe that a well-adjusted normal woman has a . . . divine composure), hasn't accused herself of being a monster? Who, feeling a funny desire stirring inside her (to sing, to write, to dare to speak, in short, to bring out something new), hasn't thought she was sick? Well, her shameful sickness is that she resists death, that she makes trouble.

And why don't you write? Write! Writing is for you, you are for you; your body is yours, take it. I know why you haven't written. (And why I didn't write before the age of twenty-seven.) Because writing is at once too high, too great for you, it's reserved for the great—that is for "great men"; and it's "silly." Besides, you've written a little, but in secret. And it wasn't good, because it was in secret, and because you punished yourself for writing, because you didn't go all the way, or because you wrote, irresistibly, as when we would masturbate in secret, not to go further, but to attenuate the tension a bit, just enough to take the edge off. And then as soon as we come, we go and make ourselves feel guilty—so as to be forgiven; or to forget, to bury it until the next time.

Write, let no one hold you back, let nothing stop you: not man; not the imbecilic capitalist machinery, in which publishing houses are the crafty, obsequious relayers of imperatives handed down by an economy that works against us and off our backs; and not *yourself*. Smug-faced readers, managing editors, and big bosses don't like the true texts of women—female-sexed tests. That kind scares them.

I write woman: woman must write woman. And man, man. So only an oblique consideration will be found here of man; it's up to him to say where his masculinity and femininity are at: this will concern us once men have opened their eyes and seen themselves clearly.[1]

Now women return from afar, from always: from "without," from the heath where witches are kept alive; from below, from beyond "culture"; from their childhood which men have been trying desperately to make them forget, condemning it to "eternal rest." The little girls and their "ill-mannered" bodies immured, well-preserved, intact unto themselves, in the mirror. Frigidified. But are they ever seething underneath! What an effort it takes—there's no end to it—for the sex cops to bar their threatening return. Such a display of forces on both sides that the struggle has for centuries been immobilized in the trembling equilibrium of a deadlock.

Here they are, returning, arriving over and again, because the unconscious is impregnable. They have wandered around in circles, confined to the narrow room in which they've been given a deadly brainwashing. You can incarcerate them, slow them down, get away with the old Apartheid routine, but for a time only. As soon as they begin to speak, at the same time as they're taught their name, they can be taught that their territory is black: because you are Africa, you are black. Your continent is dark. Dark is dangerous. You can't see anything

---

[1] Men still have everything to say about their sexuality, and everything to write. For what they have said so far, for the most part, stems from the opposition activity/ passivity from the power relation between a fantasized obligatory virility meant to invade, to colonize, and the consequential phantasm of woman as a "dark continent" to penetrate and to "pacify." (We know what "pacify" means in terms of scotomizing the other and misrecognizing the self.) Conquering her, they've made haste to depart from her borders, to get out of sight, out of body. The way man has of getting out of himself and into her whom he takes not for the other but for his own, deprives him, he knows, of his own bodily territory. One can understand how man, confusing himself with his penis and rushing in for the attack, might feel resentment and fear of being "taken" by the woman, of being lost in her, absorbed or alone.

in the dark, you're afraid. Don't move, you might fall. Most of all, don't go into the forest. And so we have internalized this horror of the dark.

Men have committed the greatest crime against women. Insidiously, violently, they have led them to hate women, to be their own enemies, to mobilize their immense strength against themselves, to be the executants of their virile needs. They have made for women an antinarcissism! A narcissism which loves itself only to be loved for what women haven't got! They have constructed the infamous logic of antilove.

We the precocious, we the repressed of culture, our lovely mouths gagged with pollen, our wind knocked out of us, we the labyrinths, the ladders, the trampled spaces, the bevies—we are black and we are beautiful.

We're stormy, and that which is ours breaks loose from us without our fearing any debilitation. Our glances, our smiles, are spent; laughs exude from all our mouths; our blood flows and we extend ourselves without ever reaching an end; we never hold back our thoughts, our signs, our writing; and we're not afraid of lacking.

What happiness for us who are omitted, brushed aside at the scene of inheritances; we inspire ourselves and we expire without running out of breath, we are everywhere!

From now on, who, if we say so, can say no to us? We've come back from always.

It is time to liberate the New Woman from the Old by coming to know her—by loving her for getting by, for getting beyond the Old without delay, by going out ahead of what the New Woman will be, as an arrow quits the bow with a movement that gathers and separates the vibrations musically, in order to be more than her self.

I say that we must, for, with a few rare exceptions, there has not yet been any writing that inscribes femininity; exceptions so rare, in fact, that, after plowing through literature across languages, cultures, and ages,[2] one can only be startled at this vain scouting mission. It is well known that the number of women writers (while having increased very slightly from the nineteenth century on) has always been ridiculously small. This is a useless and deceptive fact unless from their species of female writers we do not first deduct the immense majority whose workmanship is in no way different from male writing, and which either obscures women or reproduces the classic representations of women (as sensitive—intuitive—dreamy, etc.)[3]

---

[2] I am speaking here only of the place "reserved" for women by the Western world.
[3] Which works, then, might be called feminine? I'll just point out some examples: one would have to give them full readings to bring out what is pervasively feminine in their significance. Which I shall do elsewhere. In France (have you noted our

Let me insert here a parenthetical remark. I mean it when I speak of male writing. I maintain unequivocally that there is such a thing as *marked* writing; that, until now, far more extensively and repressively than is ever suspected or admitted, writing has been run by a libidinal and cultural—hence political, typically masculine—economy; that this is a locus where the repression of women has been perpetuated, over and over, more or less consciously, and in a manner that's frightening since it's often hidden or adorned with the mystifying charms of fiction; that this locus has grossly exaggerated all the signs of sexual opposition (and not sexual difference), where woman has never *her* turn to speak—this being all the more serious and unpardonable in that writing is precisely *the very possibility of change*, the space that can serve as a springboard for subversive thought, the precursory movement of a transformation of social and cultural structures.

Nearly the entire history of writing is confounded with the history of reason, of which it is at once the effect, the support, and one of the privileged alibis. It has been one with the phallocentric tradition. It is indeed that same self-admiring, self-stimulating, self-congratulatory phallocentrism.

With some exceptions, for there have been failures—and if it weren't for them, I wouldn't be writing (I-woman, escapee)—in that enormous machine that has been operating and turning out its "truth" for centuries. There have been poets who would go to any lengths to slip something by at odds with tradition—men capable of loving love and hence capable of loving others and of wanting them, of imagining the woman who would hold out against oppression and constitute herself as a superb, equal, hence "impossible" subject, untenable in a real social framework. Such a woman the poet could desire only by breaking the codes that negate her. Her appearance would necessarily bring on, if not revolution—for the bastion was supposed to be immutable—at least harrowing explosions. At times it is in the fissure caused by an earthquake, through that radical mutation of things brought on by a material upheaval when every structure is for a moment thrown off balance and an ephemeral wildness sweeps order away, that the poet slips something by, for a brief span, of woman. Thus did Kleist expend himself in his yearning for the existence of sister-lovers, maternal daughters, mother-sisters, who never hung their heads in shame. Once the palace of magis-

---

infinite poverty in this field?—the Anglo-Saxon countries have shown resources of distinctly greater consequence), leafing through what's come out of the twentieth century—and it's not much—the only inscriptions of femininity that I have seen were by Colette, Marguerite Duras, . . . and Jean Genet.

trates is restored, it's time to pay: immediate bloody death to the uncontrollable elements.

But only the poets—not the novelists, allies of representationalism. Because poetry involves gaining strength through the unconscious and because the unconscious, that other limitless country, is the place where the repressed manage to survive: women, or as Hoffmann would say, fairies.

She must write her self, because this is the invention of a *new insurgent* writing which, when the moment of her liberation has come, will allow her to carry out the indispensable ruptures and transformations in her history, first at two levels that cannot be separated.

a) Individually. By writing her self, woman will return to the body which has been more than confiscated from her, which has been turned into the uncanny stranger on display—the ailing or dead figure, which so often turns out to be the nasty companion, the cause and location of inhibitions. Censor the body and you censor breath and speech at the same time.

Write your self. Your body must be heard. Only then will the immense resources of the unconscious spring forth. Our naphtha will spread, throughout the world, without dollars—black or gold—nonassessed values that will change the rules of the old game.

To write. An act which will not only "realize" the decensored relation of woman to her sexuality, to her womanly being, giving her access to her native strength; it will give her back her goods, her pleasures, her organs, her immense bodily territories which have been kept under seal; it will tear her away from the superegoized structure in which she has always occupied the place reserved for the guilty (guilty of everything, guilty at every turn: for having desires, for not having any; for being frigid, for being "too hot"; for not being both at once; for being too motherly and not enough; for having children and for not having any; for nursing and for not nursing . . .)—tear her away by means of this research, this job of analysis and illumination, this emancipation of the marvelous text of her self that she must urgently learn to speak. A woman without a body, dumb, blind, can't possibly be a good fighter. She is reduced to being the servant of the militant male, his shadow. We must kill the false woman who is preventing the live one from breathing. Inscribe the breath of the whole woman.

b) An act that will also be marked by woman's *seizing* the occasion to *speak*, hence her shattering entry into history, which has always been based *on her suppression*. To write and thus to forge for herself the antilogos weapon. To become *at will* the taker and initiator, for her own right, in every symbolic system, in every political process.

It is time for women to start scoring their feats in written and oral language.

Every woman has known the torment of getting up to speak. Her heart racing, at times entirely lost for words, ground and language slipping away—that's how daring a feat, how great a transgression it is for a woman to speak—even just open her mouth—in public. A double distress, for even if she transgresses, her words fall almost always upon the deaf male ear, which hears in language only that which speaks in the masculine.

It is by writing, from and toward women, and by taking up the challenge of speech which has been governed by the phallus, that women will confirm women in a place other than that which is reserved in and by the symbolic, that is, in a place other than silence. Women should break out of the snare of silence. They shouldn't be conned into accepting a domain which is the margin or the harem.

Listen to a woman speak at a public gathering (if she hasn't painfully lost her wind). She doesn't "speak," she throws her trembling body forward; she lets go of herself, she flies; all of her passes into her voice, and it's with her body that she vitally supports the "logic" of her speech. Her flesh speaks true. She lays herself bare. In fact, she physically materializes what she's thinking; she signifies it with her body. In a certain way she *inscribes* what she's saying, because she doesn't deny her drives the intractable and impassioned part they have in speaking. Her speech, even when "theoretical" or political, is never simple or linear or "objectified," generalized: she draws her story into history.

There is not that scission, that division made by the common man between the logic of oral speech and the logic of the text, bound as he is by his antiquated relation—servile, calculating—to mastery. From which proceeds the niggardly lip service which engages only the tiniest part of the body, plus the mask.

In women's speech, as in their writing, that element which never stops resonating, which, once we've been permeated by it, profoundly and imperceptibly touched by it, retains the power of moving us—that element is the song: first music from the first voice of love which is alive in every woman. Why this privileged relationship with the voice? Because no woman stockpiles as many defenses for countering the drives as does a man. You don't build walls around yourself, you don't forego pleasure as "wisely" as he. Even if phallic mystification has generally contaminated good relationships, a woman is never far from "mother" (I mean outside her role functions: the "mother" as nonname and as source of goods). There is always within her at least a little of that good mother's milk. She writes in white ink.

Woman for women.—There always remains in woman that force which produces/is produced by the other—in particular, the other woman. In her, matrix, cradler; herself giver as her mother and child; she is her own sister-daughter. You might object, "What about she who is the hysterical offspring of a bad mother?" Everything will be changed once woman gives woman to the other woman. There is hidden and always ready in woman the source; the locus for the other. The mother, too, is a metaphor. It is necessary and sufficient that the best of herself be given to woman by another woman for her to be able to love herself and return in love the body that was "born" to her. Touch me, caress me, you the living no-name, give me my self as myself. The relation to the "mother," in terms of intense pleasure and violence, is curtailed no more than the relation to childhood (the child that she was, that she is, that she makes, remakes, undoes, there at the point where, the same, she mothers herself). Text: my body—shot through with streams of song; I don't mean the overbearing, clutchy "mother" but, rather, what touches you, the equivoice that affects you, fills your breast with an urge to come to language and launches your force; the rhythm that laughs you; the intimate recipient who makes all metaphors possible and desirable; body (body? bodies?), no more describable than god, the soul, or the Other; that part of you that leaves a space between yourself and urges you to inscribe in language your woman's style. In women there is always more or less of the mother who makes everything all right, who nourishes, and who stands up against separation; a force that will not be cut off but will knock the wind out of the codes. We will rethink womankind beginning with every form and every period of her body. The Americans remind us, "We are all Lesbians"; that is, don't denigrate woman, don't make of her what men have made of you.

Because the "economy" of her drives is prodigious, she cannot fail, in seizing the occasion to speak, to transform directly and indirectly *all* systems of exchange based on masculine thrift. Her libido will produce far more radical effects of political and social change than some might like to think.

Because she arrives, vibrant, over and again, we are at the beginning of a new history, or rather of a process of becoming in which several histories intersect with one another. As subject for history, woman always occurs simultaneously in several places. Woman un-thinks[4] the unifying, regulating history that homogenizes and channels forces, herding contradictions into a single battlefield. In woman, personal history blends together with the history of all women, as well as national and

---

[4] *Dé-pense*, a neologism formed on the verb *penser*, hence "unthinks," but also "spends" (from *dépenser*).—Tr.

world history. As a militant, she is an integral part of all liberations. She must be farsighted, not limited to a blow-by-blow interaction. She foresees that her liberation will do more than modify power relations or toss the ball over to the other camp; she will bring about a mutation in human relations, in thought, in all praxis: hers is not simply a class struggle, which she carries forward into a much vaster movement. Not that in order to be a woman-in-struggle(s) you have to leave the class struggle or repudiate it; but you have to split it open, spread it out, push it forward, fill it with the fundamental struggle so as to prevent the class struggle, or any other struggle for the liberation of a class or people, from operating as a form of repression, pretext for postponing the in-evitable, the staggering alteration in power relations and in the pro-duction of individualities. This alteration is already upon us—in the United States, for example, where millions of night crawlers are in the process of undermining the family and disintegrating the whole of Amer-ican sociality.

The new history is coming; it's not a dream, though it does extend beyond men's imagination, and for good reason. It's going to deprive them of their conceptual orthopedics, beginning with the destruction of their enticement machine.

It is impossible to *define* a feminine practice of writing, and this is an impossibility that will remain, for this practice can never be theorized, enclosed, coded—which doesn't mean that it doesn't exist. But it will always surpass the discourse that regulates the phallocentric system; it does and will take place in areas other than those subordinated to philo-sophico-theoretical domination. It will be conceived of only by subjects who are breakers of automatisms, by peripheral figures that no authority can ever subjugate.

Hence the necessity to affirm the flourishes of this writing, to give form to its movement, its near and distant byways. Bear in mind to begin with (1) that sexual opposition, which has always worked for man's profit to the point of reducing writing, too, to his laws, is only a historico-cultural limit. There is, there will be more and more rapidly pervasive now, a fiction that produces irreducible effects of femininity. (2) That it is through ignorance that most readers, critics, and writers of both sexes hesitate to admit or deny outright the possibility or the pertinence of a distinction between feminine and masculine writing. It will usually be said, thus disposing of sexual difference: either that all writing, to the extent that it materializes, is feminine; or, inversely—but it comes to the same thing—that the act of writing is equivalent to masculine masturbation (and so the woman who writes cuts herself out a paper penis); or that writing is bisexual, hence neuter, which again does away with differentiation. To admit that writing is precisely working (in) the in-between, inspecting the process of the same and of the other without which nothing can live, undoing the work of death—to admit this is first to want the two, as well as both, the ensemble of the one and the other, not fixed in sequences of struggle and expulsion or some other form of death but infinitely dynamized by an incessant process of exchange from one subject to another. A process of different subjects knowing one another and beginning one another anew only from the living boundaries of the other: a multiple and inexhaustible course with millions of encounters and transformations of the same into the other and into the in-between, from which woman takes her forms (and man, in his turn; but that's his other history).

In saying "bisexual, hence neuter," I am referring to the classic conception of bisexuality, which, squashed under the emblem of castration fear and along with the fantasy of a "total" being (though composed of two halves), would do away with the difference experienced as an operation incurring loss, as the mark of dreaded sectility.

To this self-effacing, merger-type bisexuality, which would conjure away castration (the writer who puts up his sign: "bisexual written here, come and see," when the odds are good that it's neither one nor the other), I oppose the *other bisexuality* on which every subject not enclosed in the false theater of phallocentric representationalism has founded his/her erotic universe. Bisexuality: that is, each one's location in self (*repérage en soi*) of the presence—variously manifest and insistent according to each person, male or female—of both sexes, non-exclusion either of the difference or of one sex, and, from this "self-permission," multiplication of the effects of the inscription of desire, over all parts of my body and the other body.

Now it happens that at present, for historico-cultural reasons, it is women who are opening up to and benefiting from this vatic bisexuality which doesn't annul differences but stirs them up, pursues them, increases their number. In a certain way, "woman is bisexual"; man—it's a secret to no one—being poised to keep glorious phallic monosexuality in view. By virtue of affirming the primacy of the phallus and of bringing it into play, phallocratic ideology has claimed more than one victim. As a woman, I've been clouded over by the great shadow of the scepter and been told: idolize it, that which you cannot brandish. But at the same time, man has been handed that grotesque and scarcely enviable destiny (just imagine) of being reduced to a single idol with clay balls. And consumed, as Freud and his followers note, by a fear of being a woman! For, if psychoanalysis was constituted from woman, to repress femininity (and not so successful a repression at that—men have made it clear), its account of masculine sexuality is now hardly refutable; as with all the "human" sciences, it reproduces the masculine view, of which it is one of the effects.

Here we encounter the inevitable man-with-rock, standing erect in his old Freudian realm, in the way that, to take the figure back to the point where linguistics is conceptualizing it "anew," Lacan preserves it in the sanctuary of the phallos (ϕ) "sheltered" from *castration's lack!* Their "symbolic" exists, it holds power—we, the sowers of disorder, know it only too well. But we are in no way obliged to deposit our lives in their banks of lack, to consider the constitution of the subject in terms of a drama manglingly restaged, to reinstate again and again the religion of the father. Because we don't want that. We don't fawn around the supreme hole. We have no womanly reason to pledge allegiance to the negative. The feminine (as the poets suspected) affirms: ". . . And yes," says Molly, carrying *Ulysses* off beyond any book and toward the new writing; "I said yes, I will Yes."

The Dark Continent is neither dark nor unexplorable.—It is still unexplored only because we've been made to believe that it was too dark to be explorable. And because they want to make us believe that what interests us is the white continent, with its monuments to Lack. And we believed. They riveted us between two horrifying myths: between the Medusa and the abyss. That would be enough to set half the world laughing, except that it's still going on. For the phallologocentric sublation[5] is with us, and it's militant, regenerating the old patterns, anchored in the dogma of castration. They haven't changed a thing: they've theorized their desire for reality! Let the priests tremble, we're going to show them our sexts!

Too bad for them if they fall apart upon discovering that women aren't men, or that the mother doesn't have one. But isn't this fear convenient for them? Wouldn't the worst be, isn't the worst, in truth, that women aren't castrated, that they have only to stop listening to the Sirens (for the Sirens were men) for history to change its meaning? You only have to look at the Medusa straight on to see her. And she's not deadly. She's beautiful and she's laughing.

Men say that there are two unrepresentable things: death and the feminine sex. That's because they need femininity to be associated with death; it's the jitters that give them a hard-on! for themselves! They need to be afraid of us. Look at the trembling Perseuses moving backward toward us, clad in apotropes. What lovely backs! Not another minute to lose. Let's get out of here.

Let's hurry: the continent is not impenetrably dark. I've been there often. I was overjoyed one day to run into Jean Genet. It was in

---

[5] Standard English term for the Hegelian *Aufhebung*, the French *la relève*.

Pompes funèbres.[6] He had come there led by his Jean. There are some men (all too few) who aren't afraid of femininity.

Almost everything is yet to be written by women about femininity: about their sexuality, that is, its infinite and mobile complexity, about their eroticization, sudden turn-ons of a certain miniscule-immense area of their bodies; not about destiny, but about the adventure of such and such a drive, about trips, crossings, trudges, abrupt and gradual awakenings, discoveries of a zone at one time timorous and soon to be forthright. A woman's body, with its thousand and one thresholds of ardor —once, by smashing yokes and censors, she lets it articulate the profusion of meanings that run through it in every direction—will make the old single-grooved mother tongue reverberate with more than one language.

We've been turned away from our bodies, shamefully taught to ignore them, to strike them with that stupid sexual modesty; we've been made victims of the old fool's game: each one will love the other sex. I'll give you your body and you'll give me mine. But who are the men who give women the body that women blindly yield to them? Why so few texts? Because so few women have as yet won back their body. Women must write through their bodies, they must invent the impregnable language that will wreck partitions, classes, and rhetorics, regulations and codes, they must submerge, cut through, get beyond the ultimate reserve-discourse, including the one that laughs at the very idea of pronouncing the word "silence," the one that, aiming for the impossible, stops short before the word "impossible" and writes it as "the end."

Such is the strength of women that, sweeping away syntax, breaking that famous thread (just a tiny little thread, they say) which acts for men as a surrogate umbilical cord, assuring them—otherwise they couldn't come—that the old lady is always right behind them, watching them make phallus, women will go right up to the impossible.

When the "repressed"of their culture and their society returns, it's an explosive, *utterly* destructive, staggering return, with a force never yet unleashed and equal to the most forbidding of suppressions. For when the Phallic period comes to an end, women will have been either annihilated or borne up to the highest and most violent incandescence. Muffled throughout their history, they have lived in dreams, in bodies (though muted), in silences, in aphonic revolts.

And with such force in their fragility; a fragility, a vulnerability, equal to their incomparable intensity. Fortunately, they haven't sublimated;

[6] Jean Genet, *Pompes funèbres* (Paris, 1948), p. 185 [privately published].

they've saved their skin, their energy. They haven't worked at liquidating the impasse of lives without futures. They have furiously inhabited these sumptuous bodies: admirable hysterics who made Freud succumb to many voluptuous moments impossible to confess, bombarding his Mosaic statue with their carnal and passionate body words, haunting him with their inaudible and thundering denunciations, dazzling, more than naked underneath the seven veils of modesty. Those who, with a single word of the body, have inscribed the vertiginous immensity of a history which is sprung like an arrow from the whole history of men and from biblico-capitalist society, are the women, the supplicants of yesterday, who come as forebears of the new women, after whom no intersubjective relation will ever be the same. You, Dora, you the indomitable, the poetic body, you are the true "mistress" of the Signifier. Before long your efficacity will be seen at work when your speech is no longer suppressed, its point turned in against your breast, but written out over against the other.

In body.—More so than men who are coaxed toward social success, toward sublimation, women are body. More body, hence more writing. For a long time it has been in body that women have responded to persecution, to the familial-conjugal enterprise of domestication, to the repeated attempts at castrating them. Those who have turned their tongues 10,000 times seven times before not speaking are either dead from it or more familiar with their tongues and their mouths than anyone else. Now, I-woman am going to blow up the Law: an explosion henceforth possible and ineluctable; let it be done, right now, *in* language.

Let us not be trapped by an analysis still encumbered with the old automatisms. It's not to be feared that language conceals an invincible adversary, because it's the language of men and their grammar. We mustn't leave them a single place that's any more theirs alone than we are.

If woman has always functioned "within" the discourse of man, a signifier that has always referred back to the opposite signifier which annihilates its specific energy and diminishes or stifles its very different sounds, it is time for her to dislocate this "within," to explode it, turn it around, and seize it; to make it hers, containing it, taking it in her own mouth, biting that tongue with her very own teeth to invent for herself a language to get inside of. And you'll see with what ease she will spring forth from that "within"—the "within" where once she so drowsily crouched—to overflow at the lips she will cover the foam.

Nor is the point to appropriate their instruments, their concepts, their places, or to begrudge them their position of mastery. Just because there's a risk of identification doesn't mean that we'll succumb. Let's leave it to the worriers, to masculine anxiety and its obsession with how to dominate the way things work—knowing "how it works" in order to "make it work." For us the point is not to take possession in order to internalize or manipulate, but rather to dash through and to "fly." [7]

Flying is woman's gesture—flying in language and making it fly. We have all learned the art of flying and its numerous techniques; for centuries we've been able to possess anything only by flying; we've lived in flight, stealing away, finding, when desired, narrow passageways, hidden crossovers. It's no accident that *voler* has a double meaning, that it plays on each of them and thus throws off the agents of sense. It's no accident: women take after birds and robbers just as robbers take after women and birds. They (*illes*) [8] go by, fly the coop, take pleasure in jumbling the order of space, in disorienting it, in changing around the furniture, dislocating things and values, breaking them all up, emptying structures, and turning propriety upside down.

What woman hasn't flown/stolen? Who hasn't felt, dreamt, performed the gesture that jams sociality? Who hasn't crumbled, held up to ridicule, the bar of separation? Who hasn't inscribed with her body the differential, punctured the system of couples and opposition? Who, by some act of transgression, hasn't overthrown successiveness, connection, the wall of circumfusion?

A feminine text cannot fail to be more than subversive. It is volcanic; as it is written it brings about an upheaval of the old property crust, carrier of masculine investments; there's no other way. There's no room for her if she's not a he. If she's a her-she, it's in order to smash everything, to shatter the framework of institutions, to blow up the law, to break up the "truth" with laughter.

For once she blazes *her* trail in the symbolic, she cannot fail to make of it the chaosmos of the "personal"—in her pronouns, her nouns, and her clique of referents. And for good reason. There will have been the long history of gynocide. This is known by the colonized peoples of yesterday, the workers, the nations, the species off whose backs the history of men has made its gold; those who have known the ignominy of persecution derive from it an obstinate future desire for grandeur; those who are locked up know better than their jailers the taste of free air. Thanks to their history, women today know (how to do and want) what men will be able to conceive of only much later. I say woman overturns the "personal," for if, by means of laws, lies, blackmail, and marriage, her right to herself has been extorted at the same time as her

---

[7] Also, "to steal." Both meanings of the verb *voler* are played on, as the text itself explains in the following paragraph.—Tr.

[8] *Illes* is a fusion of the masculine pronoun *ils*, which refers back to birds and robbers, with the feminine pronoun *elles*, which refers to women.—Tr.

name, she has been able, through the very movement of mortal alienation, to see more closely the inanity of "propriety," the reductive stingi-
ness of the masculine-conjugal subjective economy, which she doubly
resists. On the one hand she has constituted herself necessarily as that
"person" capable of losing a part of herself without losing her integrity.
But secretly, silently, deep down inside, she grows and multiplies, for, on
the other hand, she knows far more about living and about the relation
between the economy of the drives and the management of the ego than
any man. Unlike man, who holds so dearly to his title and his titles, his
pouches of value, his cap, crown, and everything connected with his
head, woman couldn't care less about the fear of decapitation (or castration), adventuring, without the masculine temerity, into anonymity,
which she can merge with, without annihilating herself: because she's
a giver.

I shall have a great deal to say about the whole deceptive problematic
of the gift. Woman is obviously not that woman Nietzsche dreamed of
who gives only in order to.[9] Who could ever think of the gift as a gift-
that-takes? Who else but man, precisely the one who would like to take
everything?

If there is a "propriety of woman," it is paradoxically her capacity to
depropriate unselfishly, body without end, without appendage, without
principal "parts." If she is a whole, it's a whole composed of parts that
are wholes, not simple partial objects but a moving, limitlessly changing
ensemble, a cosmos tirelessly traversed by Eros, an immense astral space
not organized around any one sun that's any more of a star than the
others.

This doesn't mean that she's an undifferentiated magma, but that she
doesn't lord it over her body or her desire. Though masculine sexuality
gravitates around the penis, engendering that centralized body (in political anatomy) under the dictatorship of its parts, woman does not
bring about the same regionalization which serves the couple head/
genitals and which is inscribed only within boundaries. Her libido is
cosmic, just as her unconscious is worldwide. Her writing can only keep
going, without ever inscribing or discerning contours, daring to make
these vertiginous crossings of the other(s) ephemeral and passionate
sojourns in him, her, them, whom she inhabits long enough to look at
from the point closest to their unconscious from the moment they
awaken, to love them at the point closest to their drives; and then

---

[9] Reread Derrida's text, "Le style de la femme," in *Nietzsche aujourd'hui* (Union
Générale d'Editions, Coll. 10/18), where the philosopher can be seen operating an
Aufhebung of all philosophy in its systematic reducing of woman to the place of
seduction: she appears as the one who is taken for; the bait in person, all veils un-
furled, the one who doesn't give but who gives only in order to (take).

further, impregnated through and through with these brief, identifica-
tory embraces, she goes and passes into infinity. She alone dares and
wishes to know from within, where she, the outcast, has never ceased
to hear the resonance of fore-language. She lets the other language speak
—the language of 1,000 tongues which knows neither enclosure nor
death. To life she refuses nothing. Her language does not contain, it
carries; it does not hold back, it makes possible. When id is ambiguously
uttered—the wonder of being several—she doesn't defend herself against
these unknown women whom she's surprised at becoming, but derives
pleasure from this gift of alterability. I am spacious, singing flesh, on
which is grafted no one knows which I, more or less human, but alive
because of transformation.

Write! and your self-seeking text will know itself better than flesh
and blood, rising, insurrectionary dough kneading itself, with sonorous,
perfumed ingredients, a lively combination of flying colors, leaves, and
rivers plunging into the sea we feed. "Ah, there's her sea," he will say as
he holds out to me a basin full of water from the little phallic mother
from whom he's inseparable. But look, our seas are what we make of
them, full of fish or not, opaque or transparent, red or black, high or
smooth, narrow or bankless; and we are ourselves sea, sand, coral, sea-
weed, beaches, tides, swimmers, children, waves... More or less wavily
sea, earth, sky—what matter would rebuff us? We know how to speak
them all.

Heterogeneous, yes. For her joyous benefits she is erogenous; she is
the erotogeneity of the heterogeneous: airborne swimmer, in flight, she
does not cling to herself; she is dispersible, prodigious, stunning, desir-
ous and capable of others, of the other woman that she will be, of the
other woman she isn't, of him, of you.

Woman be unafraid of any other place, of any same, or any other.
My eyes, my tongue, my ears, my nose, my skin, my mouth, my body-
for-(the)-other—not that I long for it in order to fill up a hole, to
provide against some defect of mine, or because, as fate would have it,
I'm spurred on by feminine "jealousy"; not because I've been dragged
into the whole chain of substitutions that brings that which is substituted back to its ultimate object. That sort of thing you would expect
to come straight out of "Tom Thumb," out of the Penisneid whispered
to us by old grandmother ogresses, servants to their father-sons. If they
believe, in order to muster up some self-importance, if they really need
to believe that we're dying of desire, that we are this hole fringed with
desire for their penis—that's their immemorial business. Undeniably (we
verify it at our own expense—but also to our amusement), it's their

business to let us know they're getting a hard-on, so that we'll assure them (we the maternal mistresses of their little pocket signifier) that they still can, that it's still there—that men structure themselves only by being fitted with a feather. In the child it's not the penis that the woman desires, it's not that famous bit of skin around which every man gravitates. Pregnancy cannot be traced back, except within the historical limits of the ancients, to some form of fate, to those mechanical substitutions brought about by the unconscious of some eternal "jealous woman"; not to penis envies; and not to narcissism or to some sort of homosexuality linked to the ever-present mother! Begetting a child doesn't mean that the woman or the man must fall ineluctably into patterns or must recharge the circuit of reproduction. If there's a risk there's not an inevitable trap: may women be spared the pressure, under the guise of consciousness-raising, of a supplement of interdictions. Either you want a kid or you don't—*that's your business*. Let nobody threaten you; in satisfying your desire, let not the fear of becoming the accomplice to a sociality succeed the old-time fear of being "taken." And man, are you still going to bank on everyone's blindness and passivity, afraid lest the child make a father and, consequently, that in having a kid the woman land herself more than one bad deal by engendering all at once child—mother—father—family? No; it's up to you to break the old circuits. It will be up to man and woman to render obsolete the former relationship and all its consequences, to consider the launching of a brand-new subject, alive, with defamilialization. Let us demater-paternalize rather than deny woman, in an effort to avoid the cooptation of procreation, a thrilling era of the body. Let us defetishize. Let's get away from the dialectic which has it that the only good father is a dead one, or that the child is the death of his parents. The child is the other, but the other without violence, bypassing loss, struggle. We're fed up with the reuniting of bonds forever to be severed, with the litany of castration that's handed down and genealogized. We won't advance backward anymore; we're not going to repress something so simple as the desire for life. Oral drive, anal drive, vocal drive—all these drives are our strengths, and among them is the gestation drive—just like the desire to write: a desire to live self from within, a desire for the swollen belly, for language, for blood. We are not going to refuse, if it should happen to strike our fancy, the unsurpassed pleasures of pregnancy which have actually been always exaggerated or conjured away—or cursed—in the classic texts. For if there's one thing that's been repressed, here's just the place to find it: in the taboo of the pregnant woman. This says a lot about the power she seems invested with at the time, because it has always been suspected, that, when pregnant, the woman not only doubles her market value, but—what's more important —takes on intrinsic value as a woman in her own eyes and, undeniably, acquires body and sex.

There are thousands of ways of living one's pregnancy; to have or not to have with that still invisible other a relationship of another intensity. And if you don't have that particular yearning, it doesn't mean that you're in any way lacking. Each body distributes in its own special way, without model or norm, the nonfinite and changing totality of its desires. Decide for yourself on your position in the arena of contradictions, where pleasure and reality embrace. Bring the other to life. Women know how to live detachment; giving birth is neither losing nor increasing. It's adding to life an other. Am I dreaming? Am I misrecognizing? You, the defenders of "theory," the sacrosanct yes-men of Concept, enthroners of the phallus (but not of the penis):

Once more you'll say that all this smacks of "idealism," or what's worse, you'll splutter that I'm a "mystic."

And what about the libido? Haven't I read the "Signification of the Phallus"? And what about separation, what about that bit of self for which, to be born, you undergo an ablation—an ablation, so they say, to be forever commemorated by your desire?

Besides, isn't it evident that the penis gets around in my texts, that I give it a place and appeal? Of course I do. I want all. I want all of me with all of him. Why should I deprive myself of a part of us? I want all of us. Woman of course has a desire for a "loving desire" and not a jealous one. But not because she is gelded; not because she's deprived and needs to be filled out, like some wounded person who wants to console herself or seek vengeance. I don't want a penis to decorate my body with. But I do desire the other for the other, whole and entire, male or female; because living means wanting everything that is, everything that lives, and wanting it alive. Castration? Let others toy with it. What's a desire originating from a lack? A pretty meager desire.

The woman who still allows herself to be threatened by the big dick, who's still impressed by the commotion of the phallic stance, who still leads a loyal master to the beat of the drum: that's the woman of yesterday. They still exist, easy and numerous victims of the oldest of farces: either they're cast in the original silent versions in which, as titanesses lying under the mountains they make with their quivering, they never see erected that theoretic monument to the golden phallus looming, in the old manner, over their bodies. Or, coming today out of their *infans* period and into the second, "enlightened" version of their virtuous debasement, they see themselves suddenly assaulted by the builders of the analytic empire and, as soon as they've begun to formulate the new desire, naked, nameless, so happy at making an appearance, they're taken in their bath by the new old men, and then, whoops! Luring them with flashy signifiers, the demon of interpretation—oblique, decked out in modernity—sells them the same old handcuffs, baubles, and chains. Which castration do you prefer? Whose degrading do you like better, the father's or the mother's? Oh, what pwetty eyes, you pwetty little girl. Here, buy my glasses and you'll see the Truth-Me-Myself tell you everything you should know. Put them on your nose and take a fetishist's look (you are me, the other analyst—that's what I'm telling you) at your body and the body of the other. You see? No? Wait, you'll have everything explained to you, and you'll know at last which sort of neurosis you're related to. Hold still, we're going to do your portrait, so that you can begin looking like it right away.

Yes, the naives to the first and second degree are still legion. If the New Women, arriving now, dare to create outside the theoretical, they're called in by the cops of the signifier, fingerprinted, remonstrated, and brought into the line of order that they are supposed to know; assigned by force of trickery to a precise place in the chain that's always formed for the benefit of a privileged signifier. We are pieced back to the string which leads back, if not to the Name-of-the-Father, then, for a new twist, to the place of the phallic-mother.

Beware, my friend, of the signifier that would take you back to the authority of a signified! Beware of diagnoses that would reduce your generative powers. "Common" nouns are also proper nouns that disparage your singularity by classifying it into species. Break out of the circles; don't remain within the psychoanalytic closure. Take a look around, then cut through!

And if we are legion, it's because the war of liberation has only made as yet a tiny breakthrough. But women are thronging to it. I've seen them, those who will be neither dupe nor domestic, those who will not fear the risk of being a woman; will not fear any risk, any desire, any space still unexplored in themselves, among themselves and others or anywhere else. They do not fetishize, they do not deny, they do not hate. They observe, they approach, they try to see the other woman, the child, the lover—not to strengthen their own narcissism or verify the solidity or weakness of the master, but to make love better, to invent.

Other love.—In the beginning are our differences. The new love dares for the other, wants the other, makes dizzying, precipitous flights between knowledge and invention. The woman arriving over and over again does not stand still; she's everywhere, she exchanges, she is the desire-that-gives. (Not enclosed in the paradox of the gift that takes nor under the illusion of unitary fusion. We're past that.) She comes in, comes-in-between herself me and you, between the other me where one is always infinitely more than one and more than me, without the fear of ever reaching a limit; she thrills in our becoming. And we'll keep on becoming! She cuts through defensive loves, motherages, and devourations: beyond selfish narcissism, in the moving, open, transitional space, she runs her risks. Beyond the struggle-to-the-death that's been removed to the bed, beyond the love-battle that claims to represent exchange, she scorns at an Eros dynamic that would be fed by hatred. Hatred: a heritage, again, a reminder, a duping subservience to the phallus. To love, to watch-think-seek the other in the other, to despecularize, to unhoard. Does this seem difficult? It's not impossible, and this is what nourishes life—a love that has no commerce with the apprehensive desire that provides against the lack and stultifies the strange; a love that rejoices in the exchange that multiplies. Wherever history still unfolds as the history of death, she does not tread. Opposition, hierarchizing exchange, the struggle for mastery which can end only in at least one death (one master—one slave, or two nonmasters ≠ two dead)—all that comes from a period in time governed by phallocentric values. The fact that this period extends into the present doesn't prevent woman from starting the history of life somewhere else. Elsewhere, she gives. She doesn't "know" what she's giving, she doesn't measure it; she gives, though, neither a counterfeit impression nor something she hasn't got. She gives more, with no assurance that she'll get back even some unexpected profit from what she puts out. She gives that there may be life, thought, transformation. This is an "economy" that can no longer be put in economic terms. Wherever she loves, all the old concepts of management are left behind. At the end of a more or less conscious computation, she finds not her sum but her differences. I am for you what you want me to be at the moment you look at me in a way you've never seen me before: at every instant. When I write, it's everything that we don't know we can be that is written out of me, without exclusions, without stipulation, and everything we will be calls us to the unflagging, intoxicating, unappeasable search for love. In one another we will never be lacking.

Translated by Keith Cohen and Paula Cohen

Bio/Bibliography

Beauvoir, Simone de. Born 1908 in Paris. Philosopher, essayist, author of novels and memoirs including: *L'invitée*, 1946 [*She Came To Stay*]; *Le deuxième sexe*, 1949 [*The Second Sex*]; *Les mandarins*, 1954 [*The Mandarins*]; *Mémoires d'une jeune fille rangée*, 1958 [*Memoirs of a Dutiful Daughter*]; *La force de l'âge*, 1960 [*The Prime of Life*]; *La force des choses*, 1963 [*Force of Circumstance*]; *Une mort très douce*, 1964 [*A Very Easy Death*]; *Les belles images*, 1966 [*Les Belles Images*]; *La femme rompue*, 1967 [*The Woman Destroyed*]; *La vieillesse*, 1970 [*The Coming of Age*]; *Tout compte fait*, 1972 [*All Said and Done*].

Chawaf, Chantal. Young writer, author of *Retable-Rêverie*, 1975; *Cercoeur*, 1975; *Blé de semences*, 1976; *Chair chaude* suivi de *L'écriture*, 1976; *Le soleil et la terre*, 1977; *Rougeâtre*, 1978.

Cixous, Hélène. Born 1938 in Algeria. Teaches at the University of Paris VIII (Vincennes) where she has founded the first research group on the theory of femininity; co-editor with Catherine Clément of a new collection "Féminin Futur"; on the editorial board of the journal *Poétique*; author of about twenty books, essays, novels, plays, and numerous articles including: *L'exil de James Joyce ou l'art du remplacement*, 1968 [*The Exile of James Joyce*]; *Le prénom de Dieu*, 1967; *Dedans*, 1969; *Le troisième corps*, 1970; *Tombe*, 1973; *Prénom de personne*, 1974; "Sorties" in *La jeune née*, 1975; *Souffles*, 1975; *Portrait de Dora*, 1976; *Angst*, 1977; *Préparatifs de noces au delà de l'abîme*, 1978; *Chant du corps interdit*, 1978.

Clément, Catherine. Teaches at the University of Paris I and at the University of Paris VIII (Vincennes); director of cultural services for *Matin de Paris*; on the editorial staff of the review *L'arc*; co-editor with Hélène Cixous of "Féminin Futur"; author of "Le sol freudien et les mutations de la psychanalyse" in *Pour une critique marxiste de la théorie psychanalytique*, 1973; author of *Le pouvoir des mots*, 1974; "La coupable" in *La jeune née*, 1975; *Miroirs du sujet*, 1975; *Les fils de Freud sont fatigués*, 1978.

Duras, Marguerite. Born 1914 in Indochina. Writer and film maker. Her works include: novels—*Le square*, 1955 [*The Square*]; *Moderato Cantabile*, 1958 [*Moderato Cantabile*]; *Le ravissement de Lol V. Stein*, 1964 [*Ravishing of Lol Stein*]; *L'amante anglaise*, 1967 [play version: *A Room Without Doors*]; *Détruire dit-elle*, 1969 [*Destroy She Said*]; film script—*Hiroshima mon amour*, 1958; film scripts and direction—*Nathalie Granger*, 1974; *India Song*, 1975; *Baxter, Vera Baxter*, 1977; *Le camion*, 1977.

Eaubonne, Françoise d'. Born 1920 in Paris. Reader for Flammarion, Julliard, and Calmann-Lévy; author of about twenty novels, essays, and collections of poetry

266   Bio/Bibliography

including: *Le complexe de Diane*, 1951; *Je m'appelle Kristine*, 1960; *Je voulais être une femme*, 1962; *Y-a-t'il encore des hommes?* 1964; *Une femme témoin de son siècle: Madame Germaine de Staël*, 1966; *La couronne de sable: vie d'Isabelle Eberhardt*, 1968; *Les écrivains en cage*, 1971; *Eros minoritaire*, 1971; *Le féminisme*, 1972; *Le féminisme ou la mort*, 1974; *Les femmes avant le patriarcat*, 1976. Directs a center of Ecology-Feminism in Paris.

Forrester, Viviane. Has been director of an art gallery; worked for radio and television; published articles in *La quinzaine littéraire*, *Le nouvel observateur*, *Le monde*, and *Tel quel*; written three novels: *Ainsi des exilés*, 1970, *Le grand festin*, 1971, *Le corps entier de Marigda*, 1975; and translated into French Virginia Woolf's *Three Guineas*, 1977.

Gagnon, Madeleine. Born 1938 in Canada. Teaches at the University of Quebec in Montreal. Author of *Les morts vivants*, 1969; *Pour les femmes et autres*, 1974; "Amour parallèle" in *Portraits du voyage*, 1975; *Poélitique*, 1975; "Mon corps dans l'écriture" in *La venue à l'écriture*, 1977; *Retailles complaintes politiques*, with Denise Boucher, 1977; as well as a large body of poetry.

Gauthier, Xavière. Born 1942 in Normandy. Teaches at the University of Paris I. Author of *Surréalisme et sexualité*, 1971; *Les parleuses* (with Marguerite Duras), 1974; *Rose saignée*, 1974; *Dire nos sexualités—contre la sexologie*, 1977; editor of the feminist journal *Sorcières*.

Groult, Benoîte. Born 1920 in Paris. Formerly teacher and journalist. Has collaborated with her sister Flora in: *Journal à quatre mains*, 1963; *Le féminin pluriel*, 1965; *Il était deux fois*, 1967; and on her own: *La part des choses*, 1972; *Ainsi soit-elle*, 1975; *Le féminisme au masculin*, 1977; one of the editors of *F Magazine* (1978–).

Halimi, Gisèle. Born 1927 in Tunisia. Lawyer, member of the Paris Bar Association; defense attorney for the Algerian and Basque Liberation Fronts; co-founder, co-president, and legal counsel for "Choisir, la cause des femmes"; author of books and articles including: *La cause des femmes*, 1973; co-author of *Le programme commun des femmes*, 1978.

Herrmann, Claudine. Born 1926 in Brussels. Practicing lawyer and teacher of French literature. Author of: *Le cavalier des steppes*, 1963; *Le diplôme*, 1965; *L'étoile de David*, 1959; *Maître Talmon*, 1961; *Le rôle judiciaire et politique des femmes sous la république romaine*, 1963; *Les voleuses de langue*, 1976.

Horer, Suzanne and Socquet, Jeanne. Authors of *La création étouffée*, 1973.

Irigaray, Luce. Psychoanalyst. Author of *Le langage des déments*, 1973; *Speculum de l'autre femme*, 1974; *Ce sexe qui n'en est pas un*, 1977.

Kristeva, Julia. Born 1941 in Bulgaria. Teaches at the University of Paris VII. Author of: *Recherches pour une sémanalyse*, 1969; *Le texte du roman*, 1970; *La traversée des signes*, 1974; *La révolution du langage poétique*, 1974; *Des chinoises*, 1974 [*About Chinese Women*]; *Polylogue*, 1977. Editor of *Essays in Semiotics*, 1971.

Laguiller, Arlette. Born 1940. Since 1956 has been a secretary for Le Crédit Lyonnais, a large Parisian bank. Long-time militant for the Communist, Socialist and Trotskyist parties. Ran as the first woman candidate for president in the 1974 election on a Trotskyist platform (*lutte ouvrière*—"workers' struggle") and won close to 600,000 votes. Author of *Moi, une militante*.

Leclerc, Annie. Teacher of philosophy. Published a first novel in 1967, *Le pont du Nord*; two volumes of philosophical and poetic essays, *Parole de femme*, 1974 and *Epousailles*, 1976, and in collaboration with Madeleine Gagnon and Hélène Cixous, *La venue à l'écriture*, 1977.

Le Dantec, Denise. Born in Brittany in the 1930s. Teacher of philosophy. Poet, author of *Le jour* and *Notes pour un scénario imaginaire*, 1975; *Les joueurs de Go*, 1977.

Macciocchi, Maria-Antonietta. Italian intellectual and writer now living in France. Has taught at the University of Vincennes. Is a regular contributor to *Tel quel*. Author of "Gramsci et la question du fascisme" and "Les femmes et la traversée du fascisme" in *Eléments pour une analyse du fascisme*, 1976; *De la France*, 1977. Is writing a book in collaboration with Jacqueline Aubenas entitled *Lutte des femmes* [Women's struggle].

Parturier, Françoise. Born 1919 in Paris. Journalist and writer. Has published *L'amant de cinq jours*, 1959; *Marianne m'a dit*, 1963; *Lettre ouverte aux hommes*, 1968 [An Open Letter to Men]; *L'amour? Le plaisir?*, 1968; *Lettre ouverte aux femmes*, 1974.

Rochefort, Christiane. Born 1917 in Paris. Author of *Le repos du guerrier*, 1958 [The Warrior's Rest]; *Les petits enfants du siècle*, 1961 [Children of Heaven]; *Stances à Sophie*, 1963 [Cats Don't Care for Money]; *Printemps au Parking*, 1969; *C'est bizarre l'écriture*, 1970; *Archaos*, 1972; *Encore heureux qu'on va vers l'été*, 1975; *Les enfants d'abord*, 1976; *Ma vie revue et corrigée*, 1978.

Sullerot, Evelyne. Born 1924 in Montrouge. Sociologist, journalist, professor; co-founder of the French movement for family planning; member of the French Economic and Social Council and of several European organizations; author of numerous works including: *Demain les femmes*, 1965; *La presse féminine des origines à 1848*, 1966; *La femme dans le monde moderne*, 1970 [Women, Society and Change]; *Les françaises au travail*, 1973; *Histoire et mythologie de l'amour*, 1976. Editor of *Le fait féminin*, 1978.

Vincent, Madeleine. Involved in Resistance movement and deported. Member of the steering committee of the French Communist party and active in defending the interests of women workers. Author of *Femmes: quelle libération?*, 1976.

Wittig, Monique. Author of *L'opoponax*, 1964 [The Opoponax]; *Les guérillères*, 1969 [Les guérillères]; *Le corps lesbien*, 1973 [The Lesbian Body]; *Brouillon pour un dictionnaire des amantes*, 1976. Contributes to the journal *Questions féministes*.

Selected Bibliography

We have listed the major texts used and referred to in this anthology and those articles relevant to our topic which have appeared in English.

Albistur, Maïté and Armogathe, Daniel. *Histoire du féminisme français du moyen-âge à nos jours.* des femmes, 1977.

Beauvoir, Simone de. *Le deuxième sexe.* Gallimard, 1949. (*The Second Sex.* Translated by H. M. Parshley. Vintage, 1974.)

"Bisexualité et différence des sexes." Special Issue. *Nouvelle revue de psychanalyse,* Spring 1973.

Brée, Germaine. *Women Writers in France.* Rutgers University Press, 1973.

Bulletin de recherches et d'études féministes francophones (BREFF). Department of French and Italian, University of Wisconsin. Madison, Wisconsin, May 1976.

Burke, Carolyn Greenstein. "Report from Paris: Women's Writing and The Women's Movement." *Signs,* Summer 1978, pp. 843–54.

Cixous, Hélène. "Le rire de la méduse." *L'arc,* no. 61 (1975), pp. 39–54. ("The Laugh of the Medusa." Translated by Keith Cohen and Paula Cohen. *Signs,* Summer 1976, pp. 875–93.)

Cixous, Hélène and Clément, Catherine. *La jeune née.* Union Générale d'Editions, 10/18, 1975.

Cixous, Hélène; Gagnon, Madeleine; Leclerc, Annie. *La venue à l'écriture.* Union Générale d'Editions, 10/18, 1977.

Collins, Marie and Weil Sayre, Sylvie, eds. *Les femmes en France.* Scribners, 1974.

Conley, Verena. "Missexual Misstery." Review of *La jeune née* by Hélène Cixous and Catherine Clément. *Diacritics,* Summer 1977, pp. 70–82.

Eaubonne, Françoise de. *Le féminisme.* Moreau, 1973.

———. *Le féminisme ou la mort.* Horay, 1974.

"Ecriture, Féminité, Féminisme." Special Issue. *Revue des sciences humaines,* no. 188 (Oct.–Dec. 1977).

"Femmes." Special Issue. *Dialectiques,* no. 8 (Spring 1975).

Les femmes aujourd'hui, demain. "Semaine de la pensée marxiste." Editions sociales, 1975.

"Les femmes s'entêtent." Special Issue. *Les Temps Modernes.* April–May 1974.

Féral, Josette. "Antigone or the Irony of the Tribe." Translated by Alice Jardine and Tom Gora. Review of *Speculum de l'autre femme* and *Ce sexe qui n'en pas un* by Luce Irigaray and of *Polylogue* by Julia Kristeva. *Diacritics,* Fall 1978, pp. 2–14.

Gallop, Jane. "The Ladies' Man." *Diacritics,* Winter 1976, pp. 28–34.

Groult, Benoîte. *Ainsi soit-elle*. Grasset, 1975.
———. *Le féminisme au masculin*. Denoël/Gonthier, 1977.
Halimi, Gisèle. *La cause des femmes*. Grasset, 1973.
———. *Le programme commun des femmes*. Grasset, 1978.
Herrmann, Claudine. *Les voleuses de langue*. des femmes, 1976.
Horer, Suzanne and Socquet, Jeanne. *La création étouffée*. Horay, 1973.
Irigaray, Luce. *Ce sexe qui n'en est pas un*. Minuit, 1977.
———. *Le speculum de l'autre femme*. Minuit, 1974.
Kristeva, Julia. *Des chinoises*. des femmes, 1974. (*About Chinese Women*. Translated by Anita Barrows. Urizen Books, 1977).
Leclerc, Annie. *Epousailles*. Grasset, 1977.
———. *Parole de femme*. Grasset, 1974.
"Libération des femmes, année zéro." Special Issue. *Partisans*, no. 106. Maspéro, 1972.
Macciocchi, M.-A. "Les femmes et la traversée du fascisme." *Eléments pour une analyse du fascisme*. Vol. 1. Union Générale d'Editions, 10/18, 1976.
Makward, Christiane; Becker, Mary Helen; Hage, Madeleine; Eisinger, Erica M., eds. *Ecrits de femmes*. Stock, forthcoming.
Marks, Elaine. "Review Essay: Women and Literature in France." *Signs*, Summer 1978, pp. 832–42.
Michel, Andrée, ed. *Les femmes dans la société marchande*. P.U.F., 1978.
Montrelay, Michèle. *L'ombre et le nom*. Minuit, 1977.
Musidora. *Paroles . . . elles tournent*. des femmes, 1976.
Parturier, Françoise. *Lettre ouverte aux femmes*. Albin Michel, 1974.
———. *Lettre ouverte aux hommes*. Albin Michel, 1968. (*An Open Letter to Men*. Translated by Joseph Bernstein. Heineman, 1968.)
Pisan, Annie de and Tristan, Anne. Preface by Simone de Beauvoir. *Histoires du MLF*. Calmann-Lévy, 1977.
La quinzaine littéraire. Special Issue on Women, no. 192 (August 1974).
Rabaut, Jean. *Histoire des féminismes français*. Stock, 1978.
Raitière, Anna. "La française devient majeure." *The French Review*, no. 1 (October 1974), pp. 47–64.
"Recherches féminines." Special Issue. *Tel quel*, no. 74 (Winter 1977).
Schwartz, Danielle. "Les femmes et l'écriture." *Nouvelle critique*, no. 116 (297) (Aug.–Sept. 1978), pp. 18–23.
"Simone de Beauvoir et la lutte des femmes." Special Issue. *L'arc*, no. 61 (1975).
Sullerot, Evelyne, ed. *Le fait féminin: Qu'est-ce qu'une femme?* Fayard, 1978.
"Textual Politics: Feminist Criticism." Special Issue. *Diacritics*, Winter 1975.
Weitz, Margaret Collins. "Cherchez la femme: recherches sur les femmes." *The French Review*, no. 3 (February 1978), pp. 415–18.
Wittig, Monique. *Les guérillères*. Minuit, 1969. (*Les guérillères*. Translated by David Le Vay. Viking, 1971.)
Yaguello, Marina. *Les mots et les femmes*. Payot, 1978.

Index

Agoult, Marie d', 164
Agrippa, Henry Cornelius: *De nobilitate et praecellentia feminei sexus* (1529), 12
Albistur, Maïté: *Histoire du féminisme français* (1977), 27
Algerian War, 23
Althusser, Louis, xii
Anastasi, Ann, 173
Anne of Brittany, 12
Antoinette. *See* Fouque, Antoinette
Apologie des femmes (Perrault), 14
"Apologie des rapports de domination, Une" (Poggi), 76–78
"Appel 343 femmes, Un," 24, 29, 190
"Apres 48 heures du cinéma des femmes à La Rochelle" (Roncier and Landy), 204–6
Arc, L', 26, 34, 197
Arc de Triomphe, 31
"Are Women Writers Still Monsters?" (Rochefort), 182–86
Aristotle, 43
Armogathe, Daniel: *Histoire du féminisme français* (1977), 27
Artaud, Antonin, 138, 165
Aubenas, Jacqueline, 121–24
Auclert, Hubertine, 20, 21; *La citoyenne*, 20
Audry, Colette, 190
August, Marilyn A. (translator), 137–41, 161–64, 165–67

Bachofen, J. J., 96

Balzac, Honoré de: *La physiologie du mariage* (1829), 17
Barre, Poulain de la, 3, 4, 7, 8, 49; *De l'égalité des deux sexes* (1673), 7, 14
Barrows, Anita (translator), 241
Barthes, Roland, 71, 73
Bataille, Georges, 69, 70, 112; *Histoire de l'oeil* (1967), 73
Baudelaire, Charles, 69
Beauvoir, Simone de, xi, 6, 7, 8, 26, 29, 34–35, 158, 183, 190, 207, 265; interview, 142–53; Introduction to "Les femmes s'entêtent," 191; *La femme rompue* (1967), 183; *Le deuxième sexe* (1949), xiii, 4, 7, 8, 23, 39–56, 142, 145, 146, 147, 149, 233; *Questions féministes* (1977), 27
Bebel, August, 28, 46
Benda, Julien: *Rapport d'Uriel* (1946), 44
Bible, The, 6
Blum, Léon, 22
Bobigny trial, 25, 209
Boileau, Nicolas: *Satire X: Les femmes* (1694), 14
Bosquet, Alain: Preface to *Hanches* (Burine), 161
Bossuet, Jacques Bénigne, 44
Bourges, Clémence de, 13
Bread Riots (Paris, 1795), 16
Brée, Germaine (translator), 188
Breton, Jean: Introduction to *Poésie féminine d'aujourd'hui*, 161
Bretonne, Rétif de la: *Les gynographes* (1777), 15
Brion, Hélène, 4; *La voix féministe: femme, ose être!* (1916), 21

Briques et tuiles (Segalen), 168–69
Brunfaut, Emilienne, 207
Burine, Claude de: *Hanches* (1971), 161

Caen, Roger de, 10
Cage, John, 138
Camille Sée Law, 20
Carmen de contemptu mundi (Caen), 10
Carrouges, Michel, 52n
Cause des femmes, La (Halimi), 25
Cavanni, Lilianna: *Night Porter*, 73
C.D. *See* Delphy, Christine
"Ce que je cherche à faire" (Sarraute), 163
"Cercle Dimitriev," 25
Césaire, Aimé: *Discourse on Politics*, 174
Ce sexe qui n'en est pas un (Irigaray), 27
C'est moi Diego (Plantier), 162
"Chair linguistique, La" (Chawaf), 177–78
Champion des dames, Le (Franc), 12
Chapsal, Madeleine, 71, 74
Charcot, Jean Martin, 133
Charlemagne, king of France, 10
Charles VII, king of France, 11
Charles VIII, king of France, 12
Chawaf, Chantal, 265; "La chair linguistique" (1976), 177–78
Chinese women, 139–40, 146, 240, 241
"Chinoises à 'contre-courant,' Les" (Kristeva), 240
"Choisir," 25, 27, 29, 208, 209
Choisir, 29
Citoyenne, La, 20
Cixous, Hélène, ix, x, xi, xii, 33, 34, 36, 37, 265; "Le rire de la méduse" (1975), 26, 245–63; "Sorties" (1975), 90–98
Classical Age, 14
Clélie (Scudéry), 13
Clément, Catherine, xi, xii, 34, 265; "Enclave esclave" (1975), 130–36
Clovis, king of France, 10
Cohen, Keith (translator), 245–63
Cohen, Paula (translator), 245–63
Colonie, La (Marivaux), 14

Condition de la française d'aujourd'hui, La (Michel and Texier), 23
Condorcet, Jean Antoine de, 3; *Déclaration des droits et l'admission des femmes au droit de cité* (1790), 15; *Lettres d'un bourgeois de Newhaven à un citoyen de Virginie* (1787), 15
Confucius, 139
Consulate, 17
Conundrum (Morris), 170
"Coordonnées féminines: espace et temps, Les" (Herrmann), 168–73
Corday, Charlotte, 5, 16
"Corps I" (Gagnon), 179–80
Courtivron, Isabelle de (translator), 121–24, 179–80, 181–82, 194–95, 204–6, 237
Création étouffée, La (Horer and Socquet), 243–44
Crusades, 10

"Debout les femmes!" (song), 188
Déclaration des droits de la femme et de la citoyenne (Gouges), 16
Déclaration des droits et l'admission des femmes au droit de cité (Condorcet), 15
De l'amour (Stendhal), 17
De l'éducation des dames (Barre), 7
De l'éducation des femmes (Laclos), 15
De l'éducation des femmes (Stendhal), 17
De l'égalité des deux sexes (Barre), 7, 14
De l'excellence des hommes contre l'égalité des sexes (Barre), 7
Delphy, Christine, 34, 35; "Pour un matérialisme féministe" (1975), 197–98
Démar, Claire: *Ma loi d'avenir* (1833), 18
Deneuve, Catherine, 190
De nobilitate et praecellentia feminei sexus (Agrippa), 12
Deraismes, Maria: *Le droit des femmes*, 20
Deroin, Jeanne: *La voix des femmes*, 19
Derrida, Jacques, xii
Desanti, Dominique, 164
Desbordes-Valmore, Marceline, 161

Descartes, René, 52; *Discours de la méthode* (1637), 13
Des chinoises (Kristeva), 26, 241
des femmes en mouvements (1978), 27, 32
Deuxième sexe, Le (Beauvoir), xiii, 4, 7, 8, 23, 39–56, 142, 145, 146, 147, 149, 233
Dialectic of Sex, The (Firestone), 146
Diderot, Denis, 50
Dien Bien Phu, Battle of, 23
Dimitrieff, Elisabeth, 20
Directory, 16
Discours de la méthode (Descarte), 13
Discourse on Politics (Césaire), 174
Dreyfus Affair, 21
Droits de l'homme et du citoyen (1789), 15
Droit des femmes, Le, 20
Drouet, Minou, 161
Dumézil, Georges, 44
Durand, Marguerite: *La fronde*, 21
Duras, Marguerite, xi, 111–13, 163, 171, 183, 238, 265; interview (1975), 174–76
Duvert, Tony: *Sur un paysage de fantaisie* (1973), 71, 72

Eaubonne, Françoise d', xii, 25, 36, 265; *Le féminisme ou la mort* (1974), 236
"Ecologie-Féminisme," 25
Écrits féministes de Simone de Beauvoir, Les (1979), 27
Eden, Eden, Eden (Guyotat), 72
Edict of Nantes, 14
éditions des femmes, 27, 31, 32, 193
Effe, 212
Égalité des hommes et des femmes (Gournay), 7, 13
Eisinger, Erica M. (translator), 199–203
Elle, 24, 29, 64
Emile (Rousseau), 15
Emma, 212
Emmanuelle (fictional heroine), 78
"Enclave esclave" (Clément), 130–36
Engels, Friedrich, 28, 139
Enigme, L' (Morris), 170
Épître au dieu d'amour, L' (Pisan), 6, 11
Erasmus, *Institutis Christiani Matrimonii* (1526), 12

Estaing, Giscard d', President of Fifth Republic, 26, 141
Etrennes nationales des dames, 16
Eustis, Helen (translator), 142–50
"Existential Marxism," 30
"Existe-t-il une écriture de femme?" (Gauthier), 161–64
Express, L', 76

Fait féminin, Le (Sullerot, editor), 27
Fanan, Jean: Avant-propos to *Poésie féminine d'aujourd'hui*, 162
Felman, Shoshana, xii
"Féminin-Masculin-Futur," 23
"Féminisme-Marxisme," 23
Féminisme ou la mort, Le (Eaubonne), 64–67, 236
"Féministes révolutionnaires," 24, 33, 35
"Femme, ce n'est jamais ça, La" (Kristeva), 137–41
Femme dans la société, La (Lauwe and Lauwe), 23
Femmes savantes, Les (Molière), 14, 61
"Femmes s'entêtent, Les," 26, 34, 191–92, 212
Fénelon, François de Salignac de la Mothe, *Traité de l'éducation des filles* (1687), 14
Ferrat, Jean, 152
Fifth Republic, 23
Figaro littéraire, 51
Firestone, Shulamith: *The Dialectic of Sex* (1971), 146
First International Congress for Women's Rights, 20
Flaubert, Gustave, 133
F Magazine, 27
Forrester, Viviane, 265; "Le regard des femmes" (1976), 181–82
Fouque, Antoinette, 32, 117–18
Fourier, Charles, 28; *Le phalanstère*, 18; *Théorie des quatre mouvements* (1808), 17
Franc, Martin Le, 3; *Le champion des dames* (1442), 12
Franchise, 41n
François I, king of France, 12
Franco-Prussian War, 20
French Movement for Family Planning, 23
French Renaissance, 8, 12

French Resistance, 22, 28
French Revolution of 1789, 3, 5, 6, 8, 16
Frère, Maude, 207
Freud, Sigmund, xii, 33, 35, 36, 69, 93, 99, 100, 108, 109, 110, 133, 166, 202, 239, 454; *The Disappearance of the Oedipus Complex* (1933), 94–95
Friedan, Betty, 144
Froissart, Jean, 11
Fronde, La (organization), 6, 13
Fronde, La (newspaper), 21

Gagnon, Madeleine, 266; "Corps I" (1977), 179–80
Garçonne, La (Margueritte), 22
Gaulle, Charles de, 5, 22, 23
Gauthier, Xavière, 266; "Existe-t-il une écriture de femme?" (1974), 161–64; interviewer, 165–67; "Pourquoi Sorcières?" (1976), 199–203; *Sorcières* (ed., 1976), 26
Gay, Désirée: *La voix des femmes*, 19
Gazette des femmes, 18
Gelfand, Elissa (translator), 59–63, 68–75, 76–78
Genet, Jean, 98; *Pompes funèbres* (1948), 255–56
Gennari, Geneviève, 28
Gérard, Juliette, 207
Gide, André, 52
Gill, Gillian C. (translator), 79–86
Giroud, Françoise, 29, 124
GLIFE, 26
Gouges, Olympe de, 3, 16; *Déclaration des droits de la femme et de la citoyenne* (1791), 16
Gournay, Marie de, 3, 4, 6, 8
Granet, Marcel, 44
"Grande donnée de notre temps, Une" (Vincent), 125–29
Grégoire, Ménie, 28
Grévy, Jules, President of Third Republic, 20
Grief des dames, Le (Gournay), 7, 13
Groult, Benoîte, 36, 207, 266; "Les portiers de nuit" (1975), 68–75
Guérillères, Les (Wittig), 24, 37, 163, 224, 242
Guitry, Sacha, 222

Guyotat, Pierre: *Eden, Eden, Eden*, 72
Gynographes, Les (Bretonne), 15

Hachette, Jeanne, 5
Halimi, Gisèle, 29, 190, 207, 266; Introduction to *Le programme commun des femmes* (1978), 208–11; *La cause des femmes* (1973), 25
Hanches (Burine), 161
Hebdo-Latin, 51
Hegel, Georg Wilhelm Friedrich, xii, 45, 52
Heptaméron (Navarre), 13
Herrmann, Claudine, xi, xii, 266; "Les coordonnées féminines: espace et temps" (1976), 168; "Le système viril" (1976), 87–89
Hippolyte, Jean, xii
Historie de la presse féminine en France des origines à 1848 (Sullerot), 23
Histoire d'O, L' (Réage), 26, 71, 76
Histoire du féminisme français (Albistur and Armogathe), 27, 32, 34
Histoires d'elles (1977), 27, 212
Histoires du MLF (Pisan and Tristan), 27, 32
Horer, Suzanne: *La création étouffée* (1974), 243–44
Hoffman, Ernst Theodor Amadeus, 250
Hules, Virginia (translator), 111–13
Humanité, L', 123
Hundred Years' War, 11
Husserl-Kapit, Susan (translator), 174–76, 238

Ibarruri, Dolores, 132n
Indiana (Sand), 18
Information des femmes, L', 212
Institutis Christiani Matrimonii (Erasmus), 12
International Tribunal on Crimes Against Women, 207n
Irigaray, Luce, xii, 37, 207, 266; "Ce sexe que n'en est pas un" (1977), 99–106; *Ce sexe qui n'en est pas un* (1977), 27; "Des marchandises entre elles" (1977), 107–10; *Speculum de l'autre femme* (1974), 26

Joan of Arc, 3, 5, 6, 11
Jones, Ernest: *Early Feminine Sexuality*, 93–94
Journal des dames, Le, 1759
Joyce, James, 138, 165, 166; *Finnegans Wake* (1939), 165; *Ulysses* (1922), 255
July Monarchy, 17
Justice dans la révolution et dans l'église, La (Proudhon), 19
Justine (Sade), 16

Kleist, Heinrich von, 249
Kojève, Alexandre, xii
Kramer, Heinrich: *Malleus maleficarum* (1486), 12, 201–2
Kristeva, Julia, xi, xii, 32, 36, 183, 266; *Des chinoises* (1974), 26, 241; "La femme, ce n'est jamais ça" (1974), 137–41; "Les chinoises à 'contre-courant'" (1974), 240; "Oscillation du 'pouvoir' au 'refus'" (1974), 165–67

Labé, Louise, 13, 161
Lacan, Jacques, xii, 32, 95, 163, 255
Laclos, Choderlos de: *De l'éducation des femmes* (1783), 15
Lacombe, Claire, 16
Lafargue, Paul: *La question de la femme* (1904), 21
La Fayette, Madame de: *La Princesse de Clèves* (1678), 14
Laguiller, Arlette, xiii, 121–24, 266
Lamber, Juliette: *Idées anti-Proudhoniennes* (1861), 20
Landy, Claudie: "Après 48 heures du cinéma des femmes à La Rochelle," 204–6
Lanson, Gustave, 4
Last Tango in Paris, The, 117
"Laugh of the Medusa, The" (Cixous), 245–63
Lautréamont, Cte de, 69, 165
Lauwe, M. J. and P. H. Chombart de, 28; *La femme dans la société* (1962), 23
League for Women's Rights, 20
Leclerc, Annie, 36, 37, 266; "La lettre

d'amour" (1977), 237; *Parole de femme* (1974), 79–86, 179
Le Dantec, Denise, 119, 266
Lederer, Wolfgang: *The Fear of Women* (1968), 66
Leduc, Violette, 190
Legislative Assembly, 16
Leiris, Michel, 69, 71
L'Enfantin, 18
Lenin, V. I., 52
Léon, Pauline, 16
"Les amyes" texts, 12
"Lettre d'amour, La" (Leclerc), 237
Lettre ouverte aux hommes (Parturier), 24, 59–63, 234–35
Lettres d'un bourgeois de Newhaven à un citoyen de Virginie (Condorcet), 15
Le Vay, David (translator), 242
Lévinas, Emmanuel: *Le temps et l'autre*, 44n
Lévi-Strauss, Claude, xii, 36, 170; *Les structures élémentaires de la parenté* (1949), 45
Liddle, Ann (translator), 90–98
"Ligue du droit des femmes," 26, 35, 150
"Ligue pour le droit des femmes, La," 29
Lilar, Suzanne, 28
Lin Piao, 139
Li-Tai-Po, 168
Livre de la cité des dames, Le (Pisan), 6
Lonzi, Carla: *Spit on Hegel*, 64, 66
Louis XI, king of France, 12
Louis XIV, king of France, 5, 13
Louis XVI, king of France, 15
Louis XVIII, king of France, 17
Louis Napoleon, President of Second Republic, 19
Louis-Philippe, 17, 19
"lutte des classes," 27
"Lutte ouvrières," 123

Macciocchi, Maria-Antonietta, xi, 120, 239, 267
Mallarmé, Stéphane, xii, 92, 161, 165
Malleus maleficarum (Sprenger and Kramer), 12, 201–2

Ma loi d'avenir (Démar), 18
Malraux, André, 83, 85
Manifesto of the 343, 24, 29, 190
Marat, Jean Paul, 16
Marchais, Georges, 123
"Marchandises entre elles, Des" (Iriga-ray), 107–10
Margueritte, Victor: *La garçonne* (1922), 22
Marivaux, Pierre Carlet de Chamblain de: *La colonie* (1750), 14
Marks, Elaine (translator), 117–18, 120, 151–53, 191–92, 193, 196, 197–98, 211, 234–35, 239, 240
Marx, Karl, xii, 28, 52, 143, 144; *Misère de la philosophie* (1847), 19
Masoch, Leopold von Sacher, 69
Mauriac, Claude, 52
Méricourt, Théroigne de, 16
Meung, Jean de, 6, 7, 49; *Le roman de la rose* (1275), 6, 11
Mexican Expeditions, 20
Michel, Andrée, 28, 34; *La condition de la française d'aujourd'hui* (1964), 23
Michel, Louise, 20
Michelet, Jules, 3, 44, 201, 221; *La sorcière* (1862), 20, 175
Mill, John Stuart, 50
Miller, Henry, 70, 71
Misère de la philosophie (Marx), 19
Mitchell, Juliet: *Woman's Estate* (1973), x, xi
MLAC, 25
MLF. *See* "Mouvement de Libération des Femmes"
MLF Song, 188
Modern Woman: The Lost Sex, 42
Molière: *Les femmes savantes* (1672), 14, 61; *Les précieuses ridicules* (1659), 14
Monde, Le, 183
Monod, Jacques: *Chance and Necessity* (1972), 154
Montaigne, Michel Eyquem de, 50
Montherlant, Henry de, 49, 51
Moreau, Jeanne, 190, 207
Morris, Jan: *Conundrum* (1974), 170
"Mouvement de Libération des Femmes," 24, 27, 30, 31, 122, 142, 143, 145, 151, 152
"Musidora," 25

Napoleon III, Emperor of France, 19
Napoleon Bonaparte, 5, 16, 17
Napoleonic code, 5, 23, 28
Navarre, Marguerite de: *Heptaméron* (1559), 13
Neel, Alexandra David: *Voyage d'une Parisienne à Lhasa* (1964), 171
Neuwirth Law, 23
Niboyet, Eugénie: *La voix des femmes*, 19
Nietzsche, Friedrich Wilhelm, 52, 138, 259
Night Porter (Cavanni), 73
Nouveau roman: hier aujourd'hui, 163
Nouvelles féministes, 35
Nouvel observateur, 32

O'Leary, Susan (translator), 125–29

Parent-Duchâtel, Alexandre Jean Baptiste, 19
Paris Commune, 20
Parker, Dorothy, 42
Parole de femme (Leclerc), 79–86, 179
Parshley, H. M. (translator), 39–56, 233
Partisan, année zéro, 24
Partisans, 34
Parturier, Françoise, xii, 36, 267; *Lettre ouverte aux hommes* (1968), 24, 59–63, 234–35
Pascal, Blaise, 83
Pasionaria, 132
Pays où tout est permis, Le (Podolski), 166
Pelletier, Monique, Minister for the Status of Women, 27
Perrault, Charles: *Apologie des femmes* (1694), 14
Pétain, Henry Philippe, 22
Pétrement, Simone, 170
pétroleuses, les, 26, 212
Phalanstère, Le (Fourier), 18
Physiologie du mariage, La (Balzac), 17
Pisan, Annie de: *Histoires du MLF* (1977), 27
Pisan, Christine de, 3, 4, 6, 7, 8, 11

Pissarjevsky, Lydia, 4; *Socialisme et féminisme* (1907), 21
Plantier, Thérèse: *C'est moi Diego* (1971), 162
Podolski, Sophie: *Le pays où tout est permis* (1975), 166
Poggi, Dominique: "Une apologie des rapports de domination" (1976), 76–78
Poirot-Delpech, Bertrand, 71, 73
Pompes funèbres (Genet), 255–56
Pompidou, Georges, President of Fifth Republic, 24
Poniatowski, Michael, 196
Popular Front, 22
"*Portiers de nuit, Les*" (Groult), 68–75
Postel, Guillaume, 12
"Pour un matérialisme féministe" (Delphy), 197–98
Précieuses ridicules, Les (Molière), 14
préciosité movement, 13, 14
"Préface au fait féminin" (Sullerot), 154–58
Presle, Micheline, 190
Princesse de Clèves, La (La Fayette), 14
Programme commun des femmes, 27
"Prostituées de Lyon parlent à la population, Les," 196
Proudhon, Pierre Joseph, 154; *La justice dans la révolution et dans l'église* (1858), 19, 20
"Psychanalyse et Politique," x, 24, 25, 26, 31–33, 35, 137–41, 193

Querelle des femmes, 5, 6, 11
Question de la femme, La (Lafargue), 21
Questions féministes (1977), 27, 35, 212
Quinze joyes de mariage, Les (Sale), 11
Quotidien des femmes, Le, 130

"Rape is an Abuse of Power," 194–95
Recherches féminines, 211
Reeder, Claudia (translator), 99–106, 107–10
"Regard des femmes, Le" (Forrester), 181–82

Reign of terror, 16
Religious wars (1562–1598), 13
Repos du guerrier, Le (Rochefort), 183, 184
Research on Women, 211
Reynaud, Colette: *La voix des femmes*, 22
Richer, Léon: *Le droit des femmes*, 20
Rimbaud, Arthur, 149, 233
"Rire de la méduse, Le" (Cixous), 26, 37, 245–63
Rochefort, Christiane, xi, 24, 31, 190, 207, 267; "Are Women Writers Still Monsters?" (1975), 182–86; *Le repos du guerrier* (1958), 183, 184
Rochette-Ozzello, Yvonne (translator), 154–58, 177–78, 212–30, 244
Roland, Pauline, 19
Roman de la rose, Le (Meung), 6, 11
Roncier, Nathalie: "Après 48 heures du cinéma des femmes à La Rochelle" (1976), 204–6
Rousseau, Jean-Jacques: *Émile* (1762), 15
Roussel, Nelly, 4, 22
Russian women, 143

Sade, Marquis de, 63, 69, 70, 73; *Justine* (1791), 16
Sagan, Françoise, 183, 190
St. Augustine, 50
Saint-Exupéry, Antoine de, 83
St. Paul, 52
Saint-Simon, Claude Henry de Rouvroy de, 17, 28
Saint-Simonian school, 18
St. Thomas, 42, 44
Sale, Antoine de la: *Les quinze joyes de mariage*, 11
Salic Law, 5, 10, 11
Sand, George, 164; *Indiana* (1832), 18
Sarraute, Nathalie: "Ce que je cherche à faire," 163
Sartre, Jean Paul, 34, 133, 146, 147
Satire X: Les femmes (Boileau), 14
Saussure, Ferdinand de, xii, 30
Schmitz, Betty (translator), 64–67, 236
Schneider, Romy, 190
Schuster, Marilyn R. (translator), 87–89, 119, 130–36

Schwarzer, Alice (interviewer), 142–53
Scudéry, Madeleine de: *Clélie* (1654), 13
S.C.U.M., 144
Second Empire, 19
Second Republic, 19
Second Sex, The. See *Deuxième sexe, Le* (Beauvoir)
Secretariat of State for the Status of Women, 26–27, 124, 141
Segalen, Victor: *Briques et tuiles* (1975), 168–69
Servan-Schreiber, Claude, 207; *F Magazine*, 27
Seven Years' War, 14
Sexus (Miller), 71
Sexual Behavior in the Human Male (Kinsey *et al.*), 43n
Seyrig, Delphine, 190, 207
Shaw, George Bernard, 51
"Simone de Beauvoir et la lutte des femmes," 34
Simone Veil Law, 208
Socialisme et féminisme (Pissarjevsky), 21
Socialisme et sexualisme (Valette), 21
Society for Revolutionary Republican Women Citizens, 16
Socquet, Jeanne: *La création étouffée* (1974), 243–44
Sollers, Philippe, 71
Sorcière, La (Michelet), 20
Sorcières, 26
"Sorties" (Cixous), 90–98
"SOS Battered Women," 151
"SOS Femmes-alternatives," 35
Soubiran, Dr., 61
Spanish Civil War, 22
Sparerib, 212
Speculum de l'autre femme (Irigaray), 26
"Spirale," 25
Spit on Hegel (Lonzi), 64, 66
Sprenger, Jakob: *Malleus maleficarum* (1486), 12, 201–2
Stendhal: *De l'amour* (1822), 17; *De l'éducation des femmes* (1822), 17
Stern, Daniel. See Agoult, Marie d'
Story of O, The. See *Histoire d'O, L'*
Stockhausen, Karlheinz, 138
Sullerot, Evelyne, 28, 267; *Histoire de la presse féminine en France des origines*

à *1848* (1966), 23; *Le fait féminin* (1978), 27; "Préface au fait féminin" (1978), 154–58
Sur un paysage de fantaisie (Duvert), 71, 72, 73
"*Système viril, Le*" (Herrmann), 87–89

"Tel quel," 32
Temps modernes, 26, 34, 68, 151
Texier, Geneviève, 28; *La condition de la française d'aujourd'hui* (1964), 23
Théorie des quatre mouvements (Fourier), 17
Third Republic, 20
Thirty Years' War, 13
Tomb of the unknown soldier (Paris), 24, 31
Torchon brûle, Le, 25, 212
Traité de l'éducation des filles (Fénelon), 14
Tribune des femmes, La, 18
Tristan, Anne: *Histoires du MLF* (1977), 27
Tristan, Flora: *Union ouvrière* (1843), 18

Union ouvrière (Tristan), 18

Valabrègue, Catherine, 25
Valette, Aline: *Socialisme et sexualisme* (1893), 21
Van Parys, Agnès, 164
"Variations sur des thèmes communs" (1977), 212–30
Veil, Simone, Minister of Health, 26, 29, 208
Vincent, Madeleine, xiii, 267; "Une grande donnée de notre temps" (1976), 125–29
"Viol est un abus de pouvoir, Le," 194–95
Violette C., 207
Voilquin, Suzanne, 18, 19; *La voix des femmes*, 19
Voix des femmes, La, 19, 22
Voix féministe: femme, ose être, La (Brion), 21
Voyage d'une Parisienne à Lhasa (Neel), 171

War of First Coalition, 16
War of Spanish Succession, 14
War of Third Coalition, 17
*Warrior's Rest, The. See Repos du guer-
rier, Le* (Rochefort)
Weil, Simone, 170, 171; *Waiting for
God* (1949–1950), 169–70
Weill-Hallé, Marie-Andrée Lagroua, 23
Wittig, Monique, xii, 24, 31, 33, 35, 37,
163–64, 267; *Les guérillères* (1969),
24, 37, 163, 224, 242
Women Arise! (song), 188

"Women Prostitutes of Lyon Speak to
the People," 196
Woman's Estate (Mitchell), x, xi
Women's Union, 20
Woolf, Virginia, 166, 171, 172; *Orlando*
(1928), 171
World Congress of Women against Fas-
cism, 22
World War I, 21

Zwang, Gérard, 70, 74